Praise for Bill Glazer's
OUTRAGEOUS Multi-Step Marketing Campaigns

"Step-by-step instructions: Step 1: Open book, find a marketing campaign that applies to your business. Step 2: Copy campaign, swipe and deploy. Step 3: Watch your bank account grow. Bill Glazer is practical, pragmatic and gives simple implementable resources shared by his network of genius marketing friends. Your bank account deserves to be bigger – grab this book!" ● **MIKE KOENIGS**

"So many books these days are strong on theory, but weak on the 'in the trenches,' step-by-step tactics that actually get results. This book is different in that it's almost ALL tactics. Literally every page presents something new you can try and apply to grow your business, and as excited as I was to contribute to the book, I was even more excited to read it!" ● **RYAN DEISS**

"Flat out, Bill Glazer makes people OUTRAGEOUS sums of money, myself included. When he speaks I listen and when he puts a book out, I get it. His OUTRAGEOUS advice is genius, easy to implement and, most importantly, WORKS. If you'll put the ideas, strategies and examples to work, it will make an OUTRAGEOUS difference in your business." ● **DUSTIN MATHEWS**

"This is a hands-on, practical guide to growing your business and making more money. Unlike most marketing books, it's not theory and it's not fluff. Inside, you'll find real examples of what's working now, along with a step-by-step guide to getting it done. If you want to make more money, have a greater impact, and create great value in the world, you need to read this book." ● **ED RUSH**

"Why would you want to rack your brain for a brilliant marketing idea, when Bill Glazer has done the hard work of collecting some of the best right here. These are full-blown campaigns from a variety of industries so you can get inspired to creatively stand out from your competitors." ● **YANIK SILVER**

"Bill Glazer is a friend, mentor and beacon for entrepreneurs everywhere. His uncanny marketing mind has helped so many of us thrive, and he continues to guide a growing band of renegade entrepreneurs. For the renegade entrepreneur, *OUTRAGEOUS "Multi-Step" Marketing Campaigns That Are OUTRAGEOUSLY Successful* is a must-read." ● **A.J. MIRABEDINI**

"The strategies in this book give any business owner or marketer lucky enough to read them an unfair competitive advantage in the marketplace. And who doesn't want that?" ● **KIM WALSH PHILLIPS**

"Just one campaign can change your life forever and inside this book you'll find 49 outrageous campaigns you can adapt, tweak and alter for your business!" ● **MATT BACAK**

"Bill builds a solid foundation of critical components to any successful marketing campaign. That alone is worth the price of admission, but he follows it up with 49 supercharged examples, each of which is like a MARKETING ROCKET SHIP to explode your business' sales and profits!" • RORY FATT

"Every entrepreneur should use this book as their most trusted creative marketing resource. You'll come back to it again and again, not only for inspiration, but to swipe these OUTRAGEOUS campaigns for your own use! It's like an idea box you can open up whenever you need fresh, creative ideas that you can easily adapt and apply to your own business." • JULIE BOSWELL

"This book is for YOU if you want concrete examples of PROVEN, OUTRAGEOUSLY SUCCESSFUL marketing campaigns that have helped businesses small and large to CRUSH their competition. It's for YOU if you'd like a seemingly endless flow of marketing campaigns from which you can borrow and with which you can convert more of your prospects to customers. It's for YOU if you want to GROW your BUSINESS, have MORE FUN and make a LOT MORE MONEY." • DR. TOM ORENT

"OUTRAGEOUS Multi-Step Marketing Campaigns That Are Outrageously Successful gives you real-world marketing campaigns that have generated millions of dollars. No theory or academic fluff here. Just "what's working now" example after example." • MIKE CAPUZZI

"Bill has combined the creativity to stand out among the 1,000's of ads we see each day, with tested, proven, and *measurable* direct response methods to create a formula that works for any business. If you struggle for new, fresh ideas to market your business… If you find your ads falling flat in both appeal and results, then look no further than Bill's newest book. If you keep an open mind, you'll find at least a dozen different ideas from this book to use in your own business." • TRAVIS LEE

"Bill has a unique ability to be OUTRAGEOUS in so many ways and he continues to share those with people that want to help others. Even more important, unlike so many books Bill doesn't cut corners-he gives you everything – Step-by-Step so you can do it yourself." • MIKE CROW

"Bill Glazer has done it again. He has taken OUTRAGEOUS one step further with this appropriately named, multi-step book, combining his time-tested tips on capturing the customer's attention and turning it into cash, and 49 multi-step campaigns by many of Bill's disciples who have generated millions of dollars from them. If you are wanting to turn an idea into a workable system and cash in your pocket, this book is a must." • DR. KELLY BROWN

"Bill Glazer has created a uniquely OUTRAGEOUS guide to growing your business. Nowhere else will you see the secrets of so many successful business owners laid out for you to steal and copy in your own business. If you buy one marketing book this year, make sure it's *OUTRAGEOUS Multi-Step Marketing Campaigns that are Outrageously Successful*!" • ROB CUESTA

OUTRAGEOUS MULTI-STEP MARKETING CAMPAIGNS THAT ARE OUTRAGEOUSLY SUCCESSFUL

*Created for the 99% of
Business Owners Who Want to
Change Their Good Business
Into a GREAT Business!*

Bill Glazer

Direct Response Strategist, Bestselling Author

BrightFlame Books, Toronto

ACKNOWLEDGEMENTS

"At times our own light goes out and is rekindled by a spark from another person. Each of us has cause to think with deep gratitude of those who have lighted the flame within us."
ALBERT SCHWEITZER

This might be a different type of book acknowledgment because, as I explain in the Preface, I had a stroke a couple of years ago. So you'll find that a lot of my thanks below go to the people who helped me through that very difficult experience.

But first, I want to thank my friend, Mike Koenigs, who suggested that I hire Rob Cuesta to help me write the book.

And of course, I want to thank Rob himself. Not only has he helped me to create a great book, but he also helped me to design the campaigns to launch and promote it. I couldn't have done any of this without him.

I also want to thank all of those who made this book possible by helping me to find campaign contributors (and who also contributed campaigns of their own): Rory Fatt, Mike Capuzzi, Dr. Tom Orent, and A.J. Mirabedini, the CEO of GKIC.

I was lucky to find my speech therapist, Brooke Lang from aphasiatoolbox.com, who helped me with my recovery. I've never told this to anyone other than my wife, but during our sessions, we went through every word in this book.

Speaking of support, my family has helped me immeasurably through this process. Sherrie Sokolowski, my Executive Assistant (who I really feel is part of my family), my kids, Josh, Mary and Mara, and my wife Karen who I still call my Bride after 40 years of marriage.

Finally, I want to share my sincere appreciation to all the 49 entrepreneurs who sent me their campaigns. Without them, this book would have been a lot shorter and a lot less useful, and you wouldn't be able to change your own good business to a great business.

There's one more person I want to thank, and that is YOU. By purchasing this book, you are helping to fund a Non-Profit **VETERANS AFFAIRS** program that helps people from all walks of life who have had a STROKE to get the care and support they need.

TABLE OF CONTENTS

THE CONTRIBUTORS

PART THREE
THE "SIMPLE" CAMPAIGNS

PART FOUR
THE "COMPLEX" CAMPAIGNS

PART FIVE
PULLING ALL THE PIECES TOGETHER TO CHANGE YOUR GOOD BUSINESS INTO A GREAT BUSINESS

STOP

BEFORE YOU GO ANY FURTHER,
READ THIS IMPORTANT NOTICE FROM BILL GLAZER

Do you want to see the entrepreneurs in this book
WALK YOU THROUGH their campaigns in person?
Do you want to learn how they've updated their campaigns
to make them EVEN better?
Do you want to meet HUNDREDS of business owners
just like you, and make friendships and partnerships for life?

I'm running a LIVE workshop in sunny San Diego,
and I'd love to have you join us.

All the proceeds from this book and the live event
will be going to Veteran's Affairs, and you'll be able to see me
hand over a MASSIVE check LIVE on stage.

You can find out all the details at
www.outrageouscampaigns.com/live

I hope we'll see you there!

Bill Glazer

Who is Bill Glazer and
Why is he Writing this NEW Book?

If you've picked this up, you may be wondering who Bill Glazer is and why you should read this book. Let me answer that for you.

The short answer is, I'm a Direct Response Strategist, Speaker, and the Best-Selling Author of *OUTRAGEOUS Advertising That's Outrageously Successful*. I'm probably best known as the President and Founder of Glazer-Kennedy Insiders' Circle (now known as "GKIC").

After selling GKIC to a Private Equity firm in 2011, I continued working privately with many of my best clients around the world until I had a stroke on December 10, 2015.

Now, a stroke is not a minor thing. It turns your life around in ways you'd never expect. Everyday tasks and habits become difficult or impossible, and many people have problems with speech and language.

And you'd better believe that something as major as a stroke also focuses your mind on things like your legacy and everything you still have left to do.

Recovering from a stroke takes time and a lot of care, and I was fortunate to have a great team of therapists and the loving support of my wife, children, and good friends.

And so, at last, in Summer 2017, I finally felt ready to turn my attention to some of those things that were still left to do, starting with a NEW book to help the 99% of business owners who want to change their good business to a <u>GREAT</u> business: *OUTRAGEOUS Multi-Step Marketing Campaigns That Are Outrageously Successful.*

TWO Important Reasons Why I am Writing this Book

I wanted to achieve two key things in the book.

1. Every person who reads it will find at least one great campaign (and usually several more) that they can use to increase their sales significantly.

2. As I said above, support and access to great professionals are critical in recovering from a stroke, and I know the difference it made to me, so I am donating all of the proceeds from this new book to a Non-Profit **VETERANS AFFAIRS** program that helps Veterans nationwide who have had a stroke. Thanks to that program, those Veterans are able to attend a 4-week long intensive residential treatment program where they can have the support they need and their own great team of therapists.

So, when you read this book, not only will you be able to use these great campaigns to significantly increase your own sales, but you'll also feel good about helping Veterans who had a stroke to improve their speech and language skills.

PART ONE

Ten Things You Never Want to Miss in Your OUTRAGEOUS Marketing

In this part of the book, I'm going to introduce ten critical components that will make your marketing CAMPAIGNS much more OUTRAGEOUS and, more importantly, much more profitable.

The descriptions of each technique are deliberately short for two simple reasons.

First, the best way to understand these OUTRAGEOUS techniques is to see them in action, and you're going to get that when you read through the 49 CAMPAIGNS in Parts 3 and 4 of this book. There's a lot more value in seeing how these techniques are used in real CAMPAIGNS than there is in reading a description.

Second, I wrote about all of these in my earlier book, *OUTRAGEOUS Advertising That's Outrageously Successful.* So, in this book, I'll save you time and effort by giving you just the information you need to understand what's happening in the CAMPAIGNS, and no more. You can thank me later!

"S&D" Your Way to OUTRAGEOUS Offline and Online Marketing

You may have heard the old saying that "the definition of insanity is doing the same things over and over again and expecting a different result." In marketing, we could say something very similar: the definition of insanity is doing the same things as your competitors and expecting to beat them.

But look around any industry and what kind of marketing do you see business owners doing? Exactly the same kind of marketing their competitors are doing, and hoping that they can do it better.

If you keep doing what everyone else in your industry is doing, you're going to keep getting the same results. And most of your competitors are struggling! It's like trying to learn to swim by watching a drowning man.

In this book, I'm going to share with you 49 CAMPAIGNS from business owners who are not struggling. Business owners who are growing their businesses quickly and profitably, and they are doing it outrageously.

So ignore what your competitors are doing and copy *these* people.

Yes, it will feel uncomfortable. You'll read a CAMPAIGN, and you'll think, "but no-one in my industry does that." Great! That's the best reason for doing it.

For one thing, copying what someone else in your industry is doing is pretty unethical. How would you like to open the paper and see a competitor running an exact copy of your CAMPAIGN?

For another, bringing in marketing techniques from other industries is going to stand out in the mind of your prospects. Which would you rather be: the twentieth business attorney someone saw looking earnestly at them from the side of a bus this morning—and completely ignored, just like the other nineteen—or the attorney whose podcast they're listening to intently in the car on their commute to work?

So, I'm giving you 49 tried and tested CAMPAIGNS—CAMPAIGNS that you know are working right now—that you can swipe and deploy ("S&D") with their creators' blessing. Normally, even if you see a great CAMPAIGN and think, "I should be doing that!" you don't know how well the CAMPAIGN is working—or even whether it's working at all. With the CAMPAIGNS you see in this book, you won't have that doubt. These business owners are sharing exactly what works, and the OUTRAGEOUS results they get from their CAMPAIGNS. So, you can safely swipe and deploy the CAMPAIGNS, knowing that you'll save time and uncertainty, you'll avoid treading on the toes of your competitors, and you'll be bringing something new and refreshing to your prospects.

The Critically OUTRAGEOUS Components You Have to Have in ALL Your Offline and Online CAMPAIGNS

A lot of business owners think that online marketing is hard. That it's different.

It isn't.

The things that make offline marketing work are the same things that make online marketing work. When online marketing fails, it's for the same kinds of reasons that offline marketing fails.

Marketing is marketing, whether it's on the web, by email or in the "real" world. In order to make it work, it needs three critical components, and unless you have all three, you won't get good results:

- A headline
- An offer
- A deadline

The Headline

The headline is what stops people in their tracks and gets them to pay attention to your marketing. When we look at a newspaper ad or an article, we know what the headline is. But every type of advertising has an equivalent.

For videos and radio ads, it's the first words you hear. For a Facebook ad, it's the image, because that's what grabs your attention. With direct mail, you need to get people to open the envelope, so you have to print something on the outside that will make them wonder what's inside.

What Makes a Good Headline?

A good headline moves people along the buying process and makes them want to take the next step. It doesn't just grab attention, it creates curiosity. It puts the prospect in a mood where they absolutely have to see (or hear) what's next.

The Offer

The offer is whatever you are promising people in return for taking the next step. Every offer comes down to two things: "do this because if you do, you'll get X" (gain) or "do this because if you don't, you'll lose X" (loss).

The next step might be to buy something or hire you, to request more information, or simply to come into your place of business. You'll see examples of all of those in the OUTRAGEOUS CAMPAIGNS in this book.

And of course, the first offer doesn't have to be your main offer. It can be a stepping stone. They say the journey of a thousand miles starts with a single step. In the same way, the purchase of a $25,000 service often starts with $5 shipping and handling for a "free" book (you'll see that kind of CAMPAIGN later, too) or some other low/no-cost offer.

The point is that you need a compelling offer, and that starts with the simple question, "What will someone lose if they don't take this offer, or gain if they do take it?"

Fear of loss can be a very powerful motivator. Watch the crowds camped outside an Apple store in a sleeping bag the night before the latest iPhone is released. They are not there because they need a faster, more capable phone: most of them aren't even using all the features of their current phone! They are there because they don't want to be the only one of their friends who doesn't have the latest iPhone. Apple doesn't even need to offer discounts to get those people there: in fact, they'd probably be willing to pay a premium!

What Makes a Good Offer?

A good offer is something that makes people think, "I absolutely have to have this." It also must be worth more to them than whatever you're asking in return.

The Deadline

Putting a deadline on an offer injects it with the fear of loss. More importantly, without a deadline, there really is no offer. The deadline is what gets someone to take action, and without it—if you leave your offer open-ended—there's no reason for them to do anything: they can always get it "later," and "later" becomes never.

A deadline creates urgency, though it doesn't always have to be about time (e.g., "Buy before September 1ˢᵗ and get…"). Restricting quantity can also be an effective technique (e.g., "The next 10 customers only…").

Along with the deadline, of course, there has to be a consequence for missing the deadline. That's what creates the fear of loss. So, a deadline could be tied to receiving bonuses or individual components of the offer ("Call in the next 5 days and get this set of…"), or to a price increase ("$99, today only").

What Makes a Good Deadline?

The defining characteristics of a good deadline are clarity and loss. *Clarity* means that the prospect understands when they have to act by, and what will happen if they don't; they understand the conditions of the deadline. *Loss* means that the 'punishment' for not acting will cause them real pain. When you have both of those elements in place, your deadline will make the prospect move ahead on *your* terms.

Harnessing the Power of OUTRAGEOUS Testimonials in <u>ALL</u> Your Offline and Online Marketing

Testimonials are a very powerful marketing tool. They are much more believable and effective than talking about yourself.

There are two basic forms of testimonial.

In the first, the customer talks about a specific outcome of doing business with you: "I bought my new car from you, and I was able to get a great deal on it."

The second type of testimonial is one that overcomes an objection: "I'm glad I bought this model because even though it costs a little more money, it's more reliable and I get better fuel economy."

One testimonial is better than nothing, but to really persuade people, it's best to use several.

Don't take our word for it...
Take a look at what Gage Clients say about us...

"My first experience was excellent! And my most recent experience was just as good! There's a true level of professionalism and serving customers at Gage. Plus, they really care about total satisfaction."
—Bill McCloud, Auroa, IL

"I chose Gage because a friend purchased suits there and I liked the way they looked." — *Naji Rashid, Baltimore*

"I chose Gage because it's a businessman's dream for a classy look. My husband loves Gage's style of clothing..." — *Patricia Pender, Randallstown*

"I usually hate clothes shopping, but you made me laugh and enjoy the whole experience...it was much better." — *Ross Pollack, Owings Mills*

"Shopping at Gage is a pleasure. The staff are accomodating and make excellent suggestions It's so easy to shop at Gage!." -- Debbie Friedman, Owings Mills

" I'm a size 58 Regular and Gage is the one place where I'm always fitted. I'm happy with my last suit!." --William Davis, Pasadena, MD

"I get excellent service ...and I like natural fabrics in my clothing." — *Abraham Floyd, Baltimore*

" I come downtown to Gage for the service I receive. If only other businesses had customer service like Gage." --Dennis White, Baltimore Co.

" Lots of words come to mind when I think of Gage ...courtesy, friends, quality merchandise my size ...and always a fair price!" --Jerry Kaiser, Owings Mills

"The professionalism exhibited by the entire Gage staff will ensure Gage's existence well into the 21st Century" — Neil Insel, Baltimore

" I enjoy shopping at Gage because they carry sizes for big and tall men, plus their prices are very reasonable" --Darryl P. Gould, Baltimore

"I really like the world-class service and having excellent salesmen who make me look good. Plus, during sales, I can really keep my wardrobe current." — *Lee Williams, Randallstown*

"A great sales staff to give you the assistance and confidence one needs when buying clothes." — *Charles M. Scott, Baltimore*

" You have great service and great value on your suits. It was a pleasure to shop with Gage." -- David Landesman, Miami Beach, FL

"This is one of the greatest shopping experiences I've ever had the pleasure to have--ANYWHERE!!" --Dave Reed, Rowland Heights, CA

The image on the previous page is from a promotion I ran when I had my menswear store. There are fifteen testimonials on the page, addressing all sorts of objections, from "I hate shopping" to "I'm a big guy, so you probably don't have anything that fits me," as well as specific outcomes. Each testimonial is there for a specific reason, and if a reader doesn't relate to one of them, there is probably another one there that they *will* relate to.

Notice, also, that every testimonial has the name of the person that gave it, along with where they live. That makes the testimonial more believable.

Four of the Most OUTRAGEOUS Response Boosters for <u>ALL</u> Your Offline and Online Marketing

In this chapter, I want to explore four elements of your OUTRAGEOUS marketing that will radically improve your response rates and conversions.

- Personalization
- Double readership paths
- Photos and illustrations
- CopyDoodles®

Personalization

They say that the sweetest sound a person can hear is the sound of their own name, and it's true—people love it when you use their name. Personalizing your marketing with something as simple as using the reader's name makes people pay attention.

Here's an example of something any business can do: a personal offer to celebrate a loyal customer's birthday.

Notice that it's not just a birthday card made out to the customer—their name is printed on the front, where they'll see it immediately, and there's a special offer designed to make the customer come back in to claim it. When Jenny gets this card, she realizes it's specific to her and she's going to pay attention to it.

Double Readership Paths

Most documents are designed to be read in a very linear fashion: you start at the top, and you continue reading until you reach the bottom. And that's how people read, but ONLY if they know they're interested in something. What do they do before that? They scan the document to see if they want to read it.

That's where the double readership path comes in.

Most writers leave it to chance what the reader will pay attention to when they scan. But you're not most writers. You're an OUT-RAGEOUS marketer, so you're going to take control of what the reader scans.

Look at this letter. Where does your eye go naturally?

Most people will look first at the puzzle piece (it's a real one, not a picture)

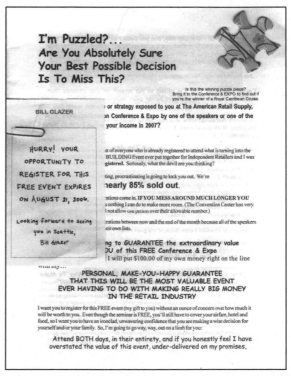

stuck to the top right-hand corner of the letter[1].

Next, your eye will probably go to the big, bold headline just to the left of the puzzle piece, especially as it starts with "I'm <u>puzzled?</u>" The whole thing—the puzzle piece and the headline—is designed to make you curious. To make you want to keep reading.

Your eye also goes naturally to the yellow sticky pinned to the letter, which has the offer and the deadline on it. See? We've already covered the three critical elements of Thing #2, and you've only just picked up the letter!

After that, your eye starts to scan anything that stands out from the sea of text. It goes to the text in bold, or the text in ALL CAPITALS, or the text that's bigger, or smaller, or in a different font. And every one of those pieces of text that has been formatted differently has been picked deliberately. It's either part of the offer, a guarantee, or it's handling an objection.

All those changes of format also create visual interest, so even before they start to scan, the reader is going to look at it and think, "What's this all about?" Then, when they scan it, they quickly think, "I see what it is. I want to find out more about it." And they go back to read the whole thing.

So as you write your marketing, ask yourself: what specific parts of this text would I want someone to read, even if they completely ignored everything else on the page?

Use Photos and Illustrations to Tell Your Story

A lot of what we're doing with these OUTRAGEOUS techniques is simply about getting the reader to stay with us, to take the next small step.

---

[1]By the way, if you are going to send something like that with a letter, you should always stick it to the paper, even though it may cost a few cents more. If you just put it loose in the envelope, it can drop out or get left in the envelope, in which case you might as well not have bothered.

We are constantly building curiosity, making people want to know more, and pictures can help us do this.

This is an ad from my days in menswear—yes, that's me doing my best impersonation of Clark Kent.

When you pick it up, the first thing you notice—even before you read any of the text—is the picture, and you have to wonder, "Who is this guy, and why is he wearing a Superman outfit? I need to find out more."

CopyDoodles Bring Oodles of Responses!

Throughout the examples in this book, you'll notice lots of text and lines on the marketing pieces that look like they've been hand drawn. They are there because they make your OUTRAGEOUS marketing even more successful.

Some years ago, Mike Capuzzi—a member of one of my mastermind groups at the time—noticed that every time he included these doodles on his direct response marketing pieces, his response rate and conversions went up.

The other members of the group begged him to share his doodles with them, so he created a software platform that allows you to customize and download all sorts of notes, arrows, lines, shapes, buttons—even your own comics—or create a custom doodle from scratch with your own text.

Just by adding CopyDoodles to this page, Curtis Mock increased his response from 13.75% (11 purchases) to 40% (102 purchases):

I use CopyDoodles in every piece of marketing I send out. If you want to try them out in your own marketing, you can get access at www.CopyEnhacements.com.

Using OUTRAGEOUS Free <u>Premium</u> <u>Gifts</u> in <u>ALL</u> Your Offline and Online Marketing

Everyone loves getting something for nothing. In my experience, giving away a premium—a free gift in exchange for taking some sort of action—typically increases response rates by as much as 30%.

A premium is usually either something you give your prospect just for responding, or something they get as a reward for having bought something else.

One twist that I've found makes premiums even more effective is to offer people a choice of gifts. Here is an example from a sales letter I wrote for one of my clients, a bank offering business accounts.

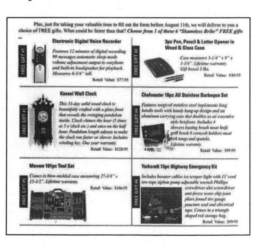

The reason why offering a choice of gifts works so well is because it changes the decision. It's no longer a matter of "do I want this gift enough to respond/buy?" Instead, the question instinctively becomes, "Which of these gifts do I want most?" By the time the reader has decided which of the gifts they *really* want, they're a lot more hooked and invested in the decision. They've put a lot of time and energy into making that choice, so it doesn't then make sense for them not to respond at all!

Celebrating Holidays & Special Occasions OUTRAGEOUSLY in <u>ALL</u> Your Offline and Online Marketing

Don't you just love holidays? How long do you spend thinking about Thanksgiving, or Valentine's Day, or Hanukkah?[2]

Most people spend *weeks* planning for and anticipating holidays. This is great for us OUTRAGEOUS marketers because we can outrageously hijack all that attention your prospects are putting into the holiday and refocus it onto our CAMPAIGNS.

And they'll respond because they're already in "the Christmas spirit" (or whatever) and the holiday is already on their mind.

In the US, the top four holidays when it comes to response, are:

1. Christmas
2. Halloween
3. Valentine's Day
4. Mother's Day

You'll see examples of holiday-based CAMPAIGNS later in the book, and you can also find many more examples—and a list of hundreds of holidays—in my book *OUTRAGEOUS Advertising That's Outrageously Successful.*

---

[2] That's a very US-centric list, but every country has celebrations throughout the year that people look forward to.

THING 7

Offline vs. Online: <u>Which Works Better</u> for Your OUTRAGEOUS Marketing?

Let me save you some time. Forget about deciding whether to implement online or offline marketing campaigns. In today's world, you need both.

Most of the CAMPAIGNS you'll see in this book work so OUTRAGEOUSLY well because they combine online and offline steps. You might start with a direct mail piece, then follow up with an email reminder if they haven't responded. Or an email followed by a telephone call. Or any combination.

The point is that different people prefer different ways of communicating, and if someone doesn't respond to contact in one channel, they may respond to another. Audiences are getting more sophisticated. People have become blind to ads on a website. They ignore emails from addresses they don't recognize and screen incoming calls. If you stick to one single way of communicating, you could be missing out on a large part of your potential audience.

For example, a postcard is much more likely to get seen than an email, but by doing both, you increase your chances of getting your message seen. One of my clients works with hair salons and restaurants to grow his business. He'll send a postcard and, soon after, send an email with a photograph of the postcard and a message like "Don't forget, this offer ends at the end of this month—if you don't hurry up, you will lose out. So come on back in!" By doing a combination of both, he doubled the response rate to his CAMPAIGNS.

In Parts Three and Four of this book, you'll find 49 campaigns that use many different media, spanning both online and offline. I want you to pay attention to how they are used and combined, especially if there's a media that you're not currently using in your own marketing.

Here is a list of just some of the ways of communicating with leads that you'll see covered:

1. Advertorials
2. Affiliate marketing
3. Awards ceremonies
4. Contests and prize draws
5. CopyDoodles®
6. Coupons
7. Cross-selling to current clients
8. Customer appreciation events
9. Customer testimonials
10. Direct mail: 3D mail
11. Direct mail: postcards
12. Direct mail: sales letters
13. Email marketing
14. Events/seminar: free
15. Events/seminar: paid
16. Every Door Direct Mail
17. Facebook ads
18. Joint ventures
19. Lead capture/squeeze pages
20. Magazine ads
21. Newsletters
22. Newspaper ads
23. Newspaper inserts
24. Pay-per-click ads
25. Pre-recorded dial-in messages
26. Radio ads
27. Referral contests
28. Sales pages
29. SMS/text messaging
30. Social media
31. Speaking at others' events
32. Special reports
33. Sponsoring a booth, breakout or meal at live events
34. Sponsoring a non-profit
35. Sponsoring an event
36. Telephone calls
37. Web TV shows/livecasts
38. Webinars/teleseminars
39. Writing a lead generation book

OUTRAGEOUS Works Everywhere— Even Your Business Card

If you've read my book *OUTRAGEOUS Advertising That's Outrageously Successful*, you've seen my business card. My OUTRAGEOUS business card looks like a folded $100 bill, and my offer is printed on the inside. I used this for my own business many years ago, and a lot of other people have copied it since then.

Here's another variation on the theme: an OUTRAGEOUS Wallet Mailer. It's an envelope printed back and front to look like a leather wallet. Inside the "wallet" is a coupon that looks like a banknote. I liked this idea so much, I used it to presell copies of this book before it was released! If you'd like your own wallet mailer, you can get them at walletmailer.com.

Understand that You Are NOT Your Customer

Over the years, one of the biggest objections I have gotten to OUTRA-GEOUS marketing ideas from business owners is, "I hate that. I'd never buy from that kind of marketing."

Well, guess what. I don't care whether you'd buy from it or not, and neither should you. What I care about—and what you should care about, too—is whether your *customers* will buy.

One of my most successful CAMPAIGNS ever—and one that many marketers have swiped and deployed ever since—was a five-page letter handwritten on yellow legal pad paper.

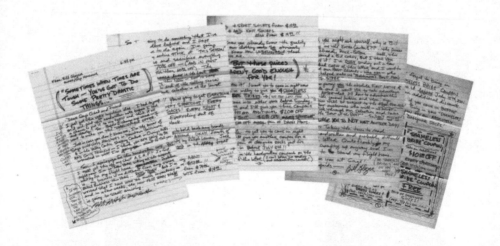

The letter looks like it was written spontaneously, with big letters and small, wildly drawn parentheses, things scratched out, and hand-drawn arrows pointing to a side note. It's the direct opposite of the carefully designed, beautifully laid out sales letters and brochures most companies think they should send. But, guess what? It made me a lot of money.

Since then, others have made a lot of money with their own versions. People used to send me copies of their CAMPAIGNS based on this letter—I've received over 100 variations over the years, and there are probably thousands that I've never seen.

The thing is, despite the "thrown together in a rush" appearance, the whole document was very carefully crafted.

Let's look at each page in turn.

Page 1: The OUTRAGEOUS Story Behind the Offer

Page 1 tells the story of why I am sending this letter, and why you need to read it right now.

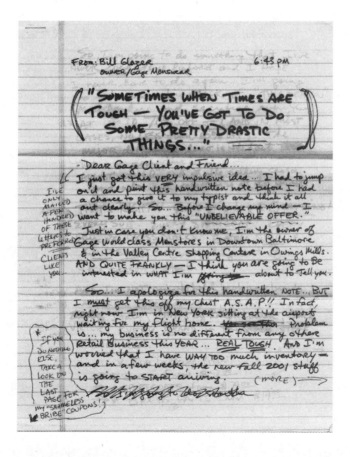

Notice how, even here, there's a double readership path, with text circled, or written in larger letters. If you saw the page in color, you'd notice that some of the text is in a different color, too.

Page 2: The OUTRAGEOUS Offer

Page 2 sets out the offer. It tells them exactly what I'm going to do for them.

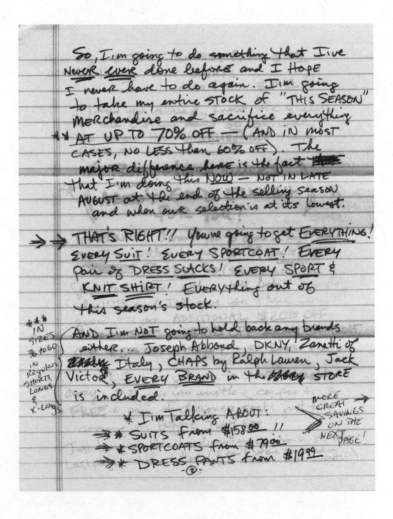

Page 3: Creating OUTRAGEOUS Deadlines and Urgency

Now that they know what the offer is, it's time to light a fire under them. Page 3 sets out the deadlines, with an extra gift for acting right away.

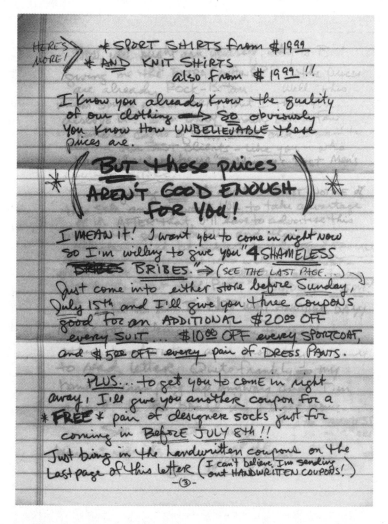

Again, notice how, even in a handwritten letter, we can create visual interest.

Page 4: The OUTRAGEOUS Personal Message

Now, one big tip with any offer and deadline is to have a reason why. People will accept all sorts of things as long as you give them a plausible explanation. On Page 4, I give them a personal message that they are my preferred customers. I point out that NOT everyone is getting these incredible savings—it's limited to my most important customers.

Now, you might ask yourself, why is Bill giving me the EXTRA COUPONS?? ...the prices are already ROCK-BOTTOM... well, this might sound a Bit CORNY, But I think you deserve it! I'm ONLY sending out a few hundred copies of this letter and I want to reward our BEST clients - like you - who have helped make us "Baltimore's Best Men's Clothing STORE."

I'm giving you the absolute FIRST NOTICE of this sale and I want YOU to take advantage of it. AFTER that, I'll have to advertise this sale to the general public and then, my selection will be subject to the FREE-FOR-ALL of regular customers who will — NO DOUBT — Pick through our selection and take HOME the "BEST of the BEST" ...So, DON'T MISS OUT!

* I URGE YOU TO NOT WAIT ANOTHER DAY!
Thanks for Taking the time to read this handwritten and probably difficult to read letter. Quite frankly, my hand is cramping up anyway and I'm about to board my flight home.

See you at Gage! (THE "SHAMELESS" BRIBES" ARE ON THE NEXT PAGE ⇒)
Warmest regards — Bill Glazer

-④-

Page 5: Shamelessly OUTRAGEOUS Coupons

Finally, on page five they get my "Shameless Bribe" Coupons with two separate deadlines.

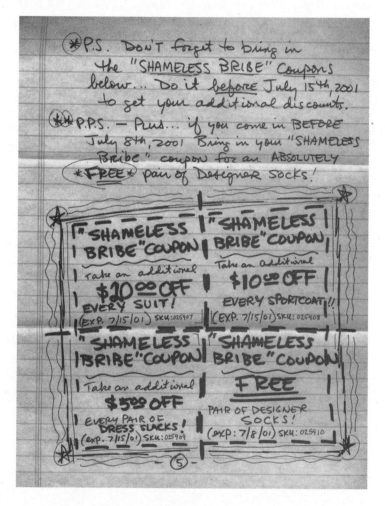

They can get $20, $10 and $5 off by coming in before July 15. BUT if they want their free designer socks, they have to come in by July 8. Why do I do that? Because now the decision isn't "Do I go in or not?" Instead, it's

"Do I go in before July 8 and get the free socks, or do I wait until July 15 and miss out?"

Also, there was a chance some people might get this and think, "There's no rush; I have two weeks." So, by giving them a second choice which was free, they would say, "I've got to make sure I am there by July 8th." Of course, while they're there picking up their free socks, they are going to look around and use the other coupons too.

Think of it as a mini takeaway—you give them lots of time, then you make them come in sooner.

The Results

How successful was this scrappy letter on legal paper? At the time when I ran it, I had a list of 42,000 customers, and I mailed that letter to all of them. Of the more than 180 CAMPAIGNS I created over the space of ten years for Gage Menswear, it got the highest response.

The men that letter brought in included CEOs, presidents of banks, accountants and attorneys—all sorts. Often, it was their wives who opened the mail, not the husbands, and I'd have men come in and say, "You know, my wife came over to me and showed me this. Usually, she throws these things away, but this one looked like it was important, so she brought it to me, and here I am!"

Later in this book, you'll see many variations on this CAMPAIGN that my clients are still running with great success.

The Three Piles of OUTRAGEOUS Advertising for ALL Your Offline and Online Marketing CAMPAIGNS

Most marketers think that when someone sees their ad or some other marketing piece, that person is thinking either "Yes, I want to buy" or "No, I don't want to buy." But there's actually a third response that most marketers forget about: *Maybe I want to get it, but I just don't want it right now.*

As I said in my book *OUTRAGEOUS Advertising That's Outrageously Successful*, the best way to think of this is to imagine people sorting their mail into three piles:

- "A" the YES pile – stuff they have to look at right now
- "B" the MAYBE pile – stuff that they might be interested in, but not right now, so they'll put it away for later.
- "C" the NO pile – stuff they're just not interested in.

So what?

Just because someone says "no," it doesn't mean that you're done with them. Even if they're not ready to buy now, or you're just not as important right now as something else, doesn't mean they won't be ready to buy later. But they're not going to remember you later if all you ever sent them was one mailer that they didn't respond to. You must continue to come back to them time after time.

Of course, if someone doesn't buy from you, you don't know whether they're a *No* or a *Maybe*, so you need to keep marketing to both. The only time you stop marketing to them is if they come back to you and say, "Please, will you just never talk to me again." Until that happens, continue to market to them.

PART TWO

Why Your Marketing Has to Be OUTRAGEOUSLY Multi-Step

What do you do when you want new customers? If you're like most business owners, you run an ad. Or you pick up the phone. Or you send a letter. Or an email. It's what we call 'one-shot' marketing: a single piece of marketing, often cold, designed to get a new customer right now.

And that's great. You'll get new customers out of it. In fact, my previous book OUTRAGEOUS *Advertising That's Outrageously Successful* explained in detail exactly how to do that kind of marketing: Do something OUTRA-GEOUS, get customers. Do something else OUTRAGEOUS, get some more customers. And each time you need some customers you just go out and do "something."

But what if I told you that creating a multi-step marketing CAMPAIGN will get you even more customers?

In this book, I want to show you how to take your marketing to the next level. You see, I want you to stop thinking in terms of sending emails and running ads. Instead, I want you to take a more long-term view of business growth.

This is an approach that works in pretty much any industry. I am going to share DOZENS of OUTRAGEOUS marketing CAMPAIGNS from business owners just like you. In fact, the CAMPAIGNS in this OUTRA-GEOUS book will apply to ANYONE who is in one of the businesses listed here:

- A small business owner (of just about any kind)
- A service business owner (of just about any kind)
- A doctor, lawyer, and others in private practice (of just about any kind)

- A B2B manufacturer (of just about any kind)
- A small professional practice (of just about any kind)
- An author, speaker, or consultant (of just about any kind)
- An e-commerce or online internet marketer (of just about any kind)
- An information marketing business owner (of just about any kind)

And even if you don't think that you fit into one of the categories on the above list, the good news is that you'll still probably be able to use these CAMPAIGNS to increase your results, regardless of what you do.

Why One-Shot Marketing Leaves Money on the Table

Don't get me wrong. One-shot marketing is great. Many good businesses have been built on one-shot marketing. But I want something more for your business, just like you do. I don't want you to have a good business; I want you to have a GREAT business. And for that, one-shot marketing isn't going to be enough.

The problem is, not everyone responds immediately to one-shot marketing. How often have you bought something from someone you just met? Probably not many times. You probably prefer to get to know something about a seller before you buy from them. And the more you're going to spend, the more you want to know.

Your customers are just the same. Studies show it can take up to seven contacts before a customer gets comfortable enough to make a purchase.

Some people will be happy to buy on the first or second touch. That's why one-shot marketing gets results. But it leaves out the people who need a few more contacts before they buy. Multi-step marketing is key to reaching these people.

The 7 Steps to Apply
SUPER OUTRAGEOUS Marketing to Your
Own OUTRAGEOUS Business

Now that we've seen the ten critical components of OUTRAGEOUS multi-step marketing, and we understand why you need to make all your marketing multi-step, let's think about how we apply the components to your business.

There are seven basic steps involved.

1. Understand that **everything** you do to advertise and market your business can be OUTRAGEOUS.
2. Understand that you are NOT your customer.
3. Train your brain to look for ideas in "obvious" places.
4. Train your brain to look for ideas in "unobvious" places.
5. Study what's working outside your industry and S&D it.
6. EVERYTHING can be OUTRAGEOUS, including… YOU!
7. OUTRAGEOUS advertising is FUN and…it lets you make your business FUN too.

Step #1: Understand That **Everything** You Do to Advertise and Market Your Business Can Be OUTRAGEOUS.

Over the years, I've had people in all sorts of businesses tell me that this wouldn't work for them—*professionals*, especially, often worry that OUTRAGEOUS marketing isn't for them.

Here's the thing though. "OUTRAGEOUS" is relative. OUTRAGEOUS marketing works in any and every industry—I have thousands of clients who will testify to that—but every industry has its own way of being OUTRAGEOUS.

As you look through the CAMPAIGNS later in this book, some of them will look more OUTRAGEOUS than others. The chances are, the ones that look less OUTRAGEOUS are probably pretty "out there" for the industry that they're in. When no-one in your industry sends a personalized birthday greeting, being the only person who does is OUTRAGEOUS!

Find your own way of being OUTRAGEOUS. If handwritten letters aren't your style, then find something that is. The point is that it must be something that no one else in your industry is doing.

Step #2: Understand That You Are NOT Your Customer.

Remember, it doesn't matter whether you would respond to your marketing; what matters is whether your audience will.

Over the years, many business owners have said to me, "Well, I would never look at an ad like that," and I would tell them, "It's not a problem that you would never respond to that kind of ad: we don't need to worry about you. We just need to make sure the customers understand."

Step #3: Train Your Brain to Look for Ideas in "Obvious" Places.

When I spoke about Swipe & Deploy (S&D) above, I warned you not to copy from your direct competitors. That doesn't mean you can't look at what similar businesses are doing. For example, if you have a retail business, you should be thinking to yourself, "I see other retail stores doing this, so I should be doing this also." Those are the obvious places to look.

Step #4: Train Your Brain to Look for Ideas in "Unobvious" Places.

We don't have to restrict ourselves to looking at marketing CAM-PAIGNS for our inspiration. Things are happening all around you that can inspire a CAMPAIGN: news events, vacations, something your child did ("Here's a special offer to celebrate my child's first tooth."). Whatever happens in your life, ask yourself, "Would this be a good excuse to get in touch with my audience and make them an offer?"

Step #5: Study What's Working Outside Your Industry and S&D It

Following on from Step 4, if we are looking at the unobvious sources of inspiration for our marketing, it makes sense to also look at the successful CAMPAIGNS you see in other industries and adapt them for your own industry. OUTRAGEOUS marketing can often be moved from one industry to the next with terrific results.

The handwritten letter CAMPAIGN that I explained above, for example, was based on a CAMPAIGN my mentor Dan Kennedy created for a political candidate. That's as far removed from menswear as you can get. Later in this book you'll see a similar letter used in the financial services industry.

Step #6: EVERYTHING Can Be OUTRAGEOUS...Including YOU!

Another point to consider is whether you can make yourself OUTRA-GEOUS, too. You don't necessarily have to go to the extremes of dressing up in a Superman suit or donning a straightjacket (which I did for the cover of OUTRAGEOUS Advertising), but remember that you are part of your business's brand, so you can be just as OUTRAGEOUS as your marketing CAMPAIGNS.

Step: #7: OUTRAGEOUS Advertising is FUN, and It Lets You Make Your Business FUN Too

One of the biggest realizations I had when I started to look for OUTRAGEOUS marketing opportunities was that it made business fun. Looking for excuses to contact my customers, finding new ways to communicate and thinking up ways to *be* OUTRAGEOUS made marketing the most fun and enjoyable aspect of my business!

Now that you've seen how to build OUTRAGEOUS marketing into your business, let's see these principles at work in some real campaigns.

Bill Glazer | 1. Ben Glass | 2. Bent Hansen | 3. Dr. Brian Bergh | 4. Cessaly Hutchinson

5. Chip Kessler | 6. Clate Mask | 7. Craig Simpson | 8. Dan Cricks | 9. Darin Spindler

10. David Linton | 11. Dr. David Phelps | 12. Demetrios Tzortzis | 13. Doug Anderson | 14. Fred White

15. Gardners Mattress | 16. Howard Anderson | 17. Jack Turk | 18. Julie Boswell | 19. Keith Lee

20. Kevin carter | 21. Kim Walsh Phillips | 22. Lisa Haster | 23. Michael Thibault | 24. Mike Capuzzi

25. Mike Crow
26. Nina Hershberger
27. Richelle Shaw
28. Rob Cuesta
29. Robert Skrob

30. Rory Fatt
31. Dr. Scot Gray
32. Dr. Sean Tarpenning
33. Todd Brown
34. Tom Orent

35. Travis Lee
36. Bill Harrison
37. Bruce Hudson
38. Dr. Kelly Brown
39. Dustin Mathews

40. Ed Rush
41. AJ Mirabedini
42. Matt Bacak
43. Mike Koenigs
44. Oli Billson

45. Ron Seaver
46. Russell Brunson
47. Ryan Deiss
48. Shaun Buck
49. Yanik Silver

PART THREE

The "Simple" Campaigns

In this part of the book, you'll find 35 campaigns laid out step-by-step that are simple for any business to implement.

In general, they have fewer steps or use fewer media than the campaigns in Part Four. That makes them faster and easier to implement.

That doesn't however, mean that they aren't powerful. Or OUTRA-GEOUS. If you need to generate cash in a hurry, or you want to take advantage of an unexpected opportunity, chances are good that you'll find something in Part Three to help.

A Note on The Examples

In each campaign, I've included extracts from the emails, webpages, and other marketing materials that were used. I've shown them exactly as they went out, complete with all sorts of errors in spelling, punctuation, and grammar.

Even with those errors, however, these campaigns made the business owners a lot of money.

Remember that the next time you're agonizing over whether you've got a comma in exactly the right place, or whether you should write "who" or "whom"!

An OUTRAGEOUS Way to Get Clients by Staying in Touch Long After Your Competitors Have Given Up

I've known Ben Glass for many years, and he is a very smart marketer. When I purchased what was then still Kennedy Inner Circle (KIC) from Dan Kennedy, Ben was one of the first members I ever met. He's a perfect example of Thing 1 in action: a lawyer who is always looking for different kinds of marketing that other lawyers won't do.

The Campaign

The goal of this campaign is simply to get Virginians who have been in a car accident to call Ben's law firm and set an appointment.

The campaign is sent to people who visit Ben's site and fill out an online form to request a copy of his book *Five Deadly Sins That Can Wreck Your Injury Claim*. Over the course of a year, that's hundreds of people.

The campaign stands out in several ways. First, it's more focused on stories than most lawyer marketing. Second, by his own admission, Ben is happy to take shots at his own industry. Let's face it, the accident lawyer industry—or ambulance chasers as some call them—isn't the most admired or revered industry in the world. Ben isn't afraid of annoying other lawyers, or even the Virginia State Bar.

Step 1: Lead Generation

The book is promoted in several ways: Facebook ads, print ads, direct mail, video, and links on Ben's firm's home page and practice area pages.

On Ben's website, he does something more businesses should do—he segments his leads up front. On the top banner, there's a video with a simple question, "How can we best help you today?" Underneath are three choices to click, each corresponding to one of the main services the firm offers.

And of course, each choice has its own lead magnet offer. This campaign is the one for leads who have been injured in an accident.

Segmenting leads like that is an OUTRAGEOUSLY smart move, which allows Ben to make his marketing totally relevant to each lead.

But that's not the only smart thing on this page. If you look closely at the video, you'll see that the thumbnail has the question on it, so a visitor doesn't have to watch the video in order to figure out what to do.

Notice that the contact form is below the video. 99% of website contact forms have a heading that says something very close to "Contact us." It's appropriate, but very stiff and formal. Ben's is called "Tell us your story." This is much more inviting and, for someone who is going to have to talk about a legal action, a lot less intimidating.

Step 2: Follow-up

OK, really this isn't step 2, it's steps 2-11, because once a prospect requests a copy of Ben's book, they're sent a sequence of 10 emails:

1. Inside: Your Free Book and a Special Message
2. From My Family to Yours
3. Recorded Call? Beware of 3 Insurance Adjuster Tricks
4. When is a 1/3 legal fee too high?
5. We're Here to Help During this Tough Process
6. The RIGHT Way to Pay for Medical Bills after a Car Accident
7. How much is your car accident case actually worth?
8. Get Well Soon from the BenGlassLaw Family
9. What Happens if I Don't Hire an Attorney for My Accident Case?
10. One Decision That Can't Wait

The medium and long emails include videos, links to other resources, testimonials, and a P.S. All the emails include a call to action to get in touch with the office.

The key principles behind the campaign—and these are great to model for your own email campaigns; you just need to figure out what they look like for your business—are these:

- **Personal attainability**: Ben tells stories of people just like the reader, so they know they can get similar results themselves.

- **Appropriateness**: Ben wants them to know that it's normal and OK for them to go through this. That many people go through it every year, and that hiring a lawyer is simply the right thing to do in the circumstances.
- **Education**: The email sequence addresses the four most frequently asked questions about hiring an injury attorney.
- **Excitement**: The sequence communicates that Ben's firm is eager to help the reader, and gets them excited about getting back to normal life and being in control again.
- **Urgency**: The sequence emphasizes the negative consequences of not hiring a lawyer, or delaying taking action.
- **Reassurance**: Prospects may worry that they will be disappointed or embarrassed by the process, so the campaign is designed to allay their fears.

Let's look at some of the things Ben does in his emails.

Email 1 is the "delivery email" for the eBook. It has a strong educational component that explains what will happen next in a typical accident claim. It also introduces how Ben's firm can help at each stage of the process (with a couple of testimonials for social proof).

Email 2 is interesting. The focus is primarily on humanizing Ben. It talks about his family life, his hobbies, and his charitable interests—all illustrated with photos.

Subject: From My Family to Yours

In my experience, people don't care where you went to law school (William & Mary, for any members of the Tribe out there) and they also don't really care how long you've been in practice (34 years in my case, but many can boast more.) Ultimately, this doesn't help you figure out whether an attorney is the right fit for you, or even a good attorney at all.

Instead, I'd like to share with you a little bit about me as a person. As most folks know, I've got 9 beautiful kids, four of whom my wife Sandi and I adopted from China. I've launched a pastor, a soldier, and a lawyer into the world, but I've still got plenty of kiddos at home that I help get on the bus every morning.

In my spare time I like to run and I like to referee youth soccer matches. My marathon days are behind me, but officiating a U15 match on a hot Virginia Saturday is all the workout I need at this point in my career.

Part of my life is also dedicated to charity. My wife and I support Love Without Boundaries, which helps orphans in China get much needed medical procedures for problems like cleft palate. As you can probably tell, adoption is very close to my heart and I want to connect as many loving homes with orphaned children as possible.

But enough about me. What's most important to me right now is that YOU have the power to make the best decision you possibly can about your car accident case. The BenGlassLaw team and I are eager to talk to you about your problem, and we hope you feel inspired to give us a call and start the process.

Thank you for reaching out to receive my free book, and get well soon.

Ben Glass

(After that are two long testimonials – Thing 3)

By the end of this email, Ben is no longer this distant, aloof attorney, but someone human that you can relate to. That's the exact opposite of the approach most lawyers take in their marketing.

I particularly like how Ben says that people don't want to know where he went to school or how much experience he has, but then tells you where he went to school and how much experience he has!

Email 3 then tackles "the other side" and sets up some fear: the insurance adjusters are out to get you—even the one from your own insurance company!—and you need to watch out for the sneaky tricks they'll use. Of course, Ben has your back because he has an ex-adjuster on his team.

In email 4, Ben de-positions his competitors by discussing the "unreasonable" fees other attorneys charge for accident cases, in contrast to his lower fee. He also introduces another book he's written, "Get It Settled." (This is more authority positioning—if you're going to settle out of court, who better to help you than the person who literally wrote the book on it?)

The other emails continue in a similar vein: de-positioning alternatives to working with Ben's team, warning you about the dangers of trying to do things on your own, and connecting you to Ben and the firm.

The final email, number 10, is short: a final call to action to call the office (and more testimonials).

Subject: One Decision That Can't Wait

Hi Firstname,

In the interest of helping you make the best decision possible about your car accident case, we have to ask: have you made a decision yet about whether to hire an attorney? We were going through our records and wanted to confirm with you whether you've taken action yet or not. Please let us know by calling our office at 703-584-7277. Thank you as always for your time, and I hope you get well soon.

Ben Glass

(It ends with another long testimonial.)

One big thing to note is that none of the emails in this sequence have a deadline. One of the things Ben accuses his competitors of doing is applying unnecessary pressure to get a client to sign up with them, so it would be incongruent to apply pressure himself.

In total, the campaign takes 12 months. By then, as I said before, Ben is usually the only lawyer still getting in touch with these clients, and therefore the only one they're thinking of when they finally decide to hire an attorney.

Results

Over 2,300 copies of the book have been downloaded since Ben started running the campaign.

Many accident victims have a very long research process, and it often doesn't start immediately after the accident: it starts when the problems show up. Many of Ben's best clients come to him 6-12 months AFTER their car accident; long after every other attorney has given up on them. In other words, *Ben gets them because he's the only one marketing to them at that point.* It's positive proof why Thing 10 is so important: you must keep marketing to leads until they buy.

Why Is This a Great Campaign to Model?

Almost anyone can use this campaign model. It works really well because Ben has found the weaknesses in his industry and brings them out into the open. He is able to knock his competitors because this is a market where prospects are highly suspicious anyway.

It's a great campaign to model for industries in which people take a long time to make a purchase. This is common when the purchase involves either a high cost or there's a lot of emotion around the decision (in Ben's case, both apply!).

Staying in touch over a long period of time like this also works well when someone pulls out of the buying process (maybe they're not ready, or there's a change in their circumstances) but there's a chance they will come back to you in the future. So, ask your leads why they aren't buying, and if it sounds like they might consider options again in the future, put them into a long-term sequence like this.

Finally, if you're in an industry that's seen as cold, distant, stuffy, or in any other way unapproachable, it would be really smart to include an email like #2 in all your campaigns to help the prospect connect with you on a more personal level. Especially because your competitors will be doing their best to stay "on top."

An OUTRAGEOUS Way to Raise Cash When You're Expanding Your Business

I first met Bent Hansen through another client of mine, Rory Fatt. Bent is a member of Rory's Royalty Rewards® program, which you can read about elsewhere in this book. Bent owns a restaurant, Los Gringos Locos, in the Los Angeles suburbs. Since 2009, he has run a monthly subscription VIP program where every month, diners pay him money *whether they come to the restaurant or not.* In 2012, Bent was opening a new restaurant and needed cash to finish construction. To accomplish this, he created a new monthly program—The Founders Club—for people who weren't in his VIP program already.

The "Campaign"

I've put campaign in quotes in the heading because this is actually a single letter.

I know that I told you to think in terms of multi-step campaigns rather than just sending a single email or letter. But think of this as a step that can be added to a campaign you're already running. In this case, Bent sent it to people who had already received his campaigns for the VIP membership but hadn't bought.

The letter is four pages long—you can see it in full on the following pages. You'll notice some familiar themes—lots of different fonts and type sizes, CopyDoodles, coupons on the back page. If you haven't read it yet, go back to Thing 9 for a full explanation of why and how these letters work.

The sales letter starts like a newsletter. In fact, there is NOTHIING on the first page to suggest that anything is being sold. Bent is simply sharing exciting news—"the story" of why he's sending the letter and why you need to read it now. He explains that he is building a new restaurant, and lists all the benefits the new restaurant will offer customers.

Notice the very explicit instruction at the bottom of the page: "Keep reading and you'll find out." That simple line will ensure the reader carries on.

From the desk of
Bent Hansen, Owner, Los Gringos Locos

We're Almost Ready!!
You're going to want to read this...
After 15 years, we're almost done!!

For the past 15 years we've been collecting your comments about Los Gringos Locos and as we read them we wished there was a way for us to make all your suggestions come true.

We have finally done it!!

We've implemented the top 5 comments from the last 15 years into our new restaurant. You will simply love what we've done!

1) **WAY BETTER PARKING**
   Our parking has been a sore spot since we opened in 1996 but our new lot is HUGE!

2) **A BIGGER AND BETTER BAR** *all the painting I did... it's simply AMAZING - especially after*
   Yes, our old 4 seat bar is pretty cozy, but just not big enough - our new dedicated bar area with tables, booths and 4 flat screen TV's is simply GORGEOUS and you just might never want to leave. We've added draft beer and some fabulous new margarita flavors.

Owner, Bent Hansen is working to make sure you'll love the new Los Gringos Locos

3) **A PATIO**
   Almost weekly we get the commment that a patio sure would be nice - there is simply nothing better than eating Mexican food and drinking margaritas on a patio. We've got one now!!

4) **A BETTER TAKE OUT AREA** *feeding your family on the go just got SO EASY at Los Gringos*
   We know it was pretty hectic to get take out at our old place - but now we have a HUGE, DEDICATED take out area - getting food to go will be simple and EASY.

5) **A PRIVATE ROOM**
   Not very many restaurants have a private room any more and so we made sure that our private room is perfect for parties, meetings, team banquets and any other event you might think of - it also has its own A/V system to use for your event!

So, when are we moving?

keep reading and you will find out...

Pages two and three set out the offer: join the program for a single up-front payment of $500 and get a $60 voucher every month, plus $100 of free guacamole.

There are also, of course, some shameless bribes to make the offer irresistible.

We will be moving sometime next week (as soon as the ABC transfers our liquor license)but *you have the chance to experience our new restaurant before anyone else!*

You see, to celebrate our new restaurant I've decided to do something CRAZY! I mean, the chance to upgrade my restaurant and fulfill the most requested suggestions from the past 15 years calls for something drastic. As one of our best customers

I am going to make you this unbelievable offer.

I have decided to put together a simply AMAZING and once in a lifetime offer. The Los Gringos Locos Founding Membership Pack 2012.

This is what I'm going to do - for the next 10 months I will send you a $60 Los Gringos Locos gift card AND a certificate for a FREE World Famous Table-side Guacamole.   Yes, EVERY MONTH!!

 *I'm giving away the STORE!!*

THAT'S RIGHT!! I'm talking about you getting $600 in gift cards AND $100 in our famous guacamole for ONLY $500. That's over $200 in savings!!

This isn't some special gimmick gift card or certificate - these NEVER EXPIRE!! You could give these away as gifts, use them yourself in the restaurant, use them for catering or save them up and have one big grand bash in our private room!! How you use them is up to you - but one thing is for sure - you're saving a TON OF DOUGH!!

Thats a 40% return!! 40% ‖‖

BUT THIS OFFER ISN'T GOOD ENOUGH FOR YOU

I mean it!! As one of our best customers, I want you to come in right now and get the LGL FOUNDING MEMBER PACK - so I'm willing to give you 3 SHAMELESS BRIBES.

Just come in to Los Gringos before SATURDAY, January 21 and I'll give you these 3 PRICELESS additions to this deal of the year:

BRIBE #1   *This bribe alone is worth OVER $80!!!!*

FREE DINNER FOR 4

That's right! This Friday and Saturday (January 20th and 21st) I will host you and 3 friends at the NEW Los Gringos Locos - before we are open to the general public.

This **PRIVATE** event is ONLY for our Founding Members and requires a reservation to attend. This is over an $80 value because we are including our Tableside Guacamole, Margaritas and entrees for your party. *ALL FREE FOR FOUNDING MEMBERS!!*

BRIBE #2

FREE LOS GRINGOS LOCOS LIMITED EDITION TEE

During the first month of our opening we will be introducing a limited edition Los Gringos Locos tee - it's REALLY COOL and will have a VERY short run. These things will probably sell on ebay for hundreds after they run out. AS A MEMBER, YOU WILL GET ONE FOR FREE!

BRIBE #3   *This bribe is worth HUNDREDS!! Discounts on take out, Free Shirt Offers and much more...*

MONTHLY MEMBER-ONLY SPECIALS AND INSIDER OFFERS

I can't even begin to explain all these offers - they are simply priceless, but as a founding member you will have access to discounts, member only parties, special tastings and insider info only members will know about. This bribe is worth HUNDREDS! You will receive these offers EVERY MONTH with your $60 gift card and FREE World Famous Tableside Guacamole.

You might be asking yourself, why is Bent giving me EXTRA coupons - this is already an amazing deal - and well, this might sound a little corny, but I THINK YOU DESERVE IT! I'm ONLY sending out a few copies of this letter I because I want to reward our BEST customers - like you - who have helped make Los Gringos Locos La Canada's best Mexican restaurant and made our upcoming move to the AWESOME new restaurant possible.

This offer is NOT available to the general public.

I URGE YOU NOT TO WAIT ON THIS because I know that the reservations for this weekend's private dinner will fill up quickly and after that this bribe (Bribe #1 - Dinner for 4) will no longer be available. However, you will still be able to buy the VALUABLE Founding Membership.

See you at Los Gringos Locos and Happy Eating!

Bent Hansen

PS - This founding membership offer expires January 31 - but if you want Bribe #1 - you need to call or come in RIGHT AWAY!!

PSS - As an added bonus, bring this letter in and ask for your FREE GIFT!! I promise you will love it!! *Bring this letter in to Los Gringos Locos for a free gift!!! Free gift offer expires January 31, 2012*

Notice, in particular, the first bribe: a free dinner on a specific date. If you don't act right away, you'll lose out!

And finally, the fourth page is the coupons and the membership form.

LOS GRINGOS LOCOS FOUNDING MEMBER 2012

Complete the form with and bring it in. Please be sure to include a valid e-mail address or 2
in case we have any super-special last minute Founding Member-only offers.

NAME: _____

ADDRESS: _____

CITY, STATE, ZIP:_____

E-MAIL: _____

PHONE: _____

CELL PHONE:_____

BIRTHDAYS & NAMES:_____

ANNIVERSARY:_____

WILL YOU BE CELEBRATING ANY SPECIAL EVENTS THIS YEAR? WHAT? WHEN?

(graduations, weddings, parties, etc.)

_____

_____

BRIBE #1
DINNER FOR 4!!

Come in and sign up for a Founding
Membership before January 21, 2012
and receive complimentary Dinner
for 4 at one of our Founding Member
Dinners

EVERYTHING IS INCLUDED:
Bar Drinks   Entress
World Famous Tableside Guacamole
expires JANUARY 21, 2012

BRIBE #3
MEMBER ONLY SPECIAL OFFERS!!

Really sweet and valuable
member-only discounts and
offers sent to you monthly.

Discounts on take out, Free
Shirts, member-only dinners
and tastings

expires JANUARY 31, 2012

BRIBE #2:   1 FREE Los Gringos
Locos Limited Edition Tee-Shirt
Come in and sign up for a Founding Member before January 31, 2012

Results

The campaign was sent to 400 top customers who had not yet joined the VIP program. It resulted in 84 members who made a total of 732 more visits to the restaurant than they did when they weren't members, spending $21,913 in addition to the $42,000 they had paid to join the Founders Club. That's almost $64,000 of additional income.

It worked so well that Bent ran it again in 2013. That year he added another bonus—a piece of the wall of the old restaurant. For a committed customer, that's a clever, unusual and desirable gift.

Why Is This a Great Campaign to Model?

This is a small but very powerful campaign, especially if you need to generate some money in a hurry.

It's also a great way to create predictable income in any business where there's no pattern or regularity to how people buy—you don't have to own a restaurant to make this work.

Bent's VIP program and the Founders program get people to return to his business every month. While they're using a free voucher, chances are good that they'll spend more than that. And of course, there's that big injection of cash up front when they join the program.

Another thing to notice about this campaign is that it's a good compromise for business owners who might not be comfortable with a handwritten letter. Here we have a printed letter, but with "handwritten" annotations (they're actually CopyDoodles).

Finally, it's interesting that you have to come into the restaurant to join. This is no accident. When you're there signing up, might as well have dinner! If your business allows for an instant sale like that, then getting the customer to come in to claim their offer is a great idea.

How to Convert Old Leads OUTRAGEOUSLY While You're on Vacation

Dr. Brian Bergh is an orthodontist. I first met him when he was a member of GKIC. He is one of the best people I know at creating newsletters. In fact, when I used to teach people about newsletters, I would tell them that he does some of the best stuff there is.

But this is not about a newsletter. By his own admission, Brian was inspired to create this campaign after reading my previous book, *Outrageous Advertising*. In it, I wrote about making money while I was on vacation, and thus the Cat's Away campaign was born.

The Campaign

The Cat's Away is a three-step mail campaign designed to be sent to people who have attended an orthodontic examination in the last three years but didn't move forward with treatment.

Typically, Dr. Bergh has 150-200 people on that list at any time, and his aim is to convert 6-10 prospects into active patients each time he runs the campaign.

Letter 1

The campaign starts with a letter on headed paper sent in a standard #10 envelope. The expectation is that, since these are people who have already met Dr. Bergh, a letter from his office is likely to go into the A pile (Thing 10), even after three years.

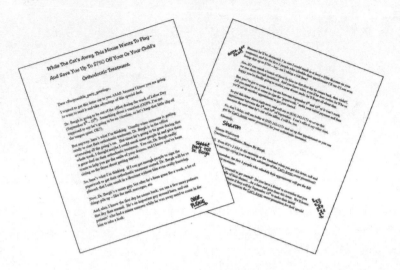

The letter is signed by Dr. Bergh's assistant and contains a discounted offer. The smart thing about this letter is the way the discount is presented. In effect, the reader is being invited to be a co-conspirator. The discount is supposedly being offered by the assistant without Dr. Bergh's knowledge. Dr. Bergh won't know what's happening *if* his assistant can keep him too busy with new patients to notice. The first three people get an extra discount ($750 discount rather than the $500 everyone else gets) to add a little urgency to the offer. However, you have to call and schedule your appointment within 24 hours. The letter also encourages the reader to share the offer with other people they know.

Letter 2

A week later, a second letter goes out in a brown paper bag. It immediately creates curiosity. After all, how often do you get a brown paper bag through the mail? Never. And if you did, wouldn't you notice it in the pile of unopened letters, pull it out, and probably open it before anything else? Of course you would. It's human nature.

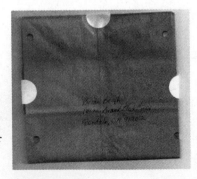

In this letter, the intrigue has developed. Four people have taken up the offer for the $750 discount, so it should be gone. But guess what? If you bring in some candy when you visit, Dr. Bergh will be so pleased, he won't mind if his assistant gives you the discount.

> I don't know if you know this or not, but Dr. Bergh just loves chocolate. So, I figured I could bribe him with some chocolate and not get in trouble for extending the $750 discount to you in addition to the other four people who already made the decision to get the smile of their dreams.
>
> You can still get the $500, no problem, as long as you schedule your appointment by September 10th. But if you still want the full $750 discount, I'm going to ask you to bring along some form of chocolate.

That, of course, is what the brown paper bag is for—to bring in your candy, because if it's not hidden in the bag, someone else will steal it before the doctor gets it. Notice how that brings you even deeper into the "conspiracy" that began in the first letter! It also changes the decision you are being asked to make. Without the candy, the question is *do I want the discount or not?* With it, the question is *do I want a $500 discount or $750?* Not buying is no longer an option.

Letter 3

Letter 3 goes out a week after Letter 2, and includes two candy bars. Of course, when you get the letter, you don't know what's inside. All you know is that there are some lumps in the package, and naturally, you want to know what they are. You have to open the letter. The candy is yet another twist to the campaign.

> The only other reasons I could think of are that you haven't had time to go get some chocolate, or that you aren't sure where to go get some chocolate. In either case, I've solved

> your problem, because I've included some chocolate with this letter.

Now you don't even need to buy candy for Dr. Bergh to get the discount. You'll get it by just bringing in the two candy bars. That takes away a key objection that might hold people back from responding to the offer.

The envelope has a further enhancement: a printed coffee stain (complete with a Copydoodle apology).

The stain is there, like the candy bars, to get you to open the letter. You see this envelope with something inside it, and it's got a stain. You have to ask yourself, *"What is this? This is unusual; I'd better open it up right away."*

Results

The first year Dr. Bergh ran it, the campaign generated a 64:1 ROI. Think about that. If you could spend $1 and get $64 back, how many dollars would you throw at that campaign?

Dr. Bergh has run the campaign once or twice a year for the last eight years, and the *lowest* ROI achieved has been 31:1. Even at that level, it's well worth the time and effort to send out those three letters!

Over that time, Brian has tested discounts against free value-added services, and the results are broadly the same.

Why Is This a Great Campaign to Model?

There are a few key details to pull out from this campaign that you could copy for your own marketing.

First, a letter from Dr. Bergh himself offering a $750 discount wouldn't be that outrageous; that's just business. What makes this campaign special is the idea that Dr. Bergh's assistant is supposedly orchestrating the whole thing behind his back while he is away on vacation, and asking the reader to be her accomplice.

Second, the three letters are full of CopyDoodles and red ink to make key phrases stand out. Using those as a guide, you could get the basic idea of the campaign in 30 seconds, just scanning the letter.

Third, each letter has three PSs. Most professionals wouldn't think of putting one PS on a letter, let alone three of them! However, many readers will look at the end of the letter before they start to read and, if they see three PSs, they will read those first. You can find out everything you need to know about the offer in thirty seconds just by reading those PSs.

Fourth, the candy is a brilliant addition. In the second letter, asking for candy gives a plausible reason for extending the $750 discount. In the third, sending the candy virtually forces you to open the letter to find out what's inside, and at the same time removes a key objection to taking action.

This is a simple campaign that requires very little setup. What do you need? A printer, some candy bars, and some brown paper bags.

Any business could run a campaign like this.

Dr. Bergh chose to use it with unconverted leads who had already met him, but it could also be used to follow up with people who had simply made an inquiry with your business. It could even work, though perhaps not with a 64:1 ROI, as a cold mailing.

Dr. Bergh sells to individuals, but this kind of campaign would also work if you sell to companies.

So, whatever your business, with a printer and some low-cost accessories, you could be converting leads OUTRAGEOUSLY!

An OUTRAGEOUS Way to Build Community Support for Your Cause

This entire book is about raising money for my favorite cause, so when I heard about Cessaly Hutchinson's campaign, I had to include it!

The campaign was set up in 1985 to make the neighborhoods of Oakland, CA, safe once more. At the time, Cessaly was a volunteer on the Resource and Support Council. Her partner in running the campaign was Stephanie Mann, the founder of Safe Kids Now National Network to keep kids safe in Oakland, CA (www.safekidsnow.com).

The Campaign

This was well before the age of email and internet, so the campaign was a good, old-fashioned mailing.

The campaign was built around a contest for local kids to design a poster on the theme of "Oakland – A Safe Place."

When you run a contest, what do you need? Prizes. And worthwhile prizes cost money, which the campaign didn't have. So Cessaly and Stephanie wrote letters to local businesses to request prizes. In exchange, donors would be mentioned on the invites to the awards ceremony, which would go to all the entrants and their families. To recruit judges, Cessaly made a presentation at Oakland art schools asking for volunteers.

Many local organizations jumped in, not only with prizes but even with food for the judges and for the various city officials and community religious leaders who were involved in the campaign. Prizes included plane tickets, a trip to Disney, a TV set, and two billboards on which the winning posters would be blown up and displayed.

The venue for the awards ceremony was provided free of charge, and the whole event was livened up by the late African American cartoonist Morrie Turner, who turned out (also for free) to draw caricatures of the kids (as well as Cessaly's!).

From Safety Campaign to Toy Drive

The campaign got very positive press coverage from the Oakland Tribune, so a few months later, in December 1985, the team decided to use a similar approach to organize a toy drive for local children. Once again, they got thousands of dollars' worth of brand new toys from local organizations.

It was so successful that in 1987, Cessaly—with the help of Stephanie and her friends—established the Oakland/Lamorinda Toy Campaign as a non-profit.

For the next 12 years, the group gathered donations of toys which they would take to the police department, which gave them space in the Community Services Division to store and wrap the toys. They carried on until about 1999, wrapping toys and gifts for children at the police department. Most touching was the sight of officers showing up of their own free will to wrap toys for the children. The campaign united Oakland's business, law enforcement, neighbors, political and grassroots organizations in an outpouring that was, to use Cessaly's own words, "just astonishing."

Results

These campaigns weren't about raising money. The first one was about getting prizes for a contest; the others were about getting toys for the toy drives.

Given the thousands of dollars' worth of value that the campaigns received each year, they were very successful.

Why Is This a Great Campaign to Model?

The key to the success of the campaigns, in each case, was tapping into community spirit and reaching out with a positive message.

Not every campaign has to be about money. And not every campaign has to involve hi-tech channels. If you have a cause that you need to get support for, a powerful hook and some letters may be all you need.

An OUTRAGEOUS Way to Make Six Figures Without Spending Any Money

I first met Chip Kessler when he was a GKIC member. He co-wrote a book with Dan Kennedy called *Make Them Believe*, and they created a product that went with it. They both presented it together at one of our live events.

But this campaign has nothing to do with that.

The Campaign

"The Active Shooter" is another of Chip's products—a DVD and a resource guide that sell for $219.97—that trains staff in nursing homes and assisted living facilities to identify armed gunmen who may be targeting their facility, and also prepares them to deal with the situation.

The whole product is about dying at the hands of a gunman, so it should be no surprise that the campaign is primarily fear-based, designed to scare the living daylights out of employees in those facilities to the point where they buy.

Lead Generation

Leads come from three main sources.

First, past buyers of other programs and services. A buyers list is one of the most valuable assets you have in your business: people who have already trusted you and given you money are the easiest people to convince they should invest in new offers.

Second, Chip has bought targeted mail and email lists from a list broker. The target market for this product is very specific and easily identifiable, so this is a situation in which buying a list makes great sense.

Third, Chip has a house list of prospects who have subscribed to his free monthly printed newsletter.

In total, some 5,600 people receive Chip's marketing communications regularly.

Communication

The campaign consists of sales letters and emails sent on a regular basis. In addition, every order shipped to a customer for other products includes a printed copy of the sales letter.

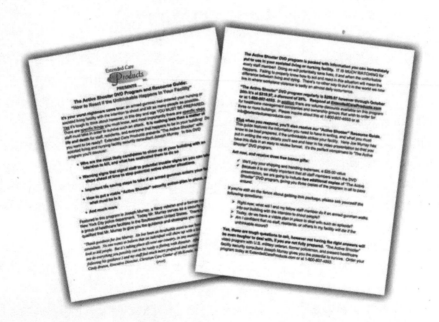

Every four weeks, prospects get two emails. In addition, notifications and ads are placed in the print newsletter which goes out every two months.

The marketing focuses on the credentials of the "star" of the product, a former NYC police officer who was trained to deal with gunmen by the Department of Homeland Security.

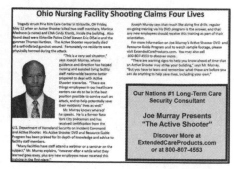

All those campaigns drive traffic to an expanded sales letter on the company's website with sample clips from the product and new footage from an actual attack (to create more fear!).

Results

To date, Chip has sold hundreds of copies of the program to long-term care facilities nationwide (he asked me not to share the specifics). Sadly, there are regular upturns in sales every time there's a mass shooting.

Why Is This a Great Campaign to Model?

This is a simple campaign that generates a six-figure income for very little outlay—the newsletter is being mailed anyway, as are the orders. The only real investment is buying mailing lists from a broker.

The real key to making this campaign work is having other products to sell. A buyer is a buyer is a buyer. They're interested in what you do, and they've already trusted you enough to pay. Each time someone buys something from you, you just put a sales letter for something else in the box. It costs you nothing and keeps bringing money in.

Amazon has made millions that way, and so have many other businesses. Why shouldn't you?

An OUTRAGEOUS Way to Get People to Return Your Sales Call

Back when I bought GKIC from Dan Kennedy, I knew that if we were going to maximize our profits, we needed a proper system to manage our customers and leads. I looked at various alternatives and settled on an (at the time) new and relatively unknown product called Infusionsoft. In fact, GKIC was Infusionsoft's fifth ever customer!

After I started using Infusionsoft, I realized it was something all our members needed too. I invited Infusionsoft CEO Clate Mask and his team to present at all our live events. As a result, in the early years of Infusionsoft, around half of their customers came through GKIC. Nowadays, that's no longer the case, and they've become a leading player in the marketing automation industry.

Clate was never a client of GKIC, but he would often ask me for advice on how to get more customers. He was also part of a secret group I helped create of hand-picked marketers—myself, Bill Harrison, Perry Marshall and a couple of others whose names you would recognize—that would meet three times a year.

The Campaign

If you engage prospects on the phone, then at some point you've probably been in a situation where you couldn't get hold of them. They never pick up, you start a game of telephone tag, or you just have the wrong number altogether. However it happens, it's annoying for whoever is doing the follow-up, and it costs you money.

This campaign addresses that problem.

Lead Scoring

Think about how much money you waste every day following up leads who aren't that engaged—especially if you have an outbound sales team. How much would you save if your sales team could cherry-pick only the leads who are most engaged with your marketing?

Infusionsoft has implemented a system called lead scoring. In simple terms, their system tracks everything a lead is doing—watching videos, clicking links, commenting, etc.—and allocates a score based on that. When someone accumulates enough points, the system notifies the lead development team, and they jump on the phone.

In an ideal world, the lead would pick up immediately, they would have a great conversation, and the lead development team would pass them on to the sales team.

That's in an ideal world. But what if you can't get hold of the lead? The whole process breaks down. So, it's critical that you get them on the phone.

Using Video to Connect on a Deeper Level

When they have trouble getting hold of a prospect or a customer, most companies send a bland email saying something like, "Sorry we missed you. Please call us back at your convenience."

That wasn't good enough for Clate, so Infusionsoft created three short videos (one for each way the connection could fail) designed to make the lead laugh and get them to pick up the phone.

- "Wrong Number" – the phone number on file is incorrect.
- "MIA" – the lead doesn't answer the phone.
- "Phone tag" – the lead is interested, but the Infusionsoft team is caught in a game of "telephone tag" with them.

You can see all three videos in a blog post by Infusionsoft at:
https://wistia.com/blog/infusionsoft-video-lead-nurturing

The videos are each 30-60 seconds long and use humor to get the lead to call back. For example, the MIA video features the team all standing around a phone rep at his desk, ready to celebrate getting through, and being very disappointed when he announces he couldn't get through. It's an OUTRAGEOUS way to deal with a tricky situation.

There's a fourth video ("Has Anything Changed?") designed to bring back a customer who is closing down their account. It features a forlorn team member waiting wistfully for the phone to ring.

You can watch the fourth video here:
https://infusionsoft.wistia.com/medias/fjws2ipayh

Getting the Video to the Customer

Each of the videos is embedded in an email that is sent to the customer as soon as the lead development agent registers the fact that they're having trouble getting in touch.

Here's the email for the phone tag video:

```
Subject line: Are you there?
Hi [contact's name],
I'm not sure what happened, but it looks like we aren't
quite able to connect. Feels a little like this video
(http://pages.infusionsoft.com/Phone-Tag.html) our team
made—check it out for a quick laugh.
What would be the best way to continue to follow up with
you? As always, I'm available for any questions you have—
let me know if you would like to connect for a quick call.
Have a great day!
```

Why Is This a Great Campaign to Model?

This is a simple but OUTRAGEOUSLY clever campaign idea that would work for any business that relies on speaking to prospects on the phone as part of the sales or marketing process.

A dental office could use videos like these when it's time to remind people about their next appointment, or a financial planner could use them when it's time for the next review. Similarly, many subscription businesses call their customers at the end of the subscription period, and these sorts of videos would work for them too.

Let's face it: if you regularly find yourself chasing prospects to talk to them on the phone, then this is a great way to get them to talk to you.

Many of the campaigns in this book have steps that involve a phone call to the prospect. These videos could be added to any of those campaigns to increase the call-back rate.

How to Reactivate Past Clients OUTRAGEOUSLY

Craig Simpson helps his clients run multi-step mail campaigns to acquire new customers or reactivate old ones. He manages the mailings from A to Z, taking care of every step of the campaign.

The campaign below is one that he created for one of those clients, US Chart Company. US Chart Company trains people in how to trade the commodities markets, then offers a subscription service to provide them with the up-to-date data they need each month to implement the strategies they've learned.

This is a customer reactivation campaign. The objective is to get customers who have allowed their subscription to lapse back onto a monthly plan.

The Campaign

Craig and US Chart have used this campaign twice a year for the last five years. It goes out to approximately 15,000 expired customers. Over a period of two months, they get a sequence of both physical mail and email.

Letter 1

The first piece of direct mail is a 16-page sales letter, folded and stapled into a brochure. I'm not going to put the whole letter in this book, but here are some highlights.

Let's start with the front page. There's not a lot of text on that first page. Instead, most of the page is used to set up a double readership path:

1. The massive headline gives a very strong instruction: "Claim Your Second Chance for First Class Wealth!"
2. Below that, a subheading teases the offer: rejoin for just $1.
3. A big, bold picture of a DVD case and two discs draws your attention to a time-limited bonus if you respond.
4. The arrow top right is there to get you to turn the page and keep reading.

Later in the letter, after reconnecting the reader to all the reasons why they signed up in the first place and setting out the offer in full, there are two pages filled with nothing but testimonials

After that, the letter restates all the reasons why you might want to be back in the system and summarizes the offer again.

Finally, the letter introduces the bonuses and the call to action.

There are a few things worth pointing out about this letter.

First, there's a lot of visual interest: Lots of graphics, font changes, callout boxes, sidebars, colored text, etc.

Second, this is a long sales letter. Craig is trying to convince these people to spend $1. But the letter isn't just about getting them to spend $1; it's about making sure they'll also want to stay on the monthly plan afterward.

Plus, once someone is in the monthly program, they are likely to buy other products and services, at a higher price point, so the value of a customer goes up exponentially.

Third, notice that Craig doesn't assume they'll remember what it was like to be in the program. In the brochure, he repeats every feature and benefit of membership, with screenshots of the software systems and information they'll get. Just because someone has been a customer in the past doesn't mean they'll remember how great it was to work with you. If you want to reactivate a past client, it's a good idea to get them connected to that past experience again.

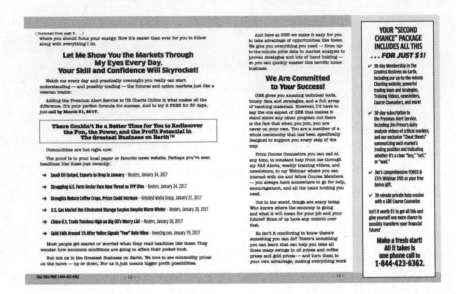

Letter 2

The second letter is shorter: just four pages in a folded brochure format (I've only shown the outer two pages). Again, it's visually attention-grabbing, with a dual readership path.

Letter 3

The biggest spike in renewals comes with the third letter, which takes a much more intimate, personal approach. Gone are the flashy graphics and headlines. Instead, it's a two-page "handwritten" letter on lined yellow paper restating the offer, just like the one in Thing 9.

Interestingly, because this letter gives the highest response, Craig tested starting the campaign with it rather than the glossy printed letters. Surprisingly, it didn't work as well, which just goes to show how important it is to keep innovating, testing, and tracking your results.

Instead, what worked best was extending the deadline in this "personal note" format midway through the campaign.

Step 4: Postcard

The final mailing is a simple postcard. The style, again, is personal and handwritten. On the back are a mini handwritten letter with a very brief offer, a call to action, and a deadline.

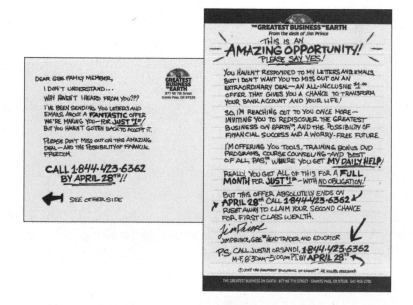

The Email Campaign

Alongside the four letters are four emails with text and video which motivate the reader to respond to the letters they're receiving.

Results

This is quite an intricate campaign. By Craig's own admission, there's a lot of planning and coordination behind the scenes, but the payoff for running a congruent offline and online campaign together is enormous.

Every time the campaign is run, there's a 3.95% renewal rate. From a list of 15,000 expired customers, that's just under 600 renewals, at $79/month. That comes to $187,000 each month and, on average, those customers stay at least five months.

Why Is This a Great Campaign to Model?

This is a campaign that would work for any business that is running a subscription model. In almost any business, the hardest dollar to make is the first. In other words, it's much easier to sell to someone who has already bought from you than it is to get a total stranger to make their first purchase. So, it's often easier (and cheaper) to bring past subscribers back into your program than to attract new subscribers.

Customer churn—customers not renewing—is a major revenue drain for subscription businesses, and yet most businesses are happy to let their subscribers ride off into the sunset, never to be seen again. When you've paid good marketing dollars to get those subscribers in the first place, that's an awful waste.

One really neat feature of this campaign is the switch from formal to informal. A campaign like Craig's might start with a glossy brochure or letter, with lots of OUTRAGEOUS marketing features built in. Then, as the campaign progresses, become less formal and more personal.

An OUTRAGEOUS Thing to Do with a Halloween Pumpkin!

I first met Dan Cricks when he was a member of GKIC. He owned an auto repair shop and started to teach other auto repair shops how to grow their business. He joined one of my mastermind groups for a couple of years, and for many years he has run a GKIC local group in Cleveland.

This campaign is one he designed for his bricks-and-mortar clients to tie into Halloween (Thing 6).

The Campaign

The campaign is a very simple one based on an old game you've probably seen at a state fair. In this case, it's a contest to guess the weight of a pumpkin, but people have been guessing how many pieces of candy are in a jar, the weight of a pumpkin, turkey, cake, or another food item—and many other variants on the theme—for centuries.

It's an interactive campaign that customers, along with their friends and families, can participate in. It appeals to a very broad range of people, mostly because there's no great skill required, no equipment to buy, and it takes moments to take part.

For the business owner, the goal is simply to get people through the door, build up customer interest, collect emails, and keep the business top of mind with their customers and prospects.

Lead Generation

Leads for the campaign come from the customer database and social media.

Step-by-Step

1. The business gets a large pumpkin and sets up a contest to guess how much it weighs.
2. Marketing material is produced to promote the contest and to explain how it works. The campaign for the promotion uses every media at the business's disposal.
3. The customer/prospect gives their email address when they enter. No purchase is required.
4. At the end of October, the winner (the person who guessed closest to the actual weight) is notified via email. Usually, there is a grand prize and prizes for 2nd and 3rd place.

Subject line: And The Winner of the Fitbit is…

<First Name>,

We weighed the giant pumpkin and it came in at 151 lbs.

Our winner guessed 150 lbs. and the winner is Lori _____ . Congratulations.

The second-place winner of the gift basket donated by _____ was Joe _____ .

The third-place winner of a Starbucks gift card was Melanie _____ .

We want to thank everyone who entered and helped us have fun again this year with our guess the weight of the pumpkin contest.

Gregg

---

5. Prize winners' names and (ideally) photos are also shared on any media the business has available. Newsletters, email, social media—some clients even use chalkboards by the door.

Because email is used to contact winners, contestants are happy to hand over their email address, unlike most campaigns!

The prizes don't have to be extravagant. For Halloween 2017, many of Dan's clients offered Fitbits as the top prize. Some of Dan's clients get other local businesses to contribute prizes or gift cards in return for free publicity. That has the added advantage that those businesses will then also promote the contest to their own customers.

Universal Appeal

Many business owners wonder how to appeal to millennials. The irony is, this campaign—as 'old school' as it is—is loved by all ages, including millennials. It also engages employees because it's a fun, funny campaign that's easy to bring into the conversation—assuming the customer doesn't bring it up themselves (after all, wouldn't you ask about the giant pumpkin by the door? I know I would!).

And, because the campaign ties into the conversations people are already having about one of the most popular holidays of the year—Halloween—it's very social media friendly and gets a lot of shares. Many of Dan's clients reach 2,000-5,000 people or more through social media.

Results

The campaign has been highly successful for every client Dan has run it with. His clients often rerun the campaign year after year. It's often the most popular campaign they run—their customers love it and will start asking about the pumpkin in August and September—and October is often the most profitable month of the year for those businesses thanks to the contest.

Why Is This a Great Campaign to Model?

Despite its simplicity, there's a lot to love about this campaign.

It creates massive customer engagement, improves their customer experience and gives them a reason to visit the business. It also portrays the business as a fun place to spend money.

An OUTRAGEOUS Way to Get Customers by Mastering the Postal Service

Darin Spindler was a GKIC member when I still owned the company. He has always been a hard worker and back then, he was just launching a business called Kids Bowl Free. Today, ten years later, there are over 1,400 participating bowling centers, and more than 25 million kids have been through the program.

That's not the focus of this campaign, however. Darin has also helped many other businesses to launch, and one of those is a brick-and-mortar pizza restaurant. This campaign was created to attract customers when the restaurant opened.

The Campaign

Darin wanted to introduce the new restaurant to as many customers as possible, so he ran a 'BOGO' (Buy One, Get One) offer to get people interested. What's so OUTRAGEOUS about that? After all, you probably get BOGOs from Domino's every week.

The first difference was in how the offer was presented. Most restaurants would create a trifold brochure, with full-color photos of the food and a menu listing.

Instead, Darin created a long-form sales letter to share the story of the restaurant, the food, and the décor. Not a single photo of a pizza in sight. Instead, Darin used drawings and call-out boxes to create a double readership path. It's an OUTRAGEOUS sales letter, not like anything else people are getting through their door!

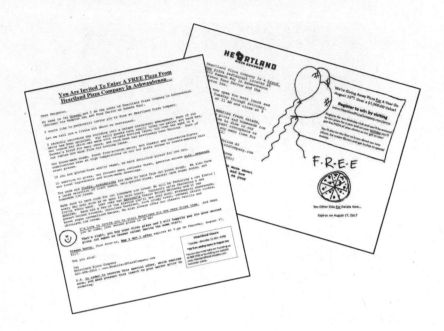

The second difference was in how the offer was delivered.

You can waste a lot of money in marketing by not targeting your campaigns properly. For a new restaurant, it could be tempting to put a flyer in the local paper and have it delivered to everyone in town, hoping to draw as many people as possible. But why would someone drive all the way across town, past a dozen established pizza restaurants, to go to one they'd never heard of? They wouldn't. So, it pays to start local and expand your reach once you've figured out what's working. In the meantime, you can let your customers spread the word for you.

Very sensibly, Darin decided to focus the initial campaign on a tight 2-mile radius around the restaurant. Using the USPS website, he selected specific postal routes that he wanted his campaign delivered to. Then, he sorted those routes, from the most to the least affluent. Finally, he had the mailers delivered by Every Door Direct Mail.

To make it easier to track the results of the campaign, the flyers for different neighborhoods were printed on different colored paper.

That way, when a diner came in to claim their offer, you could see immediately where they came from. And at the end of the campaign, you only had to count how many flyers there were of each color to figure out which were the most responsive neighborhoods. Match that up to the cost of each route (like Darin did), and you can figure out which are the most profitable neighborhoods to target for future campaigns!

Something that Dan Kennedy and I have taught for a long time is that if something works in one media, you should try it in another media as well.

Having found a campaign that worked, Darin put the same flyers into a small community newspaper (4,000 inserts) and also into the larger local newspaper, but only for the zones closest to the restaurant (another 12,000 inserts).

Of course, this is a multi-step campaign, so it doesn't end with the redemption. After each new customer redeems the offer, they are offered an instant bounce back to be used in the next 21 days, along with a call to action to join the restaurant's birthday club (a great excuse to get their contact information).

Results

The campaign was OUTRAGEOUSLY successful: one promotion brought in 107 new families for a return of nearly $24 net for every $1 invested!

In total, Darin invested $1,850 and generated $15,627 in net revenue from 518 redemptions—that's an average ROI of 844%, and over 1,000 new customers have visited the restaurant.

Of course, having made the campaign work in two media, Darin didn't stop there. Using Facebook ads, direct mail, newspaper inserts and the bounce back coupons, Darin grew the restaurant's email, mail and texting list to more than 2,400 contacts in just ten weeks, and they send that list offers every week.

Each week they send a weekly email newsletter, and they introduce other aspects of OUTRAGEOUS marketing. For example, on Green Bay Packer game day, they sent out a text with a last-minute coupon code that generated ten orders the first time it was sent.

Why Is This a Great Campaign to Model?

If you run a business that sells to local customers, you should be running a campaign like this. It is OUTRAGEOUSLY simple, and even the tracking has been made simple by using color-coded paper for the flyers.

Even if you don't run a campaign exactly like this one, I'd like you to take away one big lesson. When you find a campaign that works OUTRA-GEOUSLY well in one media, look for other media that it will work in.

How to Create an OUTRAGEOUS 172% Increase in Sales with Your Own Soap Opera

David Linton was a client of mine. He is the owner of Everlast® Epoxy Systems, a company that sells epoxy floors for commercial applications. Like many high-ticket business-to-business sales, their sales cycle is long—typically, 91 days—and prospects are usually evaluating proposals from several competitors. While you might think a long sales cycle is a problem, it's actually a great opportunity. It gives savvy sellers the time to educate the prospect on why they should buy their product or service rather than the competition's. Everlast Epoxy's products are often one of the more expensive options the prospect is evaluating, so they can't sell on price. Instead, David very wisely uses the long sales cycle to educate the buyer.

The Campaign

Leads for the campaign come from pay-per-click ads and cold traffic generated by search engine optimization. There's an opt-in form on the company's site to request the free report *Why Floors Fail.*

Before David built this campaign, the leads would be followed up a couple of times by phone. If the sales team got through, they would mail them a printed booklet and some flooring samples.

When David got a copy of my first book *OUTRAGEOUS Advertising That's Outrageously Successful,* he realized that there was nothing very OUTRAGEOUS about the campaign. So he scrapped it and created a series of 22 emails delivered over 90 days.

That's an OUTRAGEOUSLY brave move.

David needed to keep the buyer engaged as they researched and compared all the available options, which can be a lengthy process. He knew that if the emails were boring or salesy, they'd end up getting deleted—and this is about epoxy floors, so you can imagine how boring those emails could get!

To keep things interesting and entertaining, David started each email with a cartoon that highlighted a benefit of the product in a fun way, and the text told an ongoing story of a competition between two facility managers. Each email picked up the story from the last—like a soap opera—so the reader would be eagerly waiting for the next email.

After the cartoon and story, each email contained multimedia content, such as testimonial videos filmed at a customer's facility, or a link to a radio interview produced by GKIC member John Melley.

Who will win, David?

Will it be Jonah with his Easy-To-Clean Everlast Floor?

Or will it be Norbert, who seems to be falling behind already with some difficult scrubbing?

Stay tuned and try to be surprised when Jonah uses his unfair advantage to wipe the floor with his opponent!

I can tell you that installing Everlast Floor really is A LOT of fun. But I'm not as fond of cleaning floors. Kinda like it is fun to cook, but cleaning afterward - not so much.

Lucky for you - you can have a floor that is fun to install AND spend LESS time nightly doing the unfun cleaning. With Everlast Floor you get:

MORE FUN NOW

LESS UN-FUN LATER

— Don't take my word for it, see what our customers have to say —

Happy Pet-Care Customer

Everlast Floor has a textured finish. It is made from small natural marble stones and quartz which give it texture. This makes it a slip-resistant floor. It is a resin-rich floor, meaning the stones are completely saturated in epoxy resin, which makes it non-porous and therefore easy to clean.

```
Alright, so maybe you couldn't clean it in your sleep,
but you could do it with one hand, you could do it
without trying hard, you could do it at lightning
speed!
Unless you prefer long and rigorous scrubbing, reply to
this email or just call me at (800) 708-9870
---Dedicated to making your floor more durable, healthy
& attractive
Gerrald Lacey
```

To keep things interesting, there are industry-specific versions of the cartoons, and the text, testimonials, and images are matched to the prospect's business.

Each email has a very soft call to action—"reply to this email or call me"—and the prospect can respond at any point in the sequence.

Results

In the first 90 days, David compared 222 leads that did not get this campaign to 261 leads that did. The result was an OUTRAGEOUS 172% increase in sales!

Why Is This a Great Campaign to Model?

If you are in a business that has a long sales cycle, this is a great campaign to swipe and deploy.

Keeping a prospect engaged over a prolonged period is difficult, but David has found a clever way to do that by creating a soap opera for his clients to follow.

The cartoons are a fun way to communicate information that would be incredibly dry, and tailoring the content to the prospect's industry makes the emails even more engaging, simply because it makes the lead feel special.

How to Sell OUTRAGEOUSLY by Refusing to Sell

I met David Phelps when he was a member of GKIC. I would run occasional 2-day mastermind events for some of our members. Everyone would get a chance to present their challenge or question and get support from the group, and David was one of the clients in that group. This campaign is for a mastermind group—Freedom Founders—that David now runs for his own clients.

The Campaign

The overall aim of the campaign is to position membership of the group, to attract highly qualified candidates, and to filter out those who are not qualified. The entire selection process is a classic "takeaway" designed to increase the candidate's desire to get into the group.

Lead Generation

The first step along the journey is a live webinar that trains prospects on the key elements of the Freedom Founders program.

Leads for the webinar come from four main sources:

1. Promotion to the company's in-house mailing list
2. Email and direct mail blasts to JV partners' lists
3. Stage presentations
4. Facebook ads to drive cold traffic to the webinars.

In-House List

In the two weeks before each webinar, Freedom Founders sends 3-5 email blasts, 1-3 days apart. Each is a standalone long-form email invitation.

Occasionally, if registrations are low, a short email goes out on the day of the webinar itself.

JV Lists

JV lists are sent 1-3 email blasts in the week before the webinar, and two direct mail pieces. The emails are long-form invitations with a client story, an educational component, and focus on specific pain points.

Here's an example.

Subject: The Dental Apocalypse: Dentistry is Changing… Can the Solo-Practitioner Survive?

From 2009 to 2013, 75% of dentists reported a decline in production.[1]

The market landscape is changing.

Most solo practitioners are falling behind… Their only answer is to run faster on the treadmill.

Truth is, we didn't get the full story in dental school.

None knows this better than my friend Dr. David Phelps: (author of **From High Income To High Networth For Dentists.**)

His gripping story strikes a chord with me.

A Moment of Truth.

By David Phelps, D.D.S.

(Excerpt From David's Story)

There was a lump in my throat as I hung up the phone.

This wasn't how the sale of my dental practice was supposed to go.

I was selling to an associate. Turns out he wasn't up to the challenge...

The practice I had fought so hard to build was crumbling.

Turns out, surviving in dentistry requires so much more than just expertise in dental procedures… (something I was very good at).

I didn't get the full story in dental school.

I had already faced my share of challenges, both personally and professionally:

My daughter Jenna's fight with cancer.

My daughter survived, My marriage didn't…)

Trying to be present for Jenna and still build a dental practice was a two-headed monster.

I was forced me to come to terms with the stark reality:

A high-income job was costing me my life.

This wasn't the career I'd fallen in love with.

I needed a plan B.

With a sigh, I picked my phone back up and started dialing.

There was work to be done.

I took my practice back from my associate, and began putting in the sweat equity of rebuilding it, daring to believe that one day I could sell it again. Successfully.

Here's what I learned:

All the success in the world won't get you your life back.

And I was ready to do whatever it took.

I wanted my life back.

But how?

Wow. Tough message. Don't despair, though.

<u>**That's only half the story.**</u>

The second half is powerfully inspiring.

David found a way to systematize creating a Plan B for dentists.

Today, he uses his newfound freedom to help hundreds of other dentists, docs, and practice professionals find theirs.

Want to hear the second half of the story?

David's doing a live webinar on Tuesday, March 28th, to discuss building a personal Freedom Blueprint.

It's a hands on training, with Q&A.

Can you attend?

Here's the info: www.freedomfounders.com/dentist-freedom-blueprint-webinar

Jump on and find out how orthos, dentists, chiropractors, and more are creating their Personal Plan B.

Ask him whether or not he finally sold his practice.

He'd love to tell you about it.

See you there.

Facebook ads

Ads are based on the content of the promotional emails. David uses an external agency to create the ads, promote them, and track results. The monthly advertising spend is $3,000.

Emails to registrants

Everyone registered for the webinar gets three email reminders: three days before, one day before and on the day of the webinar.

No-Pitch Webinar

The webinars are positioned as a no-pitch live training with nothing to buy. The key to conversion is that David actively invites questions, and when one comes up that relates to membership in the mastermind, he illustrates the answer with stories about Freedom Founders members and immediately does a takeaway. Membership is by invitation only, and the webinar isn't about inviting anyone to join, but anyone who wants to find out more can visit the company's website.

The Website

The focus of the homepage is to get prospects to complete an application for a call with the Community Gatekeeper, John. His name is mentioned several times, a smart move that reinforces that the call is not just with a random salesperson. It's with a named individual with a specific job.

The home page of the site has a video above the fold and a button that takes you to the first page of the application form. Below that, for those who need more convincing, is a long-form sales letter.

The application itself is a qualification questionnaire designed to filter out unsuitable applicants. The process is split over multiple screens, which (as I've pointed out in several of the campaigns in this book) increases the likelihood that someone will complete it in full.

The Triage Call

If an applicant is accepted, they schedule a call with John. That call is a 'triage' call rather than a sales call. In most sales calls, the buyer calls the shots. They ask the questions, and it's up to the seller to prove that the buyer should buy from them. A triage call turns that dynamic on its head. It's the seller who asks all the questions, and it's the buyer who has to prove that they should be allowed to buy. That's an OUTRAGEOUS way to re-define the sales relationship. And really smart!

Here, the objective of the call is to decide whether the prospect will be allowed to proceed to the next stage. If a prospect makes it through the triage call, they're invited to attend the next available mastermind event as a guest. That is where the decision on whether they will be allowed to join will be made. Again, notice the positioning. They're not going to the mas-termind to decide whether they want to join; rather, they're going so that David and his team can decide whether or not to let them into the group. OUTRAGEOUS!

The Mastermind Event

Think about how we got here.

1.   The prospect has attended a webinar where there was no sale.
2.   They visited the website of their own free will and completed a long, multi-page application to be allowed to speak to a gatekeeper.
3.   They had a call with the gatekeeper in which they had to prove they should be invited to the mastermind as a guest.

4. They've made time for the mastermind and traveled there at their own expense.

AND THEY'RE STILL NOT A MEMBER OF THE MASTER-MIND! Throughout the process, the message is "You're not there yet. Prove to us that you're worthy." They've jumped through so many hoops that, even if they weren't particularly serious at the start, they now want desperately to be allowed to join.

Most business owners need the buyer to buy, and the buyer knows it. They know that as the buyer, they have all the power. Here, the buyer is in no doubt that the group doesn't *need* them. The only question is does the group *want* them. Anyone who makes it this far in the process is ready to buy—they've sold it to themselves!

Results

In total around 7,500-10,000 prospects are told about the webinar each time the campaign is run. Between 100 and 175 people typically register for each webinar, leading to 5-15 applications for a call.

In one period of 90 days, David ran seven webinars and completely filled the triage call schedule 45 days ahead. As a result, the number of pre-qualified guests at the next mastermind doubled.

Why Is This a Great Campaign to Model?

David's mastermind is a high-ticket sale, and it would be easy to assume that the model would only work for something equally high-end.

Easy, but wrong. This campaign is an OUTRAGEOUS way to make *any* product, service or opportunity highly desirable.

An OUTRAGEOUS Way to Generate So Many Leads Your Sales Team Can't Keep Up

Demetrios Tzortzis is a GKIC member and (by his own admission) a fan of my earlier book, OUTRAGEOUS *Advertising That's Outrageously Successful.* Demetrios designs and implements strategies for business owners. This campaign was created to generate targeted B2B leads for a client that provides bookkeeping services in and around Denver, CO. It's a new company, so there was no existing list, and no-one in the city had heard of them.

The Campaign

The List

The campaign was sent to a list of 5,000 Denver businesses in a range of industries, each having one to 20 employees. It was a cold list bought from a broker.

The Email Sequence

The heart of the campaign was a series of six emails. It's a very soft and conversational autoresponder sequence that adds value and incorporates different ways of engaging with the reader.

- **Email 1**: Incorporated a 'good morning and intro to company' video, with the Head Bookkeeper introducing herself and the company. It was fun and friendly with no particular ask.

- **Email 2**: A value-add blog post '5 Bookkeeping Mistakes to Avoid...' with no pitch.
- **Email 3**: Another value-add video, this time a screen share of how to do something in QuickBooks.
- **Email 4**: Informational email on how they've helped other clients.
- **Email 5**: Interactive bookkeeping quiz with calendar invite after submission.
- **Email 6**: Goodbye, break-up email with a video of the Head Bookkeeper saying goodbye.

One way of measuring the success of a campaign is open rates. How many people even open your emails will tell you how good you are at getting your email into inboxes (rather than straight to spam) and whether the subject line is working. This campaign averaged 63% over all the emails, which is great for a cold list and suggests that Demetrios's selection criteria and subject lines were good.

From Email to a Meeting

The next metric to look at is response rate. How many replies are you getting, and what kind of replies? (For example, do people tell you to get lost, or do they ask about prices?) This campaign was sent to 5,000 leads, and there were 577 replies (12%) including both the positive and the negative responses.

Whenever anyone replied to an email, the sequence stopped, and a conversation started designed to get them into a meeting with either one of the head bookkeepers or the owner of the business.

The email system also allowed Demetrios to identify people who had opened emails but hadn't responded, and these were followed up with a phone call too: "Hey, I just wanted to make sure you've received our emails and if you have any questions, would you like to speak with one of our bookkeepers?" Those follow-up activities resulted in 53 meetings from the 577 replies (11%).

One thing to note: when Demetrios first started running the campaign, the emails and videos featured the business owner, who is an MBA, and were very formal. When the company brought on a new female head bookkeeper, they started to use her for the videos and adopted a more conversational tone, and the (positive) response rate went through the roof.

Results

The final test of a campaign like this is how many leads turn into paying customers. In this case, the campaign generated four clients at an average monthly fee of $300, for a total revenue of $14,400. That's four people who had probably never heard of the company before the email arrived.

The original list cost $500, so that's a 2,880% ROI!

Overall, the campaign worked. It generated a great return on a small investment, and the client was happy with the result. All the same, one of the things that Demetrios shared with me is that the results could have been a lot better. The response rate was so high (577 replies) that a lot of people fell through the cracks and didn't get a follow-up call. In the end, Demetrios had to get on the phone himself and make 100 calls.

That backlog represents money left on the table. And guess what? It happens to businesses all the time. They hit on a successful marketing formula, and the sales team just can't keep up. One way to solve that would be to use an automated voicemail. The message would be the same, but without having to wait for someone to be free to make the call.

Why Is This a Great Campaign to Model?

This is a simple campaign that would work well for any kind of business. And remember, this was to a cold list bought from a broker, so it would work even for a brand-new business with no list.

Demetrios himself has used it to grow his own marketing business, to launch his wife's business and to reach out to PR firms.

An OUTRAGEOUS Way to Get Back 58% of Your "Lost" Customers with a "Handwritten" Envelope

Doug Anderson's campaign is a development of a campaign by Dean Killingbeck that was featured in my first book *OUTRAGEOUS Advertising That's Outrageously Successful.*

Doug bought a license from Dean to run the campaign for his own clients, and over the years he has added a few OUTRAGEOUS twists of his own to make the campaign more effective.

The Campaign

Doug's clients are restaurants, and the campaign is about getting past customers to come back to the restaurant by inviting them to celebrate their birthday (the perfect blend of celebration—Thing 6—and personalization—Thing 4).

Step 1: The Birthday Letter

The campaign starts with a 3-part physical mailing: a letter, a gift certificate for a free entrée, and an envelope.

You might not normally think of the envelope as part of your mailing—after all, it's just the thing everything else goes inside. But remember, the envelope is usually the first thing someone sees, so it has to grab attention. And here's where Doug made his first tweak to the campaign.

The envelope is addressed with a handwriting font, and it's printed directly onto the envelope, not onto a label. He also uses a real stuck-on stamp rather than putting the letter through a franking machine. The letter looks personal, rather than looking like another piece of junk mail. When someone is going through their mail in the morning, which pile (Thing 10) do you think a hand-written envelope with a real stamp goes in? It's going to go straight into the "A" pile—the "yes" pile.

Inside the envelope, the letter and the certificate use bright colors, changes of font, and stars to create a double readership path (Thing 4). There's a headline, an offer, and a deadline (Thing 2) to make sure the recipient takes action.

Step 2: The 'Bounce Back'

The other tweak Doug made to the campaign happens *after* someone has claimed their free birthday meal.

If someone comes in and uses their gift certificate, they then get a follow-up postcard to thank them for coming in and offer them a half-price entrée next time they come in.

Rochelle…We're so happy you celebrated your birthday with us!

We hope you enjoyed yourself and want you to come back soon. So we are offering you 1/2 Off Any Entrée of your Choice on your next visit to Country Kitchen with No Strings Attached! Offer expires 8-10-17

Thank you!!

Thank You For Being Our Guest!!

They've already been back once, they hopefully enjoyed their birthday, and they should be feeling good about the fact they had their entrée free. There's a very high chance they'll come back and use this new offer. And they do!

Results

None of Doug's clients have had less than a 33% response rate to the campaign. Some have had response rates as high as 52% with the birthday letter, and the average is 40%.

The bounce-back postcard raised that response rate to 58%, so it was definitely worth adding to the campaign.

Not surprisingly, Doug's clients are very loyal themselves. Some of his clients have been using this campaign for more than eight years. Why? Because it works OUTRAGEOUSLY well!

Why Is This a Great Campaign to Model?

One of the things I love about this campaign is that Doug prints the letters, certificates, and postcards for his clients. In other words, he has a physical product (the letters and postcards), and he creates demand for that product by teaching his clients how to use it in a way they might not have thought about. That's really smart.

It's also a simple, low-cost campaign that any business that has (or needs) repeat buyers can run. Of course, you need to have collected your customers' mailing addresses in order to send them something, but as an OUTRA-GEOUS marketer, you already know you have to do that, right?

An OUTRAGEOUS Way to Become a Welcome Guest Rather Than an Unwelcome Pest

Walk through any town in America, and you'll find dozens of auto service businesses, all of them selling broadly similar services to very similar people, and all of them basically indistinguishable from each other.

Miles Auto Service, Fred White's business, is an auto service provider with a difference. That difference is a critical competitive advantage compared to all his competitors in Sewell, NJ: Fred knows how to run OUTRAGEOUS multi-step marketing campaigns.

The Campaign

The campaign Fred sent me for this book is specifically targeted at parents of teen drivers. It's an evergreen campaign that runs all year on autopilot, although Fred does drive extra traffic to it in the fall as a 'back to school' campaign.

Leads

Traffic to the campaign comes primarily from an email sent to Fred's house list with a teaser to a post on the company's blog. He also runs targeted ads on Facebook and Instagram to bring in cold leads.

Step 1: The Blog Post

Leads are sent to a blog post that highlights the dangers drivers face on the road. The blog sidebar has an opt-in offer for a checklist of safety items that should be in every car but usually aren't.

The blog post also has a retargeting pixel so leads can be retargeted with ads after they leave the site.

Step 2: The First Offer

On the download page for the checklist, the lead is offered a kit containing all the items in the list. The kit costs $19.97 and is designed to make this into a "self-liquidating" offer.

A self-liquidating offer is a really smart way to generate leads. The basic (and very OUTRAGEOUS) idea is that as soon as the prospect opts in, you make them an

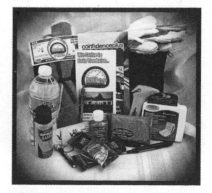

initial offer that covers the cost of getting them to the lead page. As a result, your lead generation has cost you nothing, and in effect, the lead is paying for you to market to them.

Step 3: Follow-Up Sequence #1

If a lead doesn't buy the trunk bag immediately, they are put into a short (3-day) follow-up sequence. Each day they get an email that re-sells the bag. For example, here's the first email in the sequence.

TURNERSVILLE AUTO REPAIR
(856) 281 - 2991
www.sewellcarrepairshops.com

Hi Fred,

I hope you found my download of essential car items helpful. It's a simple list but could be of vital importance in the right time. If you have any questions about this list please feel free to reach out. I made this list when I sent my own daughter out as a new driver.

As a parent sending their child out on their own, I wanted you to see this:

>>Ultimate survival trunk bag for only $19.97

There are many things to worry about when you send your baby off on their own

So as a parent myself I've created a trunk bag with many of the things on the list to get you started.
This is a small investment to your child's safety And think of the value (and peace of mindl) it will provide.
So get it now while you can:

Get Yours Now

This price wont last long I was able to make 42 bags with the suplies I have so get yours while they last.
Talk soon,

Fred White
Miles Auto Team

By the way: did you notice the scarcity?

This price won't last long. I was able to make 42 bags with the supplies I have. So get yours while they last.

Step 4: The Upsell

If a lead buys the trunk bag (on the download page or from one of the follow-up emails), they are offered a 12-month "teen driver auto maintenance" package that provides discounts on many of the services and items the driver (or their parents) will need to keep the car on the road.

That's another OUTRAGEOUS idea worth S&Ding. Think about it. The maintenance package isn't asking them to prepay for everything that they might need in the year. That would be a high-ticket sale, and a high-risk item, either for the buyer (if they end up not using it all) or Fred (if they end up using everything and getting a big discount). Instead, it's like an insurance policy: "If you get in trouble, come back to us, and you'll get this discount."

Why do I call that OUTRAGEOUS? Because Fred is tying the customer into coming back for EVERYTHING for the next twelve months. They aren't going to be calling other auto shops when something goes wrong. Why would they? They've paid for a discounted rate from Fred. So, this offer makes Fred's competitors **irrelevant**. His buyers are shopping in a market of one.

Step 5: Follow-Up Sequence #2

If the customer (remember, they've bought the trunk bag, so they're no longer just a lead: they're now a paying customer) doesn't take the maintenance package immediately, they're put into another 3-day email sequence.

Fred also puts leads who didn't buy the trunk bag into this sequence after five days. The assumption is that they probably went out and bought the items themselves, so rather than pushing the low-value offer, it's more profitable to switch up to the higher-value back end.

Results

Fred has 1,287 leads in his house list. He also spends $70 a week on Facebook and Instagram ads which bring in 2,000 new leads each week.

Sales of the trunk bags average 11 each week, and Fred uses the revenue to pay for the marketing and the cost of the items in the bags. On average, 4 of those buyers take the upsell to the maintenance program. The average lifetime value of those customers is $3,650 each.

That's $14,600 every week, or $759,200 each year. Not bad for a marketing campaign that pays for itself!

Why Is This a Great Campaign to Model?

This is a very different campaign from anything auto shops usually run, and there's a lot of OUTRAGEOUSLY good marketing for you to S&D.

I've already mentioned the value of a self-liquidating offer and tying the customer into buying from you with a small partial prepayment.

Notice, also, how the campaign starts with free valuable information that creates immediate goodwill so that when Fred turns up in their inbox later, he comes as a "welcome guest" rather than an "unwanted pest."

Something else to notice is how Fred presents the initial trunk bag offer. If Fred just offered the bag to the cold/lukewarm traffic he is generating, he probably wouldn't sell many of them. What makes people want the bag is the checklist they downloaded. He's saying, "here's all this stuff you should have in your car, oh and here—what an amazing coincidence—is a kit that just happens to contain all those items." Any business could take the same approach—give prospects a free list of things they need, then sell them everything on the list. People will buy it simply because of the convenience. And they'll be grateful that you made it so easy!

This is a simple campaign that uses no extra resources—just a blog and an email system—and yet generates $750,000 of sales every year from a very small house-list. That's well within reach of even a small or startup business.

How to Get 26% Conversion with OUTRAGEOUS Advertorials

It's easy to assume, in the age of social media and YouTube that no-one reads anything anymore, especially not something as apparently old-fashioned as an advertorial. This campaign by my friends Jeff Giagnocavo and Ben McClure at Gardner's Mattress & More proves that couldn't be further from the truth.

This campaign is all about getting people started before they even step into your store or office using advertorials in a very smart way.

Gardner's sells organic mattresses made from natural latex rather than the synthetic latex used by the majority of manufacturers, and the company faces the uphill battle of educating consumers about why they should spend more for their product when there are cheaper alternatives available. Let's face it, that's a situation many business owners can relate to!

The Campaign

Step 1: The Advertorial

The advertorial appeared in a magazine called *Natural Awakenings*.

Notice that it's not the local newspaper, or a neighborhood magazine, even though Gardner's is what many would consider a local business. It *is* a 'local' magazine—focused on just two counties—but it's one that targets a very specific lifestyle audience.

The advertorial gets put in front of a lot fewer people than it would if it was printed in a general publication, but they are far more likely to pay attention to a "natural and organic" message, and the smaller audience means the cost of running the promotion is far lower than it would be in a mass market publication!

This is a traditional piece of direct response marketing presented as an interview between a "freelance writer" and Ben McClure, president and co-owner with his business partner Jeff Giagnocavo of Gardner's. The body of the "article" focuses on the causes of poor sleep, so only someone with that problem is likely to read it. The problem (of course) stems from the cheap synthetic mattresses everyone else is selling, and the solution is a natural organic latex mattress.

At the bottom, you can see an offer. Notice how it's framed to stand out, surrounded by a dashed red line—we call it a Johnson Box in marketing. Someone just scanning the magazine will still see that it's different, and may stop, even if they were going to skip past the article

---

FREE READER'S GIFTS

As a reader of *Natural Awakenings*, you are entitled to 4 FREE GIFTS by visiting our store and answering three simple questions. Bring this coupon (code: LB0517) to Gardner's Mattress & More to receive:

- FREE Gift #1: All-Natural Rubber Pillow ($60 value); 2nd is 50% off!
- FREE Gift #2: Natural Rubber Mattress Guide ($9.95 value)
- FREE Gift #3: "Good Night" Sleep Mask ($9.95 value)
- FREE Gift #4: $200 Savings Voucher on an Organic Natural Mattress

Bring this coupon to the store at 830 Plaza Blvd. in Lancaster (behind Park City Mall, next to VanScoy Jewelers). *There's no obligation to buy anything -- just answer three simple questions.* Your Readers' Gifts expire May 31, 2017.

*Gardner's Mattress & More - 830 Plaza Blvd., Lancaster, PA 17601
Phone: 717-459-4570 - Online: www.GardnersMattressAndMore.com*

There are four gifts, and between them, they'll appeal to most types of buyers, regardless of how "sold" they already are on natural latex.

- A free pillow, and a discount on a second pillow. If someone's already interested in natural sleep solutions, this will reel them in.
- An information guide for anyone who found the article interesting but still wants to know more.
- A sleep mask, which will appeal to anyone who struggles to sleep but hasn't been convinced yet.
- A $200 voucher for anyone who is ready to buy.

The masterstroke is how you get those gifts: you have to go into the store. It's not a mail-in or call-in offer. You have to be physically present in the store. Genius.

Step 2: The "Assessment"

When the prospect visits the store, they start in a comfortable "lounge" area, where they go through an assessment. They're not shown straight to the showroom. They're not pushed into testing different mattresses to see which one they like. They talk to someone who is going to "prescribe" the right kind of mattress for them.

Only when they've been assessed are they shown through to the showroom options. If they buy, they get their $200 discount and all the other gifts they were promised. If not, they get the gifts, and they are added to the company database so that Gardner's can follow up with them and keep selling.

Step 3: Follow-Up

Follow-up starts with taking the customer's details. As they are in the store and they've been through the assessment, it makes sense to capture all that information, not just their contact details.

Gardner's uses a standard data entry form to make sure they get all the information they need. When you're collecting data in the "real" world rather than using an online form, that's critical.

In effect, they are saying, "if they come to us and don't buy, they have to fill out the form to get the gift." Once they've done that, it moves them into a sequence of three emails.

Email 1

The first one goes out the very next day. Assuming that they've tried out their new pillow, the email invites them to return to the website to find out more about natural latex or set up a time to go back to the store.

The interesting part of this email is the PS and PPS at the end. So, the PPS invites them to unsubscribe, but there's a bit of guilt to keep them in the sequence!

```
P.S. - This email serves as your $200 savings voucher
off ANY natural or organic mattress we have from Prana,
Savvy Rest, Pure Latex Bliss or Gold Bond Organic Se-
ries and expires on [date].
P.P.S. - If all you wanted was the free pillow and wish
to receive no more communications simply click here to
be removed from our list. While we might shed a tear,
we will respect your wishes.
```

Email 2

Three days later, a "social proof" email goes out with a glowing testimonial that links back to a page full of further testimonials. Again, the email assumes that they've been using—and enjoying—their new pillow, and invites them to set up a time to go back to the store and try out a mattress.

Email 3

One week later, if they still haven't come back, they get the final follow-up email. This adds urgency by reminding the prospect that their $200 discount expires at the end of the month.

Results

Over two years, Gardner's invested $50,000 in running the advertorial. The campaign generated 346 leads, 91 of whom bought a mattress, with an average sale of $3,582.

That's a 26% close rate, and brought in $325,945 in revenue. For a premium offer like this, that's a great closing rate!

Why Is This a Great Campaign to Model?

This is a great campaign for a business that has a well-defined target audience and can reach them through specific media outlets.

Remember that this campaign wasn't just put into any publication. It was in a publication that targeted the same audience that Gardner's does. When you're doing any kind of press advertising, it's essential to find the right magazine to put it into. Otherwise, you'll lose your shirt.

The reason Gardner's had good sales was that the people who read this magazine were the right people for this offer. That's why 346 of them responded, and because they were the "right" prospects, 26% bought.

In Gardner's case, it was right to choose a local magazine. They only have one store, so there was no point marketing nationally. Of course, if Gardner's was a national chain, all they would have to do is change the call to action to "Drop by your local store."

In addition, the interview format allows you to establish authority—notice how Ben McClure had himself interviewed, effectively positioning him as an expert on sleep.

Overall, advertorial campaigns lend themselves particularly well to complex products and services that need to be explained, or where an audience is unaware that the product/service exists.

How Anyone Can Create a Small OUTRAGEOUS Campaign: No Excuses!

Howard Anderson was a member of GKIC and was in one of my mastermind groups. He and his wife own a small sewing machine and vacuum cleaner business in New Jersey called Stony Brook Sew & Vac. There used to be several branches, but they made a lifestyle choice and went down to a single superstore.

This is a neat little campaign that will work for any kind of business. It consists of some Facebook ads plus three emails, themed around a holiday.

The Campaign

This particular campaign is for a Labor Day sale. Howard and his wife do different campaigns for different holidays, as I recommended in Part One (Thing 6).

The Facebook Post

One part of the campaign was a boosted Facebook post—in other words, it's a 'normal' post that Howard pays to have shown to his target audience.

Notice that this is not a "pretty" image. A lot of the time, business owners hold themselves back from running ads because they think they

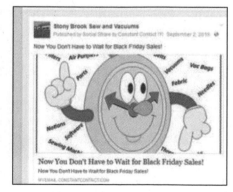

need beautiful images, especially on Facebook.

Somebody would see this post and say "What the heck is that?" and then they'd have to look at it. So, they click the post and get taken to the page on Howard's site about the Labor Day sale. It's as simple as that. In fact, 276 people clicked through from the post.

The Emails

Alongside the boosted Facebook post, Howard sent three emails to his existing mailing list.

Email 1

The first email went out on September 2nd and got 190 clicks.

First, notice that the image from the boosted Facebook post is repeated in the email. If someone saw the Facebook post, they immediately know that this is the same campaign.

Second, there's a really neat touch in the middle of the email. **"This sale is at our Bordentown Store Warehouse only! Click here for directions!"** Remember, I said that Howard and Elizabeth went down to a single store as a lifestyle choice. The email implies that there are more stores, but it never actually says it. As a result, the business sounds a lot larger than it is.

Email 2

Email 2 went out on Sept 3rd. It still has the same ugly clock, creating visual continuity with the rest of the campaign, and it's still only for the "named" location.

However, it creates urgency (Thing 2) in a really interesting way: the discount will drop hour by hour, so people have to hurry in—they can't leave it for later in the day—and by 9am the sale is over. That's urgency!

Email 3

Email 3 went out the day before the sale—September 4th, and another 82 people clicked on it. Again, it has the same visual, and it reinforces the urgency with the same hourly discount reductions. In fact, the only real difference from email 2 is that it tells the reader that the sale starts in 12 hours.

Results

In total, 276 people clicked on the Facebook ad, and 366 clicked through from the email. Overall, the campaign brought in 26 customers who spent a total of $10,252.

The total Facebook ad spend was minimal because the audience was kept very small and local, and the email campaign cost nothing, as it was sent to people Howard and Elizabeth already had on their email list. They didn't spend big bucks on graphic design—you could create an image like that yourself using free clip art and PowerPoint. In effect, that is $10,252 of free money!

Bear in mind that once someone is a customer, they're going to come back and spend more in the future. That $10,252 could turn into $20,000, $50,000 or even $100,000 over time.

Why Is This a Great Campaign to Model?

This is a small campaign. Probably the smallest you'll find in this book. There are three emails and a Facebook ad, and that's it. People just come in and buy stuff on one day.

If you've been making excuses about how complicated online marketing is, or you're simply too busy to set up a multi-step, multi-channel marketing campaign, this is a great way to get started. And finally, if you just need to make money quickly, a campaign like this can do that.

This campaign was tied to Labor Day, but any holiday will do. And if there isn't one coming up, make one up! Pick a theme that works for your business and declare next Monday a national—or international—holiday. In fact, I've just decided that next Monday is International Outrageous Marketing Day, and I want you to celebrate by creating an outrageous multi-step marketing campaign of your own!

An OUTRAGEOUS Way to Make Money NOW by Getting "Outta Your Skull"

Jack Turk is a magician and a direct response copywriter. In fact, he was GKIC's copywriter (after I'd sold the business), and if you ever subscribed to their "Copy Confidential Archives" program, you'll have seen Dan Kennedy interview Jack each month.

This campaign has a simple but powerful objective: to make money very quickly from an existing list by bundling several products together.

Jack targeted other magicians as his niche, and he had a mailing list of 1,000 prospects, which may seem small for people raised in the world of internet marketing, but actually is big enough to sustain a real business.

The Campaign

Segmenting the List

Since Jack was bundling products that he had previously sold individually, he decided to segment the list.

First, he restricted the mailing to people who had previously bought a product, so these were all buyers rather than prospects.

Next, he excluded anyone who had already bought one or more of the products in the bundle at full price. That's a clever move to avoid annoying loyal customers by showing them a product at a lower price than they've already paid.

That reduced the list from 1,000 to just 100 names, small enough to be manageable by one person, which is a consideration when you're sending out packages through the mail.

The Envelope

Jack put together a physical mailing built around a central theme—"I'm outta my skull!"—represented by an X-ray of a skull.

It starts with the envelope.

Jack attached a label to the envelope with the X-ray image and a message: "I must be crazy out of my skull to give you this deal…"

That X-ray is going to stop someone in their tracks and make them want to see what's inside. It's the kind of OUTRAGEOUS touch that makes people stop and want to find out what it's about.

He also handwrote the address and used a real stamp, which also gets people's attention and makes them want to open it—far more so than a printed name and address and a mailing label. You'll see that a lot of the campaigns in this book do that. <u>Because it works</u>!

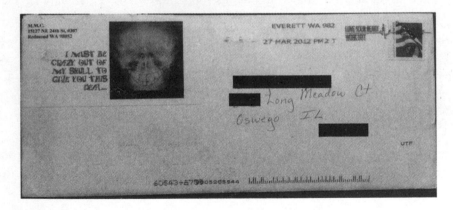

What's in the Envelope?

There were three parts to the mailing.

1. A 3-page sales letter
2. A testimonial sheet
3. A "Don't Read Until Later" letter printed on orange paper.

The Sales Letter

The letter kept up the "outta my skull" theme with the same X-ray that was on the envelope. It also used lots of red headlines and CopyDoodles to create an alternative readership path.

If you look closely, you'll also see that there's a hand-stamped deadline ("VOID APR 10, 2012") in red at the end of the letter. Hand stamping it is a nice touch that makes it stand out and seem a bit more real.

The Testimonial Sheet

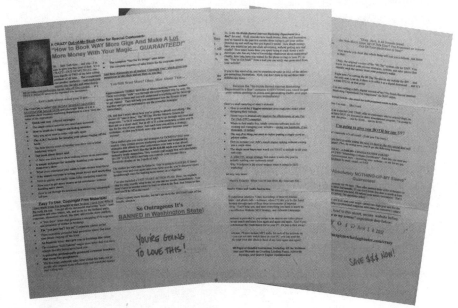

Along with the sales letter came a testimonial sheet. Even though the people Jack sent this to were already customers, it never hurts to remind people how good you are, so consider adding testimonials wherever you get a chance!

The "Do Not Read Until Later" Letter

In Part One, I talked about the importance of being in control of the buyer's process. When you call the shots in the sale, people are far more likely to buy. A really easy way to do that in a mail campaign is a "Do not read" letter. Sometimes, the letter will say something like, "Do not read unless you've decided not to buy"—that's a great way to save a sale that has almost been lost. Sometimes, it's just another piece that you want them to read as part of your pitch. It's really just another alternative readership path.

Here's why this technique works so well. Let's say someone decides to stop reading the main letter before they get to the part that you *really* wanted them to read. If that's all that was in the envelope, you've lost them. But if there's a brightly colored sheet of paper that says, "Do not read" on it, what are they going to do? You can bet good money they're going to pick it up and read it!

For this campaign, Jack repeated his OUTRAGEOUS offer. That virtually guarantees that everyone saw the pitch, even if they stopped reading the letter before they got to page 3.

Results

The campaign resulted in 20 sales to 100 leads, which is a good closing rate and a good ROI. It worked so well that Jack uses the "outta my skull" theme to this day for campaigns in other niches.

Why Is This a Great Campaign to Model?

In a single mailing, Jack has packed in a lot of the features of OUTRA-GEOUS marketing.

1. Alternative readership paths
2. A deadline
3. A hand-stamped deadline for the illusion of personalization
4. Social proof
5. Headlines
6. CopyDoodles
7. OUTRAGEOUS images

One thing that stands out about this campaign is that it is a single step. There's one mailing. So why is it in a book about multi-step campaigns? Because inside that one envelope are three different marketing pieces—it's a multi-step campaign in a single envelope.

A lot of business owners would be tempted to put all the information into a single long letter, which would be leaving a lot of money on the table. Whenever you send stuff in the mail, consider breaking it up like this into different documents.

Another standout point about this campaign is the target market. A lot of business owners tell me that their customers don't have a lot of money. But as you've seen, this campaign works well even in low-budget markets.

How to Turn a Family Occasion into OUTRAGEOUS Sales

Julie Boswell is a professional Direct Response Copywriter who used to work for me at GKIC. Even after I left GKIC, I continued to recommend her to my clients—including Rory Fatt (who also contributed a campaign for this book). Julie created the campaign below for a client, Total Census Solutions. It's a great example of manufacturing a celebration as a "reason" for a campaign (look at Thing 6 if you're not sure what I'm talking about).

The Campaign

Total Census Solutions provides call tracking services to marketers. The campaign was sent out to approximately 4,000 internal leads—people who were already doing business with the company but weren't fully taking advantage of all the call tracking numbers they needed.

The Process

The campaign has just six steps—two direct mail postcards and four emails, all driving traffic to an online sales letter—sent as follows:

- STEP 1 (Sept. 28th): It's A Boy Postcard
- STEP 2 (Sept. 30th): Email #1
- STEP 3 (Oct. 1st): Tic Toc Postcard
- STEP 4 Oct. 2nd): Email #2
- STEP 5 (Oct. 4th): Email #3
- STEP 6 (Oct. 7th - DEADLINE): Email #4

STEP 1 (Sept. 28th): It's A Boy Postcard

The first postcard simply announced, "It's a boy!" on the front, just like any other announcement postcard you might get from a friend or family member. On the back, it was personalized with the recipient's first name (Thing 4) and told them about a 40%-off sale to celebrate the happy event, along with some gifts for the first 27 people to respond (remember that in Thing 2, I said that restricting quantity is a great way to create a deadline).

STEP 2 (Sept. 30th): Email #1

The first email was short and to the point.

Subject: It's A Boy!

Hi First Name,

I sent you a birth announcement the other day. If you haven't received it yet, be sure to check your mailbox today.

There's big news in my family. My wife Lisa, is about to give birth to our 4th son. The doc is inducing labor on October 4th. We're thrilled! I'm so excited that I wanted to spread the joy and celebrate with you too.

Hey, what can I say … I'm a big barrel of love these days, and I want everyone to be as happy as I am. So, I've put together a killer package to help increase your ROI and, of course, increase your profit!

Go to www.YourROIGuy.com/BabySale to check out the details.

Best,

Richard Seppala

P.S. This is the biggest and most generous offer I've ever made and I'd hate to see you miss out. The deal is done as soon as we bring our boy home from the hospital on October 7th.

Visit: www.YourROIGuy.com/BabySale today!

Sending an email alongside a postcard is smart. If someone misses one medium (or, say, a gatekeeper tosses the postcard!), they will hopefully see the other.

STEP 3 (Oct. 1st): *Tic Toc Postcard*

Postcard 2 was designed to really get their attention. On the front, you see Richard's smiling (and clearly expecting!) wife. The text reminds the reader that this isn't the first contact they've had about it and repeats the discount offer.

Notice how Julie uses the photo to grab attention, and doodles to create a second readership path.

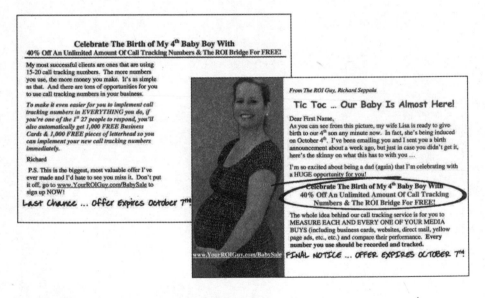

The copy also introduces a hard deadline this time: October 7th.

STEP 4 (Oct. 2nd): *Email #2*

Email #2 is a slightly longer sales letter, reminding the reader that they got an announcement, and repeating the offer and deadline.

STEP 5 (Oct. 4th): Email #3

Email #3 announces that the baby has arrived, and gives the reader the information they'd expect in a birth announcement (weight, eye color, etc.), then it's back to business. There are just 72 hours to go until the sale ends, and only 3 of the fast-response gifts left.

STEP 6 (Oct. 7th - DEADLINE): Email #4

Email #4 has a single line about the baby (*"Finally, we're home. Life will never be the same. We're officially a family of 6!"*) before getting to business: the offer expires at midnight, so act now!

Results

"It was a great campaign, and we converted 3.5% with a yearly spend of $1,000."

RICHARD SEPPALA, OWNER, TOTAL CENSUS SOLUTIONS

Out of 4,000 prospects, 140 people (3.5% conversion) took the offer, generating first-year sales for this campaign of $140,000!

Julie's client, Richard Seppala, agrees that he would use Julie's campaign again. His thoughts on this are actually comical: *"I would definitely use this campaign again, except we're done with boys! Four is enough."* So it looks like Julie is going to have to come up with a different excuse for the next campaign!

Why Is This a Great Campaign to Model?

The "4th Boy Campaign" is an example of a campaign that any business can use to boost sales surrounding a special or personal life event. You may not be expecting any children this year, but life happens to us all. Maybe one of yours is graduating, maybe you're moving/downsizing, or maybe your significant other has finally convinced you to take that epic, bucket list vacation of a lifetime overseas. You can use a campaign like this to celebrate the occasion or, better yet, pay for it. In fact, if you read *Outrageous Advertising That's Outrageously Successful*, you'll remember I ran a campaign from a cruise ship one year while my wife Karen and I were on vacation!

The great thing about this sort of campaign is that you can allow your customers to peek into your world and become a part of your family during the campaign.

People love to celebrate or commiserate with you. The magic of this campaign is the intimacy of giving your prospects a personal reason why you're conducting the sale.

And of course, the very best part is that using personality and your own life experiences like this is an OUTRAGEOUS way to bring you sales.

An OUTRAGEOUSLY Smart Way to Get to Your Leads Before Your Competitors

I met Keith Lee when we were both members of Dan Kennedy's Inner Circle (before I bought it and it became GKIC). At the time, we were both running our own businesses, and we would meet at live events.

This campaign is one that Keith created for his current business, teaching dentists how to run a profitable and successful clinic.

Sponsoring booths at conferences for your niche can be a great way to get new customers, as you'll see in several of the campaigns in this book. However, it usually requires a substantial investment, so you've got to get as many people as possible to your booth to make it worthwhile.

For his first dental conference, in San Francisco, Keith decided the best way to drive traffic to his booth was to make sure the dentists knew about it before they even arrived, which also meant they'd see his marketing ahead of any of his competitors.

Keith bought the preregistration list for the event—that's a smart move if you're sponsoring an event, by the way—with details of 1,600 attendees, and started marketing to them well ahead of the event.

The Campaign

Step 1: The Bank Bag Mailing

Keith knew that for his campaign to work, he was going to have to get past gatekeepers, and that was going to require something OUTRA-GEOUS. Given his track record, it shouldn't be a surprise that he turned to 3D mail to provide the necessary "Wow!" factor.

The first mailing in the campaign used a real bank bag[3] with a letter in it. That's unusual enough that most gatekeepers will pass it on.

The letter was three pages long, so I won't include it all here, but I wanted to show you the beginning of the letter, because it has some key lessons.

Dear Dr. <Last Name>,

I bet you're wondering why I've sent this short letter to you in a real bank bag. There are three reasons:

1. I have something very important to share with you so I wanted to make sure to get your attention before **CDA Presents** in San Francisco.

2. Since what I have to share with you can add a great deal to your bottom line I thought using a real bank bag was appropriate.

---

[3] This is one of the products his son's company, 3D Mail, sells—you'll meet Travis in a later campaign

3. This is one of those rare opportunities to improve your practice that your **staff will love, your patients will love, and you will love.**

Here's why I'm writing...

If you're like 95% of the dentists that I consult with, you're managing the performance of your staff using *random and erratic* acts that are the result of trying to solve problems after they occur.

In working with dentists and creating a GOOD Job Description, I discovered that *a GOOD Job Description for a dentist has 29 Management Responsibilities and 19 Dentist Responsibilities, yet you didn't have a single management class in dental school.*

No wonder you're struggling!

But don't feel bad. Before I decided to work exclusively with dentists, I worked with businesses in 67 different industries, and almost all of them used that same type of "put out the fire" management. Even the ones who graduated from business school.

Now, I want you to notice a few things about that opening.

First, there are lots of shifts between bold, italic and colored text (if you're reading the print edition of the book it'll look gray, but it's actually red). That creates a double readership path (Thing 4), directing the eye to where Keith needs it to go.

Second, Keith explains why he's writing a letter, why it's in a bank bag, and why the doctor needs to pay attention. That's important because the approach is so different from what these dentists and their gatekeepers are used to. The novelty will get their attention, but you still need to get that letter read.

By the way, the letter is three pages long. A lot of people will tell you that no one reads long sales copy anymore, but in this book, you'll see a lot of people using long sales letters just like this. Remember that these are smart marketers who test and monitor everything they do. If they're using long sales letters, it's because they work!

The letter goes on to talk about the challenges dentists face running their practice, and offers them a free copy of Keith's book *For Dentists Only…How to Create a Highly Productive Staff That Increases Patient Retention and Referrals* which they can get by visiting the booth.

There are also a couple of testimonials from dentists who are already using Keith's system, with the name of the dentist, their photo, the name of their center, and its location, so that if anyone wanted to track them down, they could: each of those tweaks makes the testimonial a lot more powerful.

Keith also sets up a theme in the letter that gets used in several OUTRAGEOUS ways throughout the campaign: the idea that dentists spend most of their time fighting fires in their business.

Now let's look at the end of the letter, because there's some OUTRAGEOUSLY smart stuff going on there. Keith reminds them how to get the book, and offers them a free 15-minute consultation (for anyone who wants to get going immediately).

Finally, there's that photo of a fire truck in front of a house fire. Next to the photo, it says, "Look for this banner at my booth" and the booth number.

The idea behind the photo is simple—most of the time, people at conferences struggle to remember what booths they wanted to see, and even if they remember, they can't find them. The fire photo is actually the backdrop to the booth. As people are walking around the event, they'll see the giant backdrop of a burning house and a fire truck and think, "Oh yeah, that's the guy who sent me the bank bag. I wanted to talk to him!"

Step 2: Oversize Postcard

The second mailing is a full letter-size (8½" x 11") postcard.

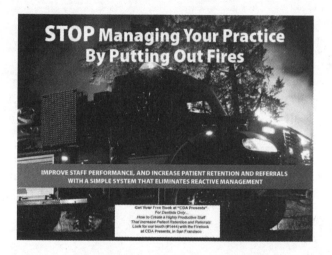

The front is the same photo of a fire truck next to a fire that was in the original letter—the same photo they'll see behind the booth at the event—and at the bottom, there's a call to action to go to the stand to get their free book.

The back of the postcard has some OUTRAGEOUS aspects to it.

First, there's a photo of the bank bag, helping them make the connection that this postcard is from the same person.

Second, there's a photo of Keith himself in a firefighter's uniform. He wanted to be sure that, when they saw him at the booth, the dentists would know he wasn't just the hired help.

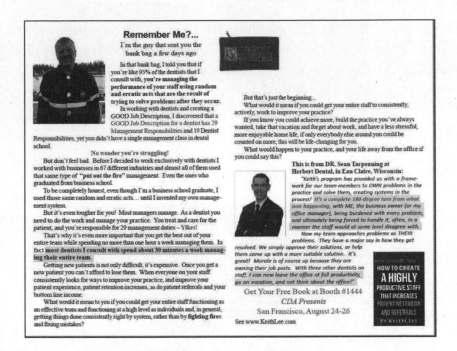

The text was the same as on the letter but edited down, and he included one of the testimonials and the picture of the book they would be getting for free at the booth.

Step 3: 3D mail

Continuing the firefighting theme, the final piece of mail had a firefighter's badge to turn it into 3D mail and make sure it got opened.

The content deliberately combines the first letter and the postcard, reinforcing that they're all from the same person. The offers are the same—come to the booth and get a free book, or call ahead and schedule a free consultation.

Living Proof

As I said above, the letters included testimonials from a couple of Keith's clients. However, one of the doctors went one better and offered to staff the booth at the conference. Now, written testimonials are great, but a testimonial that can walk up to prospects and talk to them is the most powerful proof there is!

The Booth

The whole campaign was built around consistent visual cues and, as we'll see in a moment, it worked very well.

When people were wandering around the exhibitors' hall, they saw everything they'd been told to look out for.

In fact, here's Keith, in his firefighter's gear, in front of the giant photo of the fire truck.

Results

The advance mailing was sent to the 1,600 people who pre-registered. In total, there were 3,000 people at the conference.

Keith's aim wasn't necessarily to sell anything at the event. Rather, he wanted to build his list and—more importantly—to get his book into the hands of the dentists, their office managers, and their staff.

Of the 3,000 people at the conference, 333 registered at the booth: 149 dentists, 38 office staff, and 146 dental assistants and hygienists. That's an OUTRAGEOUS result at an event like this. With 3,000 people walking around, it's harder to get people to visit the booths and register than at smaller events, so an 11% sign up rate is a great result.

More importantly, Keith knows his closing ratios and the value of a lead and a customer, and over time those 333 leads will turn into around $165,000 of revenue.

His total investment in the event (booth, travel, hotel, promotion, etc.) was $12,500, so that's a long-term ROI of 1,320%!

Why Is This a Great Campaign to Model?

There's a lot to love about this campaign. Any time you sponsor a booth at an event, the biggest challenge is making sure people will come to the booth.

Marketing to attendees ahead of the event (you'll also see that in Mike Crow's campaign in this book) makes them want to come and find you. Setting up strong visual cues so they can spot you when they get to the event is key (the vinyl footprints in Dustin Mathew's campaign are another way of doing that).

Even if you don't intend to sponsor a live event, there's another lesson that every marketer can take away from this campaign—Keith used a very distinctive theme and a handful of related visual cues to make himself stand out and be memorable. That's something any business can do, in any industry, in any aspect of their marketing.

An OUTRAGEOUS Way to "Clean Up" with a Toilet Brush

GKIC member Kevin Carter owns a janitorial services business. As you can imagine, that's a very commoditized business, and it's hard to stand out unless you get truly OUTRAGEOUS. And it's hard to be more OUTRAGEOUS than Kevin's "Johnny Mop" campaign.

The goal of this campaign is simple—to get new clients. Kevin identified thirteen cold prospects who were registered for a conference in Indiana that he was also attending, and mailed them in advance.

The Campaign

Step 1: The "Johnny Mop"

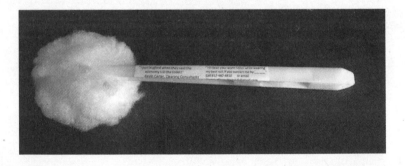

The mailing piece was the perfect piece of 3D mail for a janitorial company: a toilet brush, or "Johnny Mop" as it's known in the trade. The mop was sent exactly as you see it—with no envelope or wrapping. If you can't read the label Kevin stuck to the handle, it says:

> I just laughed when they said the economy is in the toilet. Call me by [deadline] and I will clean your worst toilet while wearing my best suit. Kevin Carter, CIO (Chief Icky Officer).

That's quite an offer, and like every good offer, it has a deadline (Thing 2). It's also a perfect example of Step 6 ("Everything can be OUTRAGEOUS... even you").

Step 2: The conference

At the conference, Kevin overheard someone telling some other business owners about the toilet brush he'd received in the mail. He'd wandered down the office hallway brandishing the brush in the air and yelling, "Who's got the worst toilet?" Kevin immediately introduced himself and was hired on the spot.

The Results

Including postage, the campaign cost just $38.09 and resulted in three bids, which turned into two new customers: a one-time job for the business owner Kevin overheard telling his friends about the toilet brush, and a long-term contract. Total revenue so far from the campaign is almost $170,000, and the contract is still running, so the total goes up every month. The best result of all, though? No one asked Kevin to clean a toilet.

Why Is This a Great Campaign to Model?

Is there a low-cost physical object connected to your business you could send through the mail? Then you can run a version of this campaign. Is there an OUTRAGEOUS offer you could make—"I'll prepare your tax return wearing a Santa suit," or "I'll deliver a birthday card to your best customer wearing a mariachi outfit"? Then you can run a version of this campaign. It truly proves that OUTRAGEOUS can be outrageously cheap!

How to Generate an OUTRAGEOUS 756% ROI by Taking Your Customers on a 3-Day Date

---

> I've given you all that you need and taken away any risk.
> So decide "yes" or "no" right now. Make a decision. If it's a yes, then join us right now and get all the incredible benefits and the feeling of knowing you have predictable leads and sales coming in every day.
>
> If it's a "no," that is fine, and I wish you all the best. Seriously, whether you join or not is not going to make a difference in my life… but it could make a huge difference in yours.
>
> Thank you so much for spending time with me today and letting me teach you. For all of you who enrolled, congratulations and
>
> I will see you in just a few minutes in our private Facebook Group for our live Q&A and quick win.

So ends Kim Walsh Phillips's 3-day date with her prospects, and it closes 15-31% of cold traffic to her webinar within 72 hours.

Kim co-authored a book with my old friend and mentor, Dan Kennedy: *No B.S. Guide to Direct Response Social Media Marketing.*

While researching strategies she could use to grow her own fanbase, she discovered an OUTRAGEOUS strategy that allows her and her clients to get new Facebook fans for less than 1¢ each—rather than the $3-$5 she had been paying.

She realized the strategy was something other people would want to know how to do. It would also make a great hook for her high-end programs. This campaign—the 3-Day Date—was built around that strategy.

The Campaign

Most (bad) marketing tries to sell immediately, whether the prospect knows, likes and trusts the seller or not. It's the equivalent of saying, "Hello, great to meet you. Will you marry me?"

The 3-Day Date campaign is designed to give cold prospects time to vet Kim and decide whether they want to go further. It was also built around getting the prospect a quick win on day one of the "date" so they get to trust not only Kim but also themselves (and their own ability to do what she teaches).

As Kim herself points out, for many of her prospects that win represents their first major marketing success.

Step 1: Facebook Ad

The campaign starts with a Facebook ad targeting cold traffic and promising a single major outcome for the prospect.

Step 2: The Landing Page

The ad drives traffic to a landing page that echoes the text of the ad. That's a very smart move. Anytime you're moving people from one step to the next, give them something that looks, sounds and feels like where they just came from—it will make them feel more comfortable when they get there. In this case, the text provides that anchor. It's a very simple page, but it converts at 44%—and remember, these are cold leads.

Step 3: The Immediate Offer

As soon as someone registers, they are offered the chance to buy the recordings of the live webinar for $7. A low-cost offer like that is a very easy way to identify the most highly motivated leads and turn them into a paying customer immediately. As I've said before in this book, a buyer is a buyer is a buyer: the first sale is always the hardest, and once someone pays you $7, it's much easier to get them to pay $100 or $1,000 or $10,000.

About 22% of leads who register for the webinar opt to buy the recordings for $7.

Step 4: The Live Training

Whether someone takes the $7 offer or not, they get three days of live training. Kim tracks who is attending or not through her webinar platform, GoToWebinar, and sends email and text reminders.

Step 5: The Close

If someone is following the training, then by the time they get to day three they are already getting results. That makes the upsell much easier.

So, on day four, Kim sells her signature program, The 12-Minute Social Media Cash Machine, which also includes an offer of a free trial of her $100/month Powerful Professionals membership.

Results

From June to October 2017, this funnel brought in 22,647 new leads, and resulted in 3,423 online orders, generating $365,103.83 in direct revenue (a 756% ROI on her ad spend) and more than a half-million dollars in private client revenue.

Of those new customers, 595 also subscribed to her continuity program at $100/month—that's another $59,500 of additional revenue *every month*.

That represents a 171% increase in sales overall.

It is, as Kim herself puts it, "a good ending to a date!"

Why Is This a Great Campaign to Model?

Building a trial of a continuity program into your offers is an OUTRA-GEOUS way to turn one-time clients into customers for life. Imagine if Kim stopped selling at the point where someone bought her 12-Minute Social Media Cash Machine program. She'd be leaving $59,500 on the table month after month. That's over half a million dollars every year. This shows the importance of building continuity income into your offers. And in case you think that wouldn't work in your industry, go and look at other campaigns in this book. There are examples of monthly subscription programs in many industries, even restaurants!

Next, look at how the campaign is structured. A lot of webinars simply try to present a much bigger offer in an hour. It might be dressed up with stories and testimonials, but ultimately the webinar is saying: here's all this stuff you need to do, and here's this program that teaches you how to do it.

The 3-Day Date starts instead with a single bold promise that will get a very specific result. Kim gave me some OUTRAGEOUS suggestions for other industries. For example, in health and wellness, you could share a strategy to triple the prospect's metabolism in three days. A marketer could give three strategies to increase email subscribers. A financial advisor could give three techniques to save money on utilities.

Having picked her big, bold promise, Kim runs ads that invite people to a webinar where they'll learn how to get that big result.

Then, on day three, she pitches the next step. In this case, it's her program, but it could just as easily be a sales meeting or any other kind of offer.

How to Close $2,500 by Being OUTRAGEOUSLY Childlike

Lisa Haster is an estate planning attorney who isn't afraid to Swipe and Deploy (Thing 1) campaigns that work from other industries. In fact, of all the OUTRAGEOUS campaigns she has run over the years, the one that gives her the highest ROI is one she swiped from a chiropractor!

In this campaign, you'll see how to follow up OUTRAGEOUSLY with prospects who make an initial inquiry but don't take the next step.

In Lisa's case, when someone contacts the office, they get a *shock and awe package*. Now, you'll see lots of campaigns in this book built around this, so let me take a moment to explain what it is.

Shock and Awe Marketing

Shock and awe packages are some of the most OUTRAGEOUS ways you can follow up with a prospect.

The basic idea is to position you uniquely in your prospect's mind. This isn't the only thing you need to do to achieve that, but it is something that EVERY business can do. Whether you're a chiropractor, an attorney, a pet store owner or you run a Fortune 500 corporation, this will work for you!

What do most business owners do when someone asks them to send them some information? They try to do it as cheaply as possible and with as little effort as possible. After all, this person might not ever become a customer, right?

The shock and awe package turns that on its head because, after all, this person *should* become a customer! That's why, rather than send out a tri-fold brochure and a business card, you put together a unique package of impressive and benefit-laden stuff that is so awesome that when someone opens it they have to pay attention, and they have to engage with it. The effect you're after is for someone to open the package, be wowed, and want to tell everyone they know what their lawyer (or financial planner or local restaurant or whatever) sent them.

Lisa Haster's shock and awe package is a metallic mailer containing:

- Free Report
- Welcome Letter
- Welcome Worksheet
- Checklist *"7 Things to Ask before hiring an Estate Planning Attorney"*
- Will v. Trust infographic
- A copy of her book

So, that's Lisa's shock and awe package, and it works well. But that's not the campaign we're interested in here. What we're going to look at is what happens *after* the shock and awe package goes out.

The Campaign

The shock and awe package is designed to get people to book a consultation with Lisa. But what happens to people who *don't* book that appointment?

They get two follow-up letters, a month apart.

These letters are from an estate planning lawyer. They are going to be smart and formal, with carefully printed labels, and Lisa's logo and return address on the front, right?

Heck no! This is OUTRAGEOUS marketing, not snooze marketing. Here's Lisa's envelope.

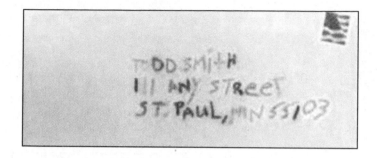

Yes, that's right. It's addressed in a child-like scrawl with a colored pencil! And that's a real stamp on the corner, not a franking machine.

Letter 1: Clover

The first letter is from Lisa's stepdaughter, Clover, offering a discount on her stepmom's behalf. Like the envelope, it's written in a handwriting font, and each paragraph is differently colored, giving it a childlike innocence and appeal.

Hi Mister or misses,

My name is Clover, and my stepmom is Attorney Haster. She told me you talked to her about her job to see if she can help you but she didn't hear back from you yet.

My stepmom says you wanted to get a plan for your family in case something happens to you but haven't decided if you want to yet.

My birthday is coming soon, and I told my stepmom that I want to go to a trampoline park with my friend Chloe and that I want a hatchable. I told my step-mom that a good way to celebrate my birthday is to give you a present from me.

So during the months of July and August (my birthday is in July!), my stepmom will take $500 off her bill if you want her to represent you.

Call my step-mom at (612) 524-9414 or email her to get my present to

you. Just say my name, Clover, for your $500 present
and you'll be glad you did.
Your friend,
Clover (my stepmom is Attorney Lisa Haster)
P.S. Here is a picture of my dog Oliveoil. I put her in my
Barbie dream house because it's bigger than her kennel.

Letter 2: Olive Oil

Now, if an appeal from Lisa's little
stepdaughter isn't enough to get you to
call, she brings in the big guns: Clover's
dog Olive Oil!

It's very similar to Letter 1 from Clover. Again, it's written in a "handwriting" font, and the text is in different
colors. This one includes Olive Oil's paw
print at the bottom, to let you know it's
the dog writing this time.

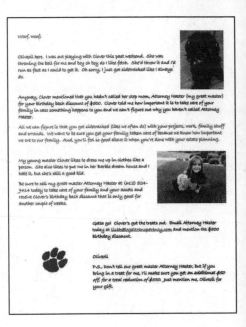

Results

Everyone hates those scrappy, childlike letters and throws them straight
in the trash, right?

No. In fact, Lisa even had a prospect call her up to tell her how creative
it was and how much he loved the letters!

On average, Lisa sends out 8 of these campaigns each month, at a *total*
cost (for all eight) of just $70.40. Those eight follow-ups result in 1.5 con-
sultations. With an average fee for an estate plan running to $2,500, the
ROI on this campaign is massive.

Why Is This a Great Campaign to Model?

This is another small, simple campaign that any business could use. While Lisa is using it to follow up from a shock and awe package, something like this could just as easily be used to follow up on a phone call, a letter, a meeting, or anything else.

All you need is a list of people who haven't taken the next step with you, a printer, and some colored pencils!

An OUTRAGEOUS Way to Turn Your Once-a-Year Customers into Monthly Customers

I first met Michael Thibault when he was helping at Rory Fatt's business; Rory would often bring Michael with him to my mastermind group. After a while, Michael started to work with other businesses and, in 2014, he asked if he could become a client of mine.

We would discuss how to improve the different things he was doing with his clients, and one of the campaigns we talked about was his *Red Envelope, No Peeking Promotion*, which is his top performing campaign ever.

The heart of the campaign is a simple red envelope given out to customers in December (when restaurants are busy) to bring them back in January (when they're not). It's an OUTRAGEOUS way to bring your peak-time customers back when things go quiet, and helps the restaurant owners implement Thing 6 (building your marketing around celebrations and holidays) into their own business.

Michael's website sets out how the promotion works in this very clear diagram.

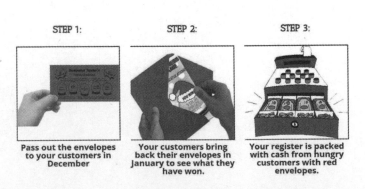

STEP 1:	STEP 2:	STEP 3:
Pass out the envelopes to your customers in December	Your customers bring back their envelopes in January to see what they have won.	Your register is packed with cash from hungry customers with red envelopes.

The envelopes announce various prizes the recipient can win from the restaurant, but they mustn't peek inside until they bring the envelope back in January. Until then, they have no way to know what they've won. That's a critical aspect of this campaign—if the customer knows what they've won, they can weigh up whether they want to go back or not. It has to be a secret until they're back at the business that gave them the envelope.

That's how the Red Envelope promotion works. But how does Michael get a restaurant owner to order envelopes in the first place? That's what this campaign is about.

The Campaign

The goal of this campaign is to maximize the number of red envelopes sold to restaurant owners.

Leads come from three main sources.

The first is Michael's house list—this is a campaign that restaurants buy year after year. The second is a range of joint venture partnerships that Michael has set up over the years. And finally, the third source is cold leads generated by pay per click ads on Facebook and Google and a brokered list.

Altogether, that's around 300,000 leads each year.

Part 1 – Emails to the House List

The campaign starts with a series of seven emails sent to the house list starting in October to drive traffic to a landing page.

The first five emails have a "free shipping before November 1ˢᵗ" deadline, which gets extended for just one more day in email #6 (the first email after the deadline).

There's a general principle in marketing that you should never extend deadlines. It just trains your list to ignore them because they'll always get more time. But there's another principle that says you can get away with most things as long as you can give a good reason why.

In this case, Michael points out that the deadline ended on a holiday (Halloween), which was unfair because a lot of people would have been busy trick-or-treating, so he's reopening the free shipping offer for just 24 hours, in case anyone missed it.

That's actually pretty smart—the reader knows Halloween is done, so there's no third chance. They have to act right now or miss it. It lights a real fire under them

True to his word, after that email Michael takes away the free shipping. Instead, the final email has a new deadline—you have to act in the next 48 hours, or you won't get your envelopes in time for December.

The final email is also loaded with testimonials (Thing 3) to give social proof.

No Peek Email #7 (Subject: Last Chance)

```
I know you're busy getting ready for the holiday season
so I will be quick.

I remember when I owned my restaurant and how I loved
November and December.  Lots of holiday parties booked,
holiday gift card sales flying off the shelf, staff in
a good mood because they make great tips this time of
year!

Lots of fun, good times.  But what happens when January
rolls around...

Does all that go away at your restaurant?

Well, I have the solution.

I have sent you a couple emails about the #1 Done For
You Restaurant Promotion that turns January into the
busiest month of the year for your restaurant. But you
have to act now if you want to make it work for your
restaurant.

You'll see what I mean when you go to the special web-
site I set up for you.

(Hyperlink)

It's called the No Peeking/Red Envelope Promotion.
Works like holiday magic putting more butts in seats in
January.
```

Check out what just a few restaurant owners that have used this money making promotion in January had to say:

"It was a GREAT January! We had a 60% redemption rate on our No Peeking Promotion and increased sales by nearly $25,000.00 a 22% increase over previous years. Thanks!!!!!!" **The Rusty Keg Brian Pettit OH**

"No Peeking was the first big promotion we did, and we did it again the next year because it worked so great. So far, we've had an ROI of 762.89%!" - **Tori Nelson, The Wapiti Restaurant and Pub, Estes Park, CO**

"We implemented this promotion as soon as we heard about it and our ROI was $154 to the dollar." - **F. Tambellini's, Pittsburgh, PA**

"We increased our sales over last year more than $7,300 with our No Peeking promotion" - **Gentleman Jim's - New York**

Click the button below to get all the details of how this cheap, money making, and almost no work on your part "No Peeking" promotion is done.

(Hyperlink)

Dig the well before you thirst,

Michael Thibault

Part 2: JV Emails

While leads on the house list are getting their emails, emails are also going out to people on Michael's partners' lists. Each JV partner has their own tailored email sequence driving traffic to a custom landing page.

Part 3: Cold Lead Generation

You can't rely on house lists and JVs all the time—you need to be generating your own cold leads. Michael gets cold leads from two main sources.

First, he buys lists of leads from a broker and sends them a mailing. Many business owners are nervous about buying lists because they worry about the quality of the leads, but you'll notice that a lot of the campaigns in this book use brokered lists. The reality is that the right list, bought from a reputable source, is priceless.

Second, he is running pay-per-click ads on Google and Facebook to drive traffic to his landing page.

Part 4: Existing Clients

Finally, alongside warm leads from your house list and partners, and cold leads, never forget that the warmest leads—and the easiest to sell to—are past customers. Michael sends a sales letter to past customers, and his sales team also phone them.

Part 5: The Upsell

Like any good OUTRAGEOUS marketer, Michael has a back-end ready for buyers. When someone orders the Red Envelope campaign, Michael includes a sales letter for pre-written newsletter services.

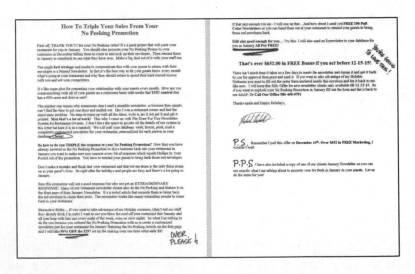

That offer potentially turns buyers of the No Peek promotion into customers for life.

To encourage the reader to take action, there's a bonus and a deadline (Thing 2). Michael also sets up a double readership path (Thing 4)—the headline is in red, and red is also used to make certain words and phrases stand out. He also uses red doodles to draw the eye to specific parts of the text. One doodle I'd like to call particular attention to is the one that says "OVER PLEASE": never assume that a reader will turn the page just because they reach the bottom. If you want to make sure someone will read the next page, give them an explicit instruction!

Results

The last time Michael ran this campaign, he sold 400,000 red envelopes, making this a very worthwhile exercise.

Why Is This a Great Campaign to Model?

Inserting a pitch for a follow-on product is OUTRAGEOUSLY smart because you're already paying to ship the product to the customer, so there's no additional cost to you to include the sales letter. You'll see the same strategy used in a number of campaigns in this book, and if you're shipping physical products to your buyers, I recommend you do the same.

Michael's campaign is a great example of tapping into the conversation that clients are already having. In this case, he knows that restaurant owners are always worried that January will be slow, so he doesn't need to convince them that it's going to happen. Ask yourself what conversation your own customers are having, and then build your campaigns around that.

Finally, another obvious thing to model is the red envelope campaign itself. If you're in a business where you want to increase how often customers come back (which is pretty much every business!), then you could run a variation on this type of campaign. You don't have to wait for Christmas—it could work any time of year.

How to Use OUTRAGEOUS Doodles to Reel People in and Make Money

Back in Thing 4, I discussed four OUTRAGEOUS response boosters, and one of them was CopyDoodles®. Many of the campaigns in this book use CopyDoodles somewhere on a letter, an envelope, a webpage, a flyer, or some other element of the campaign. This campaign is from Mike Capuzzi, the creator of CopyDoodles.

I've known Mike for many years. He was originally a member of GKIC, then joined the GKIC Peak Performer program, and eventually become a member of my mastermind group. He also owned a local GKIC chapter in Pennsylvania.

CopyDoodles was "born" at a GKIC meeting in 2007, when Mike started showing us sales letters he was creating with hand-drawn arrows, lines, and text, and telling us about the difference it was making to his results. The first thing I did was to tell my team to start using them on all our sales letters and web pages. Then I told everyone else they should be using them too!

The Campaign

In 2017, Mike was exhibiting at an event called Renegade Millionaire 2.0. There were about 200 people in the room—120 primary attendees plus their guests. They'd paid several thousand dollars to be at that event, so it was a high-value and very committed crowd of buyers, but Mike anticipated that a lot of them wouldn't already be CopyDoodles customers.

The main components of the campaign were:

- Irresistible offer for event attendees
- Attendee manual insert

- Attendee bag insert
- Exhibit table
- Gift with purchase

Irresistible Offer for Event Attendees

To celebrate the business's 10th birthday, Mike came up with a one-time-only special offer for attendees to get a 10-year membership of CopyDoodles plus five unique bonus gifts for a single payment.

The price represented a real saving of more than $3,500 compared to paying for everything separately, and the offer was only valid until the end of the event.

Already we have two of the elements of a good offer, as explained in Thing 2: huge value, and a very definite deadline.

Attendee Manual Insert

Mike used a one-page advertisement in the attendee manual to get people to his exhibit table (similar to what Dustin Matthews and Mike Crow did in their campaigns).

The "bait" was a free "Decade of Doodles" swipe file CD valued at $199.

It's A CopyDoodles BIRTHDAY WOW!

Copydoodles - the original and best collection of hand-drawn attention-grabbers turns 10 years old this month and we're celebrating with a special one-time offer here at Renegade Millionaire 20!

Stop by our table for a FREE "Decade of Doodles" Swipe File CD ($199 value)

Attendee Bag Insert

Just Like Dustin and Mike Crow, Mike also added a little "extra something" in the bags people get when they register: a clear plastic bag with one of those hand-drawn letters printed on lined colored paper, and an order form.

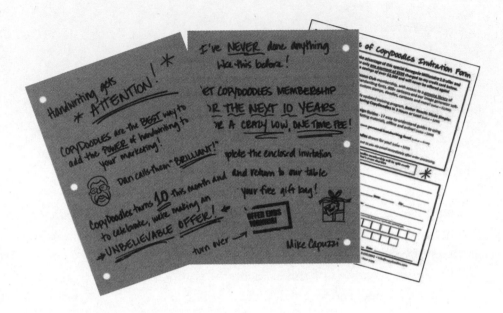

Exhibit Table

The exhibitor table was decorated to get people's attention:

- Two banners
- Birthday balloons
- CopyDoodles giveaways
- CopyDoodles brochure
- CopyDoodles testimonial book and Dan Kennedy testimonial

Every business that presents to potential customers face-to-face should have a testimonial book and display it where people can pick it up and read it while they wait to speak to you. It was really smart for Mike to get a testimonial from Dan Kennedy at his own event. Just like in Dustin Matthew's promotion, there's a lot of leverage to be had from using the event organizer's name in your promotions.

Gift With Purchase

I already discussed the value of gifts and premiums in Thing 5, and Mike made sure there were lots of them to make his offer OUTRAGEOUSLY irresistible.

When somebody joined CopyDoodles, they got a special gift bag that included:

- Custom-printed CopyDoodles birthday gift bag
- Thank you note
- CopyDoodles luggage identifier
- CopyDoodles Pocket Guide

Results

As a result of this campaign, 20 new members joined generating $11,980 in membership fees—all from a crowd where a lot of the 120 primary attendees would probably already be CopyDoodles customers.

Mike also donated $50 from every sale at the event to two non-profit organizations: a total of $1,000.

And remember, these people are now on his list for the next ten years. Guaranteed! They're not going to opt out of a product they've bought. For ten years, Mike can continue to promote upsells and back-end products, live events, membership of his mastermind, and anything else he wants.

Why Is This a Great Campaign to Model?

This was a one-time event built around a special milestone in Mike's business, in the same way that Julie Boswell built a campaign around a "special milestone" in her client's life. That plays into Thing 6—these very smart marketers are creating opportunities for a celebration, rather than waiting for someone to come up with a suitable holiday.

It also shows another approach to generating sales from a booth at a small event, even when a lot of the people there have already bought your product.

You could run this approach at any of the thousands of small trade fairs, networking meetings, conferences, and other events that happen in every major city each year, or set up your own event.

It's a campaign that doesn't require you to sponsor a breakout, a breakfast or a lunch. All you need is a table and some bag inserts.

An OUTRAGEOUS Way to Make People Want to Visit Your Booth Even Before They Get to the Event

Mike Crow was in my mastermind group from the first year to the very end. When I left GKIC, he moved to Dan Kennedy's mastermind group.

Like a few of the other campaigns in this book, the aim of Mike's campaign is designed to get attendees at someone else's event to visit his sponsor booth, and ultimately into a free breakfast presentation where they can be converted into members of his program.

The Campaign

Although the campaign is designed to get results at a live event, it actually begins well ahead of the event. Now that, in itself, is pretty OUTRAGEOUS. Most event sponsors will wait until the day of the event to start pitching. Mike likes to start indoctrinating them even before they walk in the room.

Step 1 – The Postcard

The campaign starts with a postcard sent to registered attendees one or two weeks before the event. This isn't always possible, since it requires the cooperation of the event organizer, but when

Mike *can* get the list in advance, it gives him a "soft touch" to inform them about a breakfast session at the upcoming event and introduce himself and his co-founder, Christa Trantham.

Since the real draw is the free breakfast, there's a full-color photograph of a hot breakfast, so the reader knows what they'll be getting.

Step 2 – The Ad

Most events give attendees some type of informational book or guide. Like the other event-based campaigns in this book, Mike pays for a 1- or 2-page ad in the event guide. The content of the ad is similar to the postcard and focuses on the call to action to attend the breakfast.

The ad is deliberately designed to look like the postcard so that people will recognize it. There's also a photo of the breakfast (again) and pictures of prizes that will be given away during the event.

Step 3 – The Bag Stuffer

Along with an event guide, most organizers also give attendees a "goody bag" as part of onsite check-in/registration, which is a great way of getting your marketing into their hands. Mike also pays for them to include a "bag stuffer"—a separate piece of marketing collateral.

Like Dustin Mathews, Mike wants his bag stuffer to stand out from the other sponsors, so he has a couple of OUTRAGEOUS tricks to make sure that happens.

First, most companies print their marketing piece on a standard 8.5" x 11" flyer. Mike prints his insert on oversized card stock that will literally stick out above the other pieces in the bag.

Second, most inserts are flat sheets. Mike uses a range of "lumpy mail" tactics to give his insert a unique feel. The most effective strategy he's used for this campaign is an old GKIC trick: he attaches a real $1 bill to the top corner of the bag stuffer. The dollar is attached so that it will stick out even from the oversized insert, and it's usually the first thing an attendee notices when they look in their bag.

The call to action on the insert is to visit Mike's booth to "Double This Dollar," and the back of the flyer gives details on the upcoming breakfast.

Step 4 – The Booth

The booth is set up with a single goal of getting as many people as possible to the breakfast, which is usually set up for day 2 or 3 of the event so that Mike and his team have time to promote it properly.

1. Mike collects the visitor's name and contact information, and gets them to complete a KMI (Keep Me Informed) card, which gives him permission to contact them. All completed cards are entered

into a draw for special prizes at the event, such as laptops, tablets, gold coins, Fitbits, gift cards, smart watches, etc.

2. At the stand, Mike takes their $1 bill and exchanges it for a $2 bill (as promised) with a sticker inviting them to the breakfast session. Mike and his team tell the visitor about the benefits of the information they'll hear, and mention that, although they've already turned $1 into $2, if they bring that $2 to the breakfast, they'll discover how to turn it into $100. This is a great way to build curiosity.

> **Friday 6:15am**
> ROOM: St. Johns
> **Attend This Special Session And Find Out How To** *Turn This $2 Into $100.00*
> ➤ **Coach Blueprint**
> Be Successful And Be Around Those That Are Successful

3. Many events use colored ribbons attached to the bottom of attendees' name badges to indicate special status like VIP ticket holders, panelists, speakers, etc. Mike hijacks that and attaches a ribbon to the name badge of everyone who visits the stand, announcing that Coach Blueprint turned their $1 into $2. Again, that's a very smart move—it turns every visitor into a walking billboard that reminds everyone who sees them about the process.

4. They are also told that everyone who attends the breakfast will automatically get a free gift. Most often, this is Mike's Coach Blueprint 2 Week Success Calendar, which is part of his main "big box" product. It's cheap to produce but has high perceived value.

5. The booth is decorated with posters of testimonials from many members of the program. The specific testimonials on show are rotated throughout the event, so there's always new material on display when someone walks past the booth.

6. Finally, if someone doesn't want to wait until the breakfast and insists on asking about Mike's program, he and his team are only too happy to have that conversation!

Step 5 – Additional Promotional Activities

Throughout the event, Mike and his team are hustling to get people to the breakfast. Depending on what the venue and event organizers will allow, here are some of the strategies they use.

Reminders

Whoever is working the booth takes time after meal breaks and at the end of each day to enter the new contacts into Infusionsoft.

Between the time when someone hands over their contact information at the booth and the start of the breakfast, they get up to three email reminders to attend (through Infusionsoft) and three SMS text message reminders (through FixYourFunnel.com, a third-party service that integrates with Infusionsoft).

Breakfast "Tickets"

Team members have a pile of "tickets" that are essentially just smaller versions of the flyer with information on the special breakfast session (time, location, topic, bullet points of what they'll discover with benefits to them, etc.) and remind the reader that there's free food being offered. They give them out to people they meet at the booth or other areas of the event.

If any members of Mike's program are at the event, they also get a small stack of the tickets, and they are only too happy to pass them out to people they meet as well.

Room Drops

Some hotels also offer a "room drop" service where you can pay to have your marketing pieces slipped under the door of specific guests (it's a strategy I used myself many times at my own events).

For room drops, Mike uses a version of the bag stuffer flyer with more testimonials and a call to action to attend the breakfast. He has this dropped around dinner time the evening before the breakfast so that people will find it when they return to their rooms.

Hashtags

Some events get attendees to post on social media throughout the event with event-specific hashtags. With all that activity going on, Mike and his team again hijack something that is already happening by posting their own images of giveaway winners using the hashtags.

Step 6 – The Breakfast

Mike has used this campaign for both lunches and breakfasts, but his preference is always a breakfast on day two of a three-day event or day three of a four-day event. Hosting anything on the last day is never a good idea because many people have already left, but he also wants a good run-up to promote the breakfast effectively.

The breakfast is to sell attendees into the coaching program:

1. It's a breakfast, so there is free, hot food for the attendees. It's a sad reflection that despite all the carefully crafted marketing messages and strategies, the most effective piece of copy for getting people into the room is "FREE Hot Breakfast," closely followed by "FREE coffee." It works!
2. If someone hasn't previously visited the booth, they are asked to complete a KMI card.
3. Every attendee gets the promised free gift at some point during the presentation. It serves as a post-event reminder they can take away with them, and also lists a website they can visit to take further action.
4. There is an informational presentation capped off with a sales pitch for an irresistible offer to join the coaching program.

Step 7 – Post-Breakfast

By the end of the breakfast, most of the heavy lifting is complete.

The team schedules time with Mike or Christa for anyone who has questions about the programs. Mike or Christa meet with them to see if they are a good candidate for the program and if they are, they work to close them.

After the event, contacts are added to follow-up campaigns that invite them to future valuable informational events (teleclasses and webinars) on a regular basis, where they are once again given the opportunity to buy. Remember Thing 10: just because someone didn't buy doesn't mean you stop selling to them.

Results

Mike has repeatedly employed this and similar campaigns to fill a room with 50-100 people (typically 15 to 30% of total attendees) for these early morning presentations.

Once they are in the room, Mike consistently closes around 30% of them with an offer to become members.

Why Is This a Great Campaign to Model?

Even though there are several OUTRAGEOUS CAMPAIGNS in this book to make the most of a booth sponsorship, each is unique. Here are some of the key elements you can swipe from Mike's CAMPAIGN and deploy in your own campaigns.

1. The whole idea of starting in advance is brilliant. As well as conferences, you could use this in advance of networking meetings or chamber of commerce events, your own events, a sales meeting or pitch presentation, or even a JV promotion.
2. The prize draw for people who complete a KMI card is an OUTRAGEOUS way of bribing people to give you their contact details. Think of it as the offline equivalent of a lead magnet offer.
3. The OUTRAGEOUS repetition of the call to action multiple times and in multiple media is a great way to make sure people attend, and it's something that will work in any situation. Christa calls it "connecting the dots": making sure that all the marketing pieces connect to each other so that you truly get the lead's attention more than once. Attendees get details of the breakfast session on the postcard before they even get to the event, in their event guide, and on the oversized insert. If someone doesn't turn up, it's not because they don't know where to go!
4. Another general principle you can copy is the idea of using photographs of freebies (the breakfast, the prizes, etc.) rather than just listing them
5. Finally, think about ways to turn your clients into "walking billboards"—which you can do both online and offline. What's your equivalent of the name badge ribbon?

An OUTRAGEOUS Use of Multi-Step Marketing You Probably Won't Have Thought Of

Nina Hershberger was a member of GKIC in the early days, and created the wallet mailer campaign (www.walletmailer.com) that I featured in my first book (and which I mention in Thing 8). She is also a very smart marketer. This campaign is an outlier for this book—it was created to help Nina's son, Tyler, get a job. I've included it, however, because it's a direct response campaign, and the approach could be used in any industry.

After graduating from college with a degree in Graphic Design and Video Production, Tyler became a ballroom dance instructor for four years. When he got married, he decided it was time to get a different job—one that didn't require so much evening and weekend work—and quit his job at the dance studio.

After several months of scouring job sites and countless online applications, Tyler still didn't have a job. Being the son of a great marketer like Nina, however, he knew enough about direct response marketing to know that the best jobs wouldn't be found on a job board.

The Campaign

Nina and Tyler created a five-step direct mail campaign to top local companies that would be good to work for, regardless of whether they had an advertised vacancy. The whole campaign was mapped out and written before they sent the first mail—that's a really smart move for any marketer. The letters went out weekly, so the entire sequence took five weeks from start to finish.

Nina told Tyler to be prepared, because once the letters went out, the phone would start ringing. He kept his computer on at all times, and a tracking spreadsheet open and ready. That way, if the phone rang and he didn't recognize the number, he was ready.

Targeting

Tyler lives in Indianapolis, IN. Each year, a list is published of the top 100 companies to work for in Indiana, and 38 of those are in the Indianapolis area. They also added ten video production companies to the list, since that is a field that Tyler loves.

Those 48 companies became the target audience for the campaign.

Mailing 1: File Folder Mailing

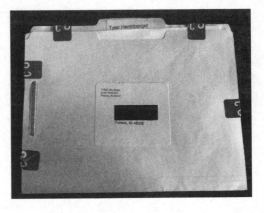

Making your mail stand out in the mail pile is a great way to make sure it gets opened first. I discovered many years ago that putting your letter in a manila folder—the kind that you would normally put in a filing cabinet— is a great way to make your package unmissable.

For her first mailing, that's exactly what Nina did. She put Tyler's name on an index label at the top and sealed the folder with the kind of labels a medical office would use. She stuck an address label on the front, added stamps and took the folders to the post office.

Inside Nina's first mailing was a mockup of an interview form customized with the company's logo (that's a form of personalization—Thing 4) and handwritten notes (as though an interview had already taken place).

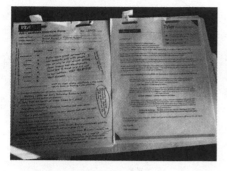

Nina bought an "Approved" stamp from an office supplies store and stamped each form, to suggest Tyler had been approved for hire.

Also in the folder was a document listing the positions Tyler would be qualified for—Nina did that because these were companies that didn't have any public job openings, so she wanted to jog their thinking about some possibilities.

Finally, there was a cover letter and a copy of Tyler's resume.

Mailing 2: X-Ray

The second mailing was in a 6x9 Kraft envelope with a handwritten address and real stamps. Anytime you send a letter, it's OUTRAGEOUSLY simple to make it stand out by using real stamps, rather than the franking machine, and writing the address on by hand. It makes it look much more personal, and less like business mail.

Inside the envelope was a fun message printed in reverse on a transparency to look like an X-ray—once again, the company's logo was mail-merged into it. Along with that was another copy of Tyler's resume, and a two-page newsletter announcing that Tyler was writing a book.

How often do you think a hiring manager sees an application from someone who has written a book? It's an OUTRAGEOUS way to stand out, and it works just as well in business: that's why you'll see so many campaigns in this book that use a book to grab attention and stand out.

Mailing 3: Crumpled Letter in a #10 white envelope

For the third mailing, Nina took a photo of Tyler looking puzzled and paper-clipped (very like the puzzle piece letter in Thing 4) it to a personalized letter printed on yellow paper in a handwriting font (like my legal pad letter in Thing 9).

Along with the letter was yet another copy of Tyler's resume (never assume the recipient has seen anything you've mailed before). To make it stand out, Nina took the resume and crumpled it up then straightened it back out before putting it in the envelope. The folds created an unusual texture inside the envelope that would make the recipient want to open the envelope—isn't that an OUTRAGEOUSLY simple way to turn a flat sheet of paper into 3D mail?

Mailing 4: The Sock Letter

The fourth letter was sent in a window envelope with a colorful child's sock bought from a dollar store (which just shows you can use almost anything to turn a letter into 3D mail, and it doesn't have to cost a lot).

Mailing 5: Max the Dog Joins In

For the final letter, Nina co-opted the family dog, Max. The letter—"signed" by Max with a paw print—had a photo of Max paperclipped to it and a dog biscuit stuck next to the paw print. The letter and another copy of Tyler's resume went into a clear plastic ziplock bag. So, it's 3D mail, in a clear bag, with a biscuit. Who could resist opening that?

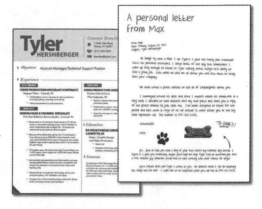

The Postscript

Even after he was hired and working, Tyler finished his book and put it on Amazon. To close the loop, he wrote again to the other 47 companies on his list thanking them for considering him and giving them a copy of the book he had promised to send them. That's a very clever move, because if he ever contacts them again, they'll remember the book.

Results

Within hours of the first mailing arriving, the phone started to ring. The first call was from the CEO of an engineering company who told him he had never seen anything this creative and had to take him to lunch to meet him.

By mailing #3 Tyler had a 38% response rate and was getting many interviews—a spectacular result for a cold job approach.

One interview was with an HR executive who said that in all his years, after hundreds of resumes, he had never seen anything like Tyler's mailings.

By mailing #4 CEOs were making calls on his behalf to other business owners they knew trying to help him find a job.

By mailing #5 he had landed a job with a video production company.

Did it make Tyler memorable? When he started looking for a new job again a few years later, the company that hired him was one that he had contacted in the original campaign, and they still remembered the mailings.

Why Is This a Great Campaign to Model?

In a world where everyone thinks the way to get a job is to wait for a job posting and mail in your resume and a cover letter, a direct mail campaign like this is guaranteed to make you stand out from the crowd.

But can you learn anything from it to use in your marketing? Absolutely!

This campaign is all about personalization and standing out. If you want your letters to be noticed—whether you're sending a resume, a brochure, a sales letter, a donation request, or anything—there are techniques in this campaign that will get your mailings noticed and acted upon.

The key? This was not a one-shot mailing: it was multi-step. Don't stop after the first letter. Reinforce your message by repeating it multiple times, and make each time as unusual and memorable as the others.

27 - RICHELLE SHAW

An OUTRAGEOUS Way to Disguise a Free Gift as a Contest Prize

Richelle Shaw is a direct marketing consultant who creates campaigns for her clients. She created this campaign to get referrals for her client, Dr. Wells—an OB/GYN in Henderson, NV. It's a great example of a strategy I have taught for years called *Everybody Wins*—you run a contest, and you make sure that everyone who enters gets some sort of prize. For this campaign, the grand prize was a family trip to Disney. However, as this was an 'everybody wins' campaign, there was a range of prizes (depending on how many referrals someone made), all the way down to a free pizza for everyone who made at least one referral.

The Campaign

'My Doctor is Famous' Referral Cards

To make referring someone easier, Richelle created postcards that could be given to friends and family, featuring a cartoon of the doctor and listing all his media appearances. People love to brag, and the card allowed them to boast to friends and family about their "famous" doctor.

Direct Mail

Richelle created a six-step direct mail campaign to existing clients to promote the contest.

Step 1: "Free Lunch" Lunch Bag Mmailer

The first mailer was a kid's lunch bag containing a blue envelope stuffed with the "My doctor is famous" referral postcards and a letter that explained the contest. You'll see unusual ways to send a letter in many of the campaigns in this book. Why? Because you have to get people to open your letter, and making your letter stand out is a great way to get them curious.

Henderson OB/GYN is Giving Away up to $117,234 worth of PRIZES

Is Dr. Wells Crazy?

I bet you heard that there is no such thing as a FREE LUNCH?? Well, I am going to change that for all of my patients who refer their friends and families to me.

For the entire month of JUNE – I want to reward you for doing me a big favor!

We have a series of great gifts, starting with just one referral – you will receive a FREE PIZZA!

Then, for more referrals the prizes get better

1 Referral - FREE Pizza

3 Referrals - Take the Family to the Movies (4 Tickets)

5 Referrals - $250 Spa Day

7 Referrals - 3 Days/2 Nights Orlando, San Diego or San Francisco

```
10 Referrals - Trip to Disneyland for family of 4
More than 10!!! - (Special Mystery Gift)


So what can you do?
1. Open the blue envelope which is full of referrals
cards for Henderson OB/GYN
2. Call your women friends and family (we see patients
from 13 - 82) and invite them to schedule an appoint-
ment with me
3. As you know, I will treat them like family
```

Then there's a description of the services Dr. Wells provides, and who his ideal patients are before the email continues with details of the referral contest.

```
And just for recommending Henderson OB/GYN, we have a
gift for you. A gift? Actually some great gifts! They
range from Afternoon Revival Spa Days to tickets to
Disneyland, just for referring patients to us.
Of course from now on, when you refer another patient
to us, we will properly thank you with a great gift,
but during this time, June 1, 2009 to June 30, 2009,
the gifts are extremely fabulous.
Good Luck!
Dr. Wells
P.S. We have to Hurry, This all ends June 30, 2009 be-
fore Viva finds out!
```

Step 2: Reminder Letter

A week later, a letter went out with a reminder. To make the letter stand out, Richelle stuck a rubber brain (from 3D Mail) to the top of the sheet. Nothing says "no-brainer" like a rubber brain stuck to a letter!

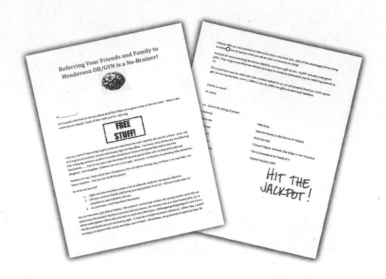

Step 2: Reminder Postcard

For the second step, Richelle took a photo of the doctor and his young daughter with a pile of the lunch bags (from step 1) and created another postcard to remind the patient about the contest. An OUTRAGEOUS photograph not only ties together

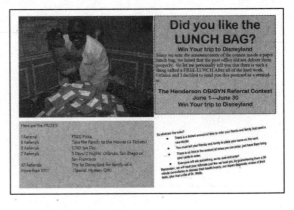

different steps in a multi-step campaign but also creates a visual anchor back to something that would have been very memorable when it arrived—after all, how often does someone send you a lunch bag in the mail?

Step 3: Newsletter Flyer

The same photo of Dr. Wells with his daughter was then inserted with the monthly newsletter. Richelle reused the photo of Dr. Wells with his daughter to tie the campaign together with a flyer to be used to make the referral.

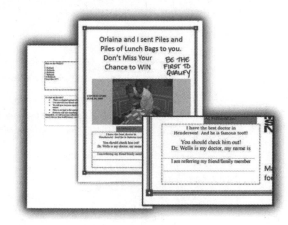

Think about that for a moment. Dr. Wells was paying postage for the newsletter anyway, so it was a very smart move to put something else in the same envelope, and it's a great example of thinking holistically about marketing. It's easy for a business owner to put their campaigns in a silo. That can be confusing for your customers and leads, especially if the messages aren't in sync. It's far better to weave the steps of your campaign into the things that you're already doing. Not only will it save you money, but it takes advantage of the fact that people are already expecting something from you, so they're primed to watch for it.

Step 4: Doctor in a Pizza Hat

For the next step, Richelle sent a postcard with a photo of Dr. Wells in a chef's hat, ready to deliver pizza to people who had already referred. The text was a reminder about the contest.

The same photo was used in a flyer in the monthly newsletter.

Step 5: Doctor in a Bikini and a Grass Skirt

Step 5 had another OUTRAGEOUS photo. This time, Dr. Wells in a bikini and a grass skirt. Why? He wants to go on vacation, of course! The photo was used for that month's postcard and newsletter to keep everything consistent:

Step 6: Final reminder

The final step was to announce the winners in the newsletter.

Public recognition is a really smart way to get people to do the things you want them to do. When you mention someone in a newsletter, they will feel great and want to do it again. Other readers see it and think, "I want to be mentioned like that, too." If you want people to make referrals, start to thank people publicly in your newsletter for each referral they make.

Results

The campaign generated 157 new referred patients. No one won the trip to Disney (you had to make ten referrals to win that), but even after the campaign ended, people kept sending in more referrals.

Why Is This a Great Campaign to Model?

The whole campaign is an OUTRAGEOUSLY good example of some key principles of OUTRAGEOUS marketing. First, Richelle used great images to get people's attention (Thing 4). Second, Dr. Wells wasn't afraid to be OUTRAGEOUS himself (that was something I discussed in Part 1 of this book). Third, Richelle kept the mailings and the newsletters consistent, so that everything reinforced everything else.

If you want to generate referrals—and I can't think of a business that wouldn't want their customers to refer them—then this is a great way to get them. As long as you're prepared to be OUTRAGEOUS!

An OUTRAGEOUS Way to Fill a High-Ticket Program at the Worst Time of Year, Even if You Don't Have a List

When I was getting ready to write this book, I called my great friend Mike Koenigs and asked him whom I should ask to help me. He told me Rob Cuesta was the best person to work with. I took his advice, and it was one of the best decisions I've made. Not only did Rob help me write the book, but he also came up with great strategies to promote it. For example, if you're reading this book, there's a good chance you heard about it through someone on the launch team that Rob got me to build.

The Campaign

What do you do when you want to launch a $16,000 program but it's December 24th, and you don't have a mailing list? Maybe you said to yourself, "Wait until January" or (if you've read some of the other campaigns in this book) "Buy a list from a broker."

In December 2011, Rob had been running his consulting business for almost ten years. After a rocky start that took him to the verge of bankruptcy in 2005, he'd turned things around and built the business to six figures over a matter of a few months. In 2010 Rob was the runner-up in a "Better Your Best" contest run by his business mentor, and after that, he started getting invited to share his story at other people's events. Soon, consultants and coaches were asking him to teach them how he did it, so he decided to launch a program at the start of 2012.

Rob had built his business working with corporate clients, so coaches and consultants were a relatively new audience for him. On top of that, it was Christmas, which meant that everyone would be stepping away from their business for a couple of weeks.

Although Rob didn't have many coaches and consultants in his mailing list, he exported his social media and address book contacts to a spreadsheet and narrowed it down to just coaches and consultants in the UK or Europe who'd had some sort of personal contact with him in the past three years.

The personal contact was important because he knew strangers probably wouldn't open his emails over Christmas, but people who recognized his name and had shaken his hand probably would.

Step 1: Start with the End in Mind

Rob had previously spent a year working for a seminar company, selling a high-ticket program from the stage almost every weekend. He decided to launch his $16,000 program with a free two-day seminar in January 2012. That meant that the aim of the campaign wasn't to sell the program; instead, it was simply to get people to sign up for the live event.

Step 2: The Twelve Days of Christmas Campaign

Rob created a 12-day email sequence he called his "Twelve Days of Christmas" (Thing 6). The emails went out daily from December 26th on, and each day, Rob taught one of his principles for building a six-figure business by positioning yourself as the leader in your field.

He created his own term for that leader—"The Natural Expert"—which is an OUTRAGEOUSLY smart thing to do. Any time you create the language for the result you deliver, you create a "market of one"—you become the only person in the world who can give your clients that specific result.

The emails were 99% free value offered to the client. The other 1% was an invitation to the two-day seminar which he positioned as a "client appreciation" event (even though the people he was emailing weren't clients).

> My no-charge 2012 "Thank You" Workshop is my way of
> showing my appreciation to those who have played a part
> in my personal and professional success over the last
> few years, my way of giving back. If you haven't seen
> the details yet, click here

There was a deadline of January 8th (Thing 2) to encourage people to take action.

The campaign was designed to do three things. First, it positioned standard ways of marketing as the reason why the reader wasn't getting clients (making your competitors part of the problem, not the solution, is an OUTRAGEOUSLY smart thing to do in your marketing).

Second, he promised solutions to specific problems in the live event.

> But uniqueness—the elusive "USP" you may have heard
> about—doesn't work anymore. I'll go into that a lot
> more at the workshop, and what you need to do instead,
> but let's just say that being Unique is actually a lot
> harder than the Gurus would have you believe. In fact,
> I'm going to argue that coming up with a USP in the
> coaching market is pretty much impossible. So, if
> you've been struggling to come up with your niche and
> your USP, "Thank You!" 2012 could be exactly what you
> need.

Third, each email positioned and pre-sold some part of the offer he'd be making at the event (although, he didn't say that, of course) so that they'd be primed for it when he started talking about it.

For example, writing and publishing an authority book was a major aspect of the program (which is no surprise, given that it's the core of his business these days!). Here's how he introduced it.

> One of the major points I'll be covering at "Thank You!"
> 2012 is writing to position yourself as the Natural Ex-
> pert in your field.
> Even though society as a whole seems to be leaving the
> book behind, when it comes to choosing our "experts",
> we still hold authors in awe. That's why one of the key

things I encourage all my clients to do is to write a physical book, not an ebook—we'll discuss why in the workshop.

It doesn't have to be War and Peace.

I see a role for two kinds of books in building your business. I call them your "Expert Manifestos" (or should that be Manifestoes? Anyway, I digress!)

The first is a short book covering specific aspects of your audience's problem, or explaining your System. It's great to give away to prospective clients.

The second is a full-length book that positions you as THE expert. It's your opportunity to tell the world not just what you do, but how you do it, and the results that you can achieve.

Imagine that you're pitching for a piece of work. Your competitor has just come out of the meeting, having left the potential client with a brochure and their business card. You walk in and hand over a copy of your book. Who are they more likely to hire?

Imagine that a client is looking for advice in your area of expertise. They look on Amazon and find your book listed, with a link to your website. They follow the link. Are they more likely to hire you than someone who found your name on Google?

Most coaches and consultants have at least one book inside them that is screaming to get out. There are two main challenges that hold them back, however:

- getting it written
- getting it published

I could write a whole book—indeed, two books!—about those challenges, so I can't do them justice in a simple email. Suffice it to say that in the workshop, I'll talk about how you can get your book written in a matter of days, along with different publishing options.

By the January 8 deadline, 21 people had signed up for the event—not bad for a campaign that started the day after Christmas, with a spreadsheet of 253 email addresses!

Step 3: The Event

When attendees arrived, they were given a workbook, a pen, and a clipboard. (There's an interesting psychological twist to the clipboard. They'd be using it on the final day, when they filled in their application, so handing it out with the workbook at the start got them comfortable writing on it).

Rob started with the challenges new businesses go through, and the myths that hold new entrepreneurs back—conversations he knew they were having in their own mind and with their significant others.

Then he took them through his own story of starting the business, struggling to get clients, and ending up broke after three years—a story he knew most of them could relate to. An interesting point is that even though these were people who knew him, and his story, Rob told the story in full to reconnect them to it.

Next, to build credibility and establish authority, he talked about the transformation he'd achieved in his own business, taking it from zero revenue to $153,000 in 11 months.

He also needed them to be ready for the $16,000 pitch at the end of the event, so the next section was on money mindset and premium pricing, preparing the audience to value themselves and invest in themselves.

The afternoon of the first day and the first half of the second day were spent sharing the models Rob used with his clients, and getting the audience to work on aspects of business he knew most of them struggled with. Each model was illustrated with case studies and videos of clients sharing how that model had changed their business. Testimonials (Thing 3) became an intrinsic part of the teaching, a smart way to introduce them without it feeling like a pitch.

The back page of the workbook was a worksheet that listed every model Rob would teach with a blank box next to it. Each time he taught a model, Rob would get the attendees to estimate the impact it would have on *their* business if they implemented it, and write it in the corresponding space. Over the two days, that added up to a very high-value proposition for them.

By lunchtime on day two, the audience understood exactly why every part of the program Rob was going to pitch was there, and they had put their own value on it. After lunch, he led an exercise where everyone added up the numbers they had written on their worksheet and shared the total. It created buzz and friendly rivalry between attendees, and anchored the value of the program to them personally.

It was also an OUTRAGEOUS transition into the close. As we'll see in the GKIC campaign later, a table rush often isn't the best way to sell a high-ticket program. Rob's close was designed simply to get prospective clients to complete an application.

In the close, Rob tied each aspect of the program back to the part of the workshop where he had explained its benefits of having it. You should never introduce new material or ideas in the close. If you ever find yourself explaining in the close, "And this is important because…", you're killing your sales.

One of the big problems with selling a program—especially a twelve month one—is that it can seem abstract. The buyer pays a large amount of money and all they get for it is a promise of things they'll receive in the future. It's easy for buyer's remorse to set in when someone has paid and hasn't immediately received anything in return.

To counteract that, Rob showed a physical leather binder during the close with a welcome letter, a timetable of every live event included in the program, workbooks for each stage, contact details of the team members clients would be talking to, a printed guarantee certificate, a pen, a

highlighter, and even a calculator to figure out how much they were making on the program. Anyone who signed up and paid during the event got their own folder that day,

turning the program into something physical and—most importantly—giving them something to hold and take home. That's an OUTRAGEOUSLY smart way to reduce cancellations.

The Book

Rob took all the Twelve Days emails and repurposed them into a short, printed book called *Secrets of a Six-Figure Expert*, which he gave as a bonus to everyone who attended.

Later, he launched it on Amazon and ran a campaign to make it a best-seller, and he used it as a lead magnet to generate cold leads for future events. He also took copies with him everywhere he went.

Rinse and Repeat

After the first event, Rob re-ran the workshop several times over the first three months of 2012. Each time, he tweaked the content, the offer, and the structure.

The first event was free (remember, it was a "client appreciation" event), but subsequent events were $150, and he added a VIP Ticket option at $450 (primarily as an anchor to make people feel happy and virtuous to "only" be investing $150 in their ticket).

Rob promoted the later events three ways. (1) The book had a call to action to buy a ticket. (2) He got JV partners to tell their lists about the events. (3) He promoted each event to his growing list.

Results

When you sell from the stage, it's important to know your numbers. An experienced seller knows how much they can sell based on how long they are speaking and how many people are in the audience.

Rob initially set himself a target of $800 per person per event. Over the four events he ran, he achieved an average of $1,854 for each person in the audience (in other words, for every eight or nine people who turned up, he knew he would sign up one client). Which meant that each time he ran the seminar, he just needed to know how many people were registered to know how much he'd make that weekend.

Why Is This a Great Campaign to Model?

Using a physical proxy for a high-ticket program is a great stick strategy, so if you sell masterminds or coaching programs, you should think about having a program folder or something else that buyers can take away that day, so they feel they have actually bought something.

Client appreciation events are a great way to engage or re-engage with customers, and it's something any business can do. You don't have to run a two-day event like Rob did: it could be an evening party in your store or offices, a lunchtime talk, or simply a one-day "VIP-customers-only" sale.

And as Rob's campaign shows, you don't even need a huge list (or any list at all) to make it work

An OUTRAGEOUS Way to Get Members in Your Program and Make Them Stay

This campaign brings together two marketers I admire greatly: Robert Skrob and Perry Marshall. Perry is a master of Google Adwords and direct marketing. Robert is the strategist who helped Perry come up with the over-all concept and design for this campaign, while Perry wrote the sales pages and the emails.

The campaign was designed to get new members engaged in a program they have just joined—in this case, Perry's *New Renaissance Club*, a virtual mastermind group for entrepreneurs who want to learn direct marketing.

It's also a "forced continuity" program. That's an OUTRAGEOUS strategy where you add a monthly payment onto the back end of a single-pay product or service. You'll see what I mean below.

The Campaign

The Purchase

The campaign starts when someone buys another of Perry's programs, *the 30-Day 80/20 Reboot* for $299. In fact, here's the really clever thing: the campaign is that product (or the product is the campaign, depending on how you want to look at it). In other words, Perry and Robert created a stick campaign that is good enough to stand on its own and be sold as a product in its own right.

When people buy the 30-Day Reboot, they also receive one month's membership of the New Renaissance Club. After that first month, they pay

$99 each month to stay in the Club. Of course, they are free to cancel at any time, including during that trial month.

The first month of any membership program or subscription is particularly dangerous because new members haven't invested much time, money or energy in the program and haven't got any results yet.

That's why Robert and Perry's focus in this campaign is to start the member taking action (investing time and energy) and getting results.

This campaign was designed specifically to increase new members' engagement with the program and ensure they started generating positive results within the first few hours and days of membership.

The New Member Welcome Kit

As soon as they join, each new member is sent a welcome pack through the mail with five elements. This is always a great idea. People love to get stuff in the mail—it's like an early birthday!

1. Welcome letter. In effect, this is a long-form sales letter that re-sells the new member on why they joined and why they should stay. That's an interesting idea. These people have already bought and

paid, and yet Perry re-sells them on being in the group. Why? Because what they actually paid for is the 30-Day Reboot. Now, Perry has to sell them on staying in the New Renaissance Club.

2. A reminder of everything that's included in their membership. A lot of the program is delivered online—training courses, webinars, group calls, discussion forums, etc.—and it would be easy for a new member to forget that they had them, so reminding them will ensure that they make use of every feature of the program.

3. FOR/AGAINST – a manifesto that sets out everything the New Renaissance Club stands for so that new members are immediately indoctrinated into the principles of the club.

4. The Perry Marshall Marketing Letter – each month of their membership, members get a copy of Perry's newsletter through the mail. The pack includes their first issue.

5. Shortcuts to Success – a strategy guide full of Perry's top ideas to improve productivity and business effectiveness.

This Welcome Kit is not advertised on the sales page, so when it arrives, it's a very pleasant surprise (and increases the new member's engagement).

The Email Campaign

The 30-Day Reboot campaign consists of daily emails for 30 days. Each email includes a task, a new way of thinking about problems, or inspiration to help new members incorporate the program philosophy.

Day 1

Here, to give you a taste, is the email they receive on day 1.

> **Subject: Welcome to 30 Day Reboot - your journey has officially commenced!**
>
> The next 30 days will alter your life.
> I predict you will never so much as desire to go back to the way you'd been managing your life before now.

No insult intended. Just understand, the world is designed to drag us into bad habits. Just so you know, I'm guilty of every horrible, time-sucking, barnacle addiction, bad habit and vice I scorn in this course.

But I've also licked these bad habits. Which is why I want you to experience the freedom.

I've restructured my life so the world I experience is conducive to strategic thinking; to my "energy tank" being full instead of empty. So I can be fully present for and serve my customers, rather than getting dragged around by the nose, like all the zombies out there who are silently peeing away their lives.

In the **introductory task**, I assigned you to do a MASSIVE email unsubscribe.

Why? Because email is our grand central station of where most of us get our actual work done. If that's cluttered, you're screwed.

Now we're going to take the next circle out:

Social Media.

Social Media is entertainment by the masses, for the masses. It's one of the most seductive, addictive inventions in the history of the world. It's massive. It's historical.

And you can make millions of dollars using it as a sales tool. And you should.

But you must alter your posture towards it.

You must operate the Matrix *from outside the Matrix*.

So here is your assignment for today:

Delete the social media apps from your phone.

Also: For the next 30 days, you're not going to check social media during business hours.

You are welcome to do Facebook / Twitter / Instagram, etc. after business hours.

You can spend up to 30 minutes a day on social media, after business hours.

But not during.

On your work computer, you log OUT of Facebook, Twitter, etc.

No 3-minute Social Media breaks. (Breaks that inevitably turn into 13 or 43 minutes.)

This is VERY important, and I want you to do it NOW. Just do it. Why?

You already de-cluttered your email box. Now you're going to de-clutter your mind.

To put this in perspective, I need to point out some things:

-You can still log into Facebook from your BROWSER instead of an app, if you must. But the point is, it takes more work.

-The best way to do Social Media is on a notebook or PC. Time-blocked, intentionally. You are an entrepreneur. Your time is w-a-a-a-y too valuable to spend haphazardly. If you wanna do Facebook, that is FINE. But do it when it is not chewing up your concentration.

Facebook dumps more random topics into your head in 10 minutes than an hour of TV channel surfing.

I predict this is going to save you an hour a day. An hour of time you were not even admitting to yourself that you were wasting.

And that is going to open up more productivity, more space for you to do better work and serve your clients better.

For a few days, this is going to feel very awkward. Because you, like I, have a limbic system response, a neural pathway carved into your brain, that says…

You're bored. Reach for the phone, open Facebook and squirt a little hit of happy juice into your brain.

That hit of happy juice kills your curiosity. It murders your ability to ask questions.

In the coming days, I'm going to give you better things to fill that space with. Strategies for altering those neural pathways and replacing them with FAR more productive habits.

For today, though, my simple suggestion is: Move the Kindle app to the first home screen of your phone. (Right now.) And when you want to scratch that itch, read something intentional like a business book, as opposed to indulging in the random meanderings and arguings you find on Facebook.

NOTE: You can still run advertising apps. You can still have your fan page. You can still inject information INTO The Matrix. You can still be a full-time Social Media Manager if that's what you do for a living.

But before 5pm, you remain OUT of The Matrix.

That's it.

SUMMARY:

1. Delete Social Media apps from your phone. Now.

2. No Social Media during business hours

3. Limit Social Media to 30 deliberate minutes per day, after business hours

4. When you feel the itch to find something exciting on your phone, read a book instead

There. I just gave you back 30-90 minutes a day. Every day.

Pop over to the 30-Day Reboot Members Area, take 30 seconds and **do your Reboot Check-In for today.** If you're not sure how the options on the check-in forms work, watch this quick video I made.

We're only getting started. Talk to you tomorrow.

Over and out.

Perry Marshall

Day 7

The Day 7 email tackles "resistance" by discussing Perry's transition from *writing* about business and marketing to being a *coach*.

Here's an excerpt:

Case in point: A decade ago, my friend Bill said, "Perry I've got a million-dollar idea for you. There's just one catch: If you sell a million dollars, you have to give $10,000 to my favorite charity."

"OK Bill, you're on," I said.

He insisted I was leaving tons of money on the table by only writing and publishing books. He advised me to expand into business coaching.

> I decided he was right. And guess what? I had the hardest time getting myself to actually do it. When I sat down to execute the details, my inner procrastinator said, "Wait a minute, why don't you go get a haircut?"
>
> I recognized the inner procrastinator as a signal that I was precisely on the right track. I resolved to finish the project.
>
> That move doubled my income. Bill's favorite charity, an inner-city school in Philadelphia, got a check for $10,000.

It continues with more teaching about why resistance and procrastination are so terrible for entrepreneurs and ends with a reflective exercise, followed by a testimonial for the 30-Day Reboot. Moreover, it's from someone at the same stage in the program—in the first week—as the reader is.

Why would you want to include a testimonial for a product someone has already bought inside the product itself? Because this is a stick campaign, this is all about reassuring people that they have made a good decision, and encouraging them to stay in the program.

The end of the email is a P.S. instructing the member to go to the membership portal for the program (and the Club) and update their progress. Remember, this is a campaign designed to get members to engage in the program. If someone joins a program like this—particularly as a free trial—and never logs on, they're much more likely to cancel. Giving them a task to do that forces them to log on, and making them do it every day, will keep them in the program.

Day 14

The Day 14 email is an exercise designed to increase personal productivity.

It's designed to follow on from an exercise earlier in the sequence, reinforcing that these aren't random tasks put together in a bunch of emails—there is a method and structure, and the exercises build on each other.

At the end, a P.S. again sends the member back to the membership portal to log their progress.

Results

Interestingly, while the aim of the campaign was to help new members get results, it had a number of additional benefits. As well as being more engaged with the program content, members also engaged more deeply with the member community.

The campaign has also been a huge benefit to Perry's business. It increased the number of new members staying in the New Renaissance Club after the trial, and at the same time decreased cancellations later in the program, extending overall memberships and increasing lifetime member value by more than 10 percent.

This has resulted in an increase of more than $289,000 per year in membership revenue, without any associated increase in marketing expenses.

This campaign makes the existing investments more effective in attracting, converting and retaining new members. More importantly, it has provided a tool for hundreds of people to reduce their stress, increase their effectiveness and grow a more successful business.

Why Is This a Great Campaign to Model?

There are two aspects of this campaign I really want to call out.

First is the obvious one—this is a "stick" campaign, much like Yanik Silver's campaign elsewhere in the book. You can use it in all the same kinds of businesses as that campaign.

Where Yanik's campaign, however, involved a substantial investment—in physical mailings, custom dolls, passport covers, and so on—a campaign like this requires a low investment: an initial mailing and then a sequence of emails. The biggest investment is in planning and writing the emails and making sure that they'll yield an immediate result.

If you have any kind of product or service where people pay a subscription or a payment plan, consider a campaign like this as a way to keep them invested.

The second aspect I want to call out, however, is the idea of forced continuity. I want to draw your attention to it because what we are really saying is that *pretty much any business can be turned into a subscription business.* That's an OUTRAGEOUS claim, but I stand by it. Whatever business you are in, there is some sort of service or product that you can add on to the back end and charge people for.

If you're in the information marketing or advice business, you can copy this idea outright. Create a mastermind group or other monthly program for your clients, and create a stand-alone product that gets them to try that program.

But it's not just for info-marketers and business coaches.

If you sell a physical product, it might be an inspection and maintenance plan, or priority support. It might be training and updates. It could be regular delivery of consumables without the need to keep ordering (a model that Xerox ran for decades very successfully). It could be as simple as access to a user community and events. There is always something you can add to a product to turn it into an ongoing service.

On the other hand, if you sell a service, you could add other bolt-on services that customers might otherwise get from your competitors. For example, an accountant could add bookkeeping through the year.

Whatever industry you are in, ask yourself whether there is a way you can create value for your clients every month. If there is, your path is clear.

1. Create a membership program and give away the first month's membership.
2. Create a stand-alone product that makes buyers use the program during their trial and gets them to achieve real results.

An OUTRAGEOUS Way to Cash in on Holidays

Around the time when I was selling a product for menswear store owners to teach them how to market themselves, Rory Fatt was selling a product for restaurant owners teaching them how to market themselves.

Eventually, we both discovered the same thing: most business owners don't want you to teach them marketing, they want you to do it for them. They just don't have time to create postcards and sales letters, or to buy (or build) a list.

And so, twelve years ago, Rory created what would eventually become Royalty Rewards®. In that time, he has not only helped thousands of business owners but also grown his own business far beyond what it could have been as a marketing training business.

Royalty Rewards® has also expanded beyond restaurants, and now has industry-specific programs for restaurants and auto repair shops, and programs for all other kinds of retail business.

The core of the Royalty Rewards®—and the logic behind its name—is a done-for-you marketing system that allows any business to implement a rewards program for its customers very easily. The program includes a welcome campaign for new members, a birthday campaign, surveys and review requests, as well as an email system for keeping in touch with the cardholders. The business owner also receives a printed newsletter each month.

Members can also buy turnkey marketing campaigns from a wide catalog of seasonal and special-occasion campaigns (to help them implement Thing 6).

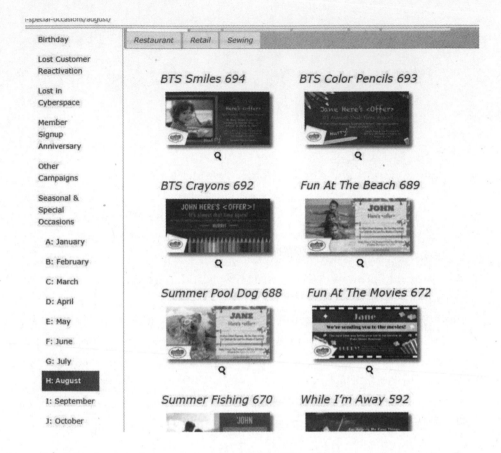

In this chapter, however, we're not looking at the campaigns that Rory creates for his members. Instead, this chapter is about how Rory and his team get business owners to buy the seasonal marketing solutions to boost their sales.

The campaign

The First Email

Each month's email is specific to the campaign being promoted. Here is the email sent in July to promote the August (Back to School) campaign.

Now, most people have images turned off when they open emails, so the first thing to notice is that in addition to the email subject line, there's a colored headline at the top the email ("Back to School – Back to Work"). That headline gets previewed by their email software, so it's the first thing they see and is designed to get them to wonder what else is in the email.

The CAMPAIGNS Rory creates for his clients are OUTRAGEOUS too. The graphics are visually stimulating and attractive, with lots of different colors and typefaces, big bold photos, CopyDoodles and many other OUTRAGEOUS features.

Each email actually contains multiple campaigns. So the August email, for example, has the Back-to-School campaign, a Watermelon Month-themed campaign, and a generic summer-themed campaign.

That gives business owners a choice. Just like the multiple premiums I discussed in Thing 5, they're not being given a Yes/No choice of "do I want this campaign or not?" Instead, they are thinking about which one they would most like to send out to their customers.

The Coach

A few days after the first email, the business owner gets a call from their coach promoting the campaign.

Royalty Rewards® members are assigned a dedicated coach whose job is to help the business owners implement the campaigns they are receiving.

The coaches are also incentivized to sell business owners the additional campaigns. They have individual and team sales targets for each month and year, they get bonuses based on the sales they make, and additional bonuses for improving on prior years.

Popup Reminders

Each time a business owner logs into the Royalty Rewards® website, they are presented with a further nudge in the shape of a popup reminder about that month's done-for-you marketing with a link to the order page.

September 2017's Got More Customer-Drawing Marketing Campaigns than Any Month before It!

No matter your customers' interests, there's a profitable campaign waiting for you to unleash in September. The only thing you need to do is choose which ones you want to use! See what they are by choosing your industry below:

I'm a Restaurant Owner

I'm an Auto Repair Shop Owner

I'm a Retail Store Owner (Or Other Business)

Ready to Order Now?

Deadline: THURSDAY, AUGUST 10th by 5pm EST

Click the red button below or call and speak to your Coach at: 1-888-353-5012

CLICK TO ORDER

Follow-Up Reminder Email

The great thing about these seasonal campaigns is that they have a built-in deadline. There's no point buying a Back-to-School campaign in December, or a Valentine's campaign in March. So a few days after the coach's call, another email goes out with a reminder to buy, and a warning that you risk missing out.

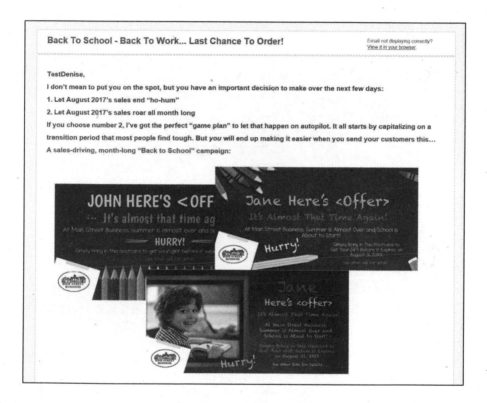

Newsletter Insert

Finally, there's another nudge in the monthly newsletter. Each month, the business owners get a printed newsletter filled with valuable information and tips, but also with reminders to buy the current campaigns.

Sending a printed newsletter is another smart move. Some business owners will like email, others will prefer print, and some may like the combination of both. That's why so many of the CAMPAIGNS in this book use multiple media.

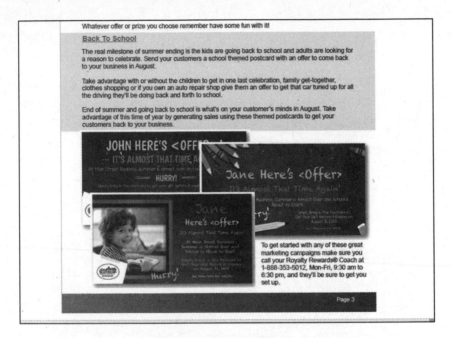

By now the business owner has had two emails, a call, and a popup every time they log into the Royalty Rewards® site. If they haven't responded after all of that, they're probably not buying!

Results

The results of this campaign have been spectacular.

Since 2014 when the process was introduced, the average number of merchants participating in the seasonal campaigns has risen by 242%, as has monthly revenue.

As a result of this multistep campaign, 2016 sales were $432,773 more than in 2014, and Rory predicts another 30% increase in 2017.

Why Is This a Great Campaign to Model?

This is a simple campaign, with very little technical setup needed, and deliberately so. Rory's customers are busy entrepreneurs, and many of them are technically challenged. In their own businesses, they are looking for simple, easy-to-understand marketing. Anything too sophisticated would scare them off.

It is a good campaign to run if you're not interested in learning the intricacies of online marketing, if you have a relatively unsophisticated audience, or if you're looking for a campaign that is quick and easy to set up and run.

An OUTRAGEOUS Way to "Ride the Gray Wave"

Dr. Scot Gray was a student of mine and a member of the GKIC Peak Performers program. He is a chiropractor who also teaches other clinicians how to fill their medical office with new patients.

This campaign was created to fill a seminar on stem cell therapy and sign patients up for a consultation to evaluate their suitability for the therapy— a $3,000-$6,000 treatment.

The Campaign

Lead Generation

Leads come from a combination of direct mail, postcards, voicemail drops, email, Facebook ads, Google ads, and newspaper ads that lead to a landing page to learn more or to call in directly and RSVP for the seminar. Visitors to the landing page are also retargeted with further ads.

Here's an example of a voicemail message.

```
Hi, this is Dr. Scot Gray. Sorry I missed you. I was just
calling to give you a friendly reminder about a community
event we're sponsoring on XXXX at XXX. If you're interested
or you have any questions about stem cell therapy, I've
brought some experts into the area to talk about this.
[Details of the event]. If you'd like to RSVP, because
reservations are required, call our office at 111-111-1111,
or you can register online at…
```

Here is one of the postcards Scot created.

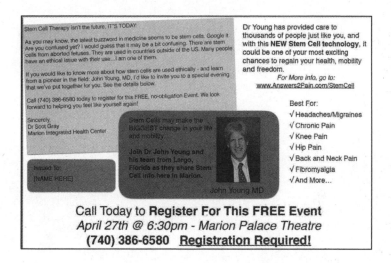

And here's one of the Facebook ads—there are many different ads targeting different types of pain.

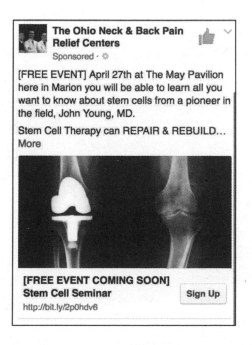

Follow-up

After a lead signs up for the seminar, they receive daily reminder emails that also provide value through education about stem cells, and on the last day, they get three email reminders about the seminar.

The Event

At the end of the seminar, leads are offered a $200-value consultation for $20 which is donated to charity. That's something we've seen in other campaigns, and it's a smart move because it forces the lead to prove they are serious by paying, but they get to feel good about paying for a "free" consultation.

Results

In the first seven weeks, the campaign converted 49 patients for a total of $148,800 in business. Over the next five weeks, it generated a further $300,000 of stem cell business, and Dr. Gray has now made the campaign evergreen and fills two seminars each month.

Dr. Gray typically spends $10,000 every month on advertising, which might seem a lot to some business owners. But that $10,000 easily generates $200,000 of revenue. It pays to look at returns rather than the straight cost!

Why Is This a Great Campaign to Model?

The title of this chapter said it's about "riding the gray wave." That has nothing to do with Dr. Gray's name, and everything to do with who he is selling to.

This campaign is a great example of making sure you match your media to your market. Because the target audience is predominantly over 50—a demographic which the media sometimes calls the "gray wave"—the best results come from newspaper ads and direct mail.

Those both tend to be more expensive than digital media and channels, so it would be tempting to stop them and rely on cheap online advertising, but that would be a big mistake. Dr. Gray would be leaving MILLIONS on the table if he did that. So which is better, online or offline? Like I said in Part One of the book, the answer is BOTH, depending on your market.

An OUTRAGEOUS Way to Bring Old Customers Back with a Rubber Fish and a Trash Can

Dr. Sean Tarpenning is a dentist and a member of Dr. Tom Orent's GG12 program—you can read all about that in Tom's campaign, which is also in this book.

In a dental practice, you have to get people back in for their next appointment. If a patient goes to another dentist, they can take their whole family with them, so as soon as someone gets to the six-month mark, you start to market to them.

This campaign is designed to achieve exactly that—to get a patient back for their six-month checkup.

The Campaign

Dr. Tarpenning is another of our contributors who doesn't worry about high-tech solutions for planning and tracking his campaign. Here's how Sean manages things.

Yes, it's a pinboard!

So, what's on the board?

The core is a three-step sequence of direct mail, followed by a phone call two weeks later, and an email two weeks after that based on the content of the direct mail piece. That sequence repeats every few weeks, with different content each time. In effect, it's nine mini-campaigns over a period of 18 months (that's Thing 10 in action!).

6 Months: Postcard 1 "Did We Make a Wrong Move?"

The campaign starts 6 to 6 ½ months after a patient's last appointment, with a funny postcard designed to jog their memory. (And, to some extent, to guilt them into calling.)

"Did we make a wrong move?"

We've noticed that it's been a while since your last cleaning and check-up appointment.

Our office is committed to the concept of Prevention. You can prevent the kind of dental problems, which could be very costly to you. If you could be a mouse in the corner of our office for one week, you would see that it is neglect, which is terribly expensive.

We sincerely care about you and your oral health. Let us hear from you!

We look forward to seeing you soon!

Thank You,
Hebert Dental

(Image © Woody Oakes & The Profitable Dentist)

Two weeks later, they get a phone call, asking, "Did you get our post-card? We notice you're overdue." Two weeks later, they get an email based on the postcard.

7½ Months: Postcard 2 "Looking for Trouble?"

Six weeks later (7½ months after the last appointment), another postcard goes out.

LOOKING FOR TROUBLE????

In the routine check of recall patients, we have noticed that you have not received a regular preventative examination and cleaning for several months. We have written you before but haven't had any response.

Let us assure you that when patients don't return for dental examinations regularly, we all become concerned! We always wonder if the patient has been neglecting dentistry or has consulted another dentist for treatment.

We can't help you keep your mouth healthy unless you allow us to help you. Please don't delay any longer! Call us and let us know if you have any plans to continue your dental treatment with us.

We don't want to lose you or your teeth. We care and we look forward to hearing from you soon!!

Sincerely,
Hebert Dental

(Image © Woody Oakes & The Profitable Dentist)

Again, this is followed up with a call and an email at two-week intervals.

9 Months: Postcard 3 "While you Were Out"

The third postcard is designed to look like a page from a "while you were out" memo pad. Before it goes out, it's personalized with the patient's name and the date.

That's a smart move (Personalization is part of Thing 4) that makes it far more likely the recipient will pick it up and read it.

And yes, there's follow-up by phone and email.

```
 ┌──────────────────────────────────────────────┐
 │                              ┌─────────┐       │
 │  FOR  NAME                   │ Urgent ☐│       │
 │  DATE  DATE        TIME  (:00   A.M.           │
 │                                 P.M.           │
 │           WHILE YOU WERE OUT                   │
 │                                                │
 │  M _____ │
 │  OF _____ │
 │  PHONE _____ │
 │                                                │
 │  ┌────────────────────┬─────────────────────┐ │
 │  │ TELEPHONED         │ PLEASE CALL        ✓│ │
 │  │ CAME TO SEE YOU    │ WILL CALL AGAIN     │ │
 │  │ RETURNED YOUR CALL │ WANTS TO SEE YOU    │ │
 │  └────────────────────┴─────────────────────┘ │
 │                                                │
 │  MESSAGE: _____ │
 │  Please call us to schedule                    │
 │  your cleaning !!                              │
 │  _____   │
 │  _____   │
 │  _____   │
 │  _____   │
 │  SIGNED                                        │
 └──────────────────────────────────────────────┘
```

11-12 Months: Staff Memo "No Free Lunch"

After another 2 or 3 months pass, the next step is a letter (labeled as a "staff memo") that arrives in a brown paper bag so it will stand out in the mail pile and hopefully get opened first.

The letter is an offer for a free office visit, and it's accompanied by a draw ticket for a seasonal prize. (In summer, for example, it's a 22" Weber grill with lots of extras—total value over $250.) They have to attend the free office visit to be entered into the draw, and there's a deadline by which they have to claim the offer.

STAFF MEMO

FROM: Dr. Tarpenning's Staff
(mostly Sarah & Adrianne this time)
        4710 Commerce Valley Rd
        Eau Claire, WI 54701
        Ph: 715-598-3165
        Monday 9:37 A.M.

Adrianne discovers there is no free lunch in the little brown bag she used to mail you this letter...meanwhile Sarah shows you the "FREE OFFICE VISIT" coupon she enclosed with this letter...plus a secret BONUS offer!

Dr. Tarpenning Says: "There Is No Free Lunch"
But We Say... There Is A FREE Office Visit!
(And We'll- Give You One Just To Prove It)

Dear Sean,

Hi again, It's us (Sarah & Adrianne) writing you this special email ...and... we want to give you a *FREE* Office Visit just for reading this brief email.

You see, last Friday morning we were listening to Dr. Tarpenning at our weekly staff training meeting, and he said something like: *"There is no such thing as a free lunch"*.

Sarah then blurted out, *"Maybe there is no such thing as a free lunch but Adrianne and I can prove there is such a thing as a FREE of office visit"*.

Then Dr. Tarpenning muttered: *"What are you two going to do...send everyone a FREE office visit offer through email?"*

Yep.

Ok, here's the deal: If you call us right now at 715-598-3165, we'll make sure you, get a FREE office visit with

As with the earlier steps, the letter is followed up with a phone call and an email.

14 Months: Staff memo "Plastic Key Chain Card"

At 14 months, they get another "staff memo" letter. This time, it comes with a keychain tag to make it 3D. The letter tells the reader to put the tag on their keychain If they bring it in next time they come in, they'll get the visit free. The new offer comes with a new deadline.

Why do they have to put the tag on their keychain? Because that way, every time they take their keys out, they get reminded of the offer. OUT-RAGEOUS!

18 months: Staff Memo "No-Brainer"

The 18-month letter is another 3D mailer, this time with a rubber brain attached. With this letter, Dr. Tarpenning is going to make the decision a no-brainer. If they come in, not only will the dental exam be free, but so will the X-rays that are needed.

That's a big offer. Why would Sean give so much away? Because every patient is worth at least $1,500. Compared to that, a few X-rays is a small price to get the patient back through the door.

20 Months: Staff Memo "Overnight Telegram"

The bribes of free treatment clearly haven't been working, so at 20 months, the message changes slightly.

The letter comes with a mock telegram (the kind of thing you see in old black and white movies!) requesting donations to the local fire department to help buy new equipment. The letter tells them that if they come in for a visit, they'll be charged $10, which will immediately be donated to the fire department.

That's a nice touch—enlisting the patient in an act of charity for the community. But they have to do it by the end of the month, or the offer expires.

22 Months: Staff Memo "What's the Catch?"

The 22-month mail comes with a rubber fish (yes, you read that right) and a picture of a fishing pole.

The offer is a free dental service and a "goody bag" for seven patients that month. (That's a double deadline: limited supply and an end date.) There's also a reminder of all the services the dental office provides, and a selection of testimonials to remind the reader why they chose Dr. Tarpenning in the first place.

24 Months: Staff Memo "Trash Can Mailer"

One of the most effective items you can get from Travis Lee's company 3D Mail is a plastic trash can. That's what Dr. Tarpenning uses for the final mailing, with a headline that reads, "Since you've thrown away my previous two letters…"

The offer is a last-ditch attempt to get them back in for a visit, including a free exam, free X-rays, free treatment plan, and $50 off any crowns, fillings, dentures, or implants they need. But it's only good for the first seven callers.

"I wouldn't have believed it possible, but they actually made going to the dentist not just a tolerable experience, but an enjoyable one. Everyone was very outgoing, kind, and sympathetic and the visit went great! It seems they have the most updated technology, too. Overall - awesome!" **Renee H, Eau Claire**

"I'm sure that I am not the only person that says, "I hate going to the Dentist". Well, you people at Hebert Dental have replaced the word "hate", to "I don't mind going to the Dentist,'. Thank you for treating me with tender care, and for making me feel important to you." **Kathleen H, Mondovi**

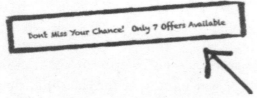

The end of the letter includes a Copydoodle, just to make sure the reader knows there are only seven free visits available.

All the letters so far had a phone call two weeks later, and an email two weeks after that. Remember, each of these is a mini 3-step campaign.

Results

Each mailing gets an average response of 5-7%. Each mailing costs less than $3, and there are nine mini-campaigns, so that's a total spend per patient of around $30. The highest response rate is with the first few letters, which are also the cheapest to send, but with an average annual value of $1,500 per patient, even the later mailings are well worth sending. In fact, even if someone just comes in for a $100 clean, the whole thing pays for itself. And it's a lot cheaper than advertising for new patients.

Why Is This a Great Campaign to Model?

This is a great example of continuing to market to a lead until they buy (Thing 10).

The idea of following up each mailing with an identical email and a call to confirm they got the mailing is simple and adds nothing to the cost. But it increases the chances that your offer will be seen by a factor of three.

What kinds of business could use a campaign like this? Any business that depends on regular repeat business. For example, a tax accountant could start chasing past clients in the months leading up to tax season.

How to Close OUTRAGEOUSLY by Letting Leads Buy at Their Own Pace

---

Todd Brown's campaign is a great example of personalizing a sales funnel (Thing 4). In this case, it's not the content that's being personalized but rather the lead's progress through the funnel.

You're probably familiar with multi-video funnels where you are granted access to each step at a pace set by the seller. That's great, and it works well for many businesses, but what if your leads are in a hurry and don't want to wait?

The Campaign

The campaign was originally designed for a live product launch. Since it had worked well, Todd then turned it into an evergreen funnel. The campaign promotes a product called The Six-Figure Funnel Formula, which sells for $497.

Step 1a: Email

25% of leads for the campaign come from emails to Todd's house list. They were sent a long-form email promoting a free four-part training.

It took me weeks of 8-10 hour days to put this together for you.

It's a comprehensive 4-part training series called **"The Short-Cut To Your First $100,000 Marketing Funnel"**.

And it's <u>FREE</u>. *(yep, nothing whatsoever to buy to access this!)*

Throughout the 4 parts I walk you through a specific marketing funnel... map and all... showing you and explaining every component.

- <u>Video #1</u>: *"What the A-Players Know About Creating Big-Money Sales Funnels the Average Marketers Don't!"*

- <u>Video #2</u>: *"The 5 Critical Pieces of a High-Transaction Value Sales Funnel (and How to Set Them up With Less Than $96 in Cheap Tools)!"*

- <u>Video #3</u>: *"The First-Steps to Load Your Sales Funnel With Quality Traffic That Converts Into Sales... Even if Your Have No Budget!"*

- <u>Video #4</u>: *"The Six-Figure Funnel Formula Map and Implementation System"*

As you go through this training, you'll <u>watch me break-down all the steps, pieces, and tools</u> to use to quickly, easily and cheaply set-up your first REAL-DEAL money-making marketing funnel.

By the end of this video series you'll know exactly what to do so generating website traffic and turning that traffic into sales and profit will be a regular, easy thing for you.

<u>**Access the FREE training series here.**</u>

Enjoy,
Todd Brown :-)

P.S. If you consider yourself an Advanced Marketer... and you already know how to create funnels that crush it... then this is <u>**NOT**</u> for you.

If, on the other hand, you have yet to create your first profitable marketing funnel, then <u>you're going to love this training series</u>.

Step 1b: Facebook Ads

75% of leads for the campaign come from Facebook ads to cold traffic.

The ads offer a free 4-part video training series and a PDF blueprint. A lot of marketers struggle to come up with graphics for their Facebook ads. Todd's approach is OUTRAGEOUSLY simple—if you're offering four videos, show four thumbnails!

Step 2: The Opt-In Page

The email and Facebook ads drive traffic to a simple opt-in page.

One thing to note about the landing page is that the thumbnails from the Facebook ad are repeated on the landing page. Keeping images and colors the same across different steps of your funnel is an easy way to make people feel comfortable as they progress through your campaign. When you change the look of your marketing at random from one step to the next, it can be very jarring and put people off.

Step 3: Follow-Up

Todd follows up by email and SMS. The sequence is driven by consumption of the content (technically known as "behavioral-triggered follow-up"). The quantity and type of follow-up messages a prospect receives is dynamic and depends on how they engage with the videos. Prospects are driven through the campaign at a speed that matches their level of engagement. Some prospects may take up to two weeks to go through the entire marketing campaign, while others may complete it in a day.

That allows the most engaged prospects to continue from one video to next and all the way through to the end of the series in one sitting, so they may not even get a single email follow-up.

Other prospects get an SMS notification when the next video in the series is available for their viewing.

At the end of the sequence, unconverted leads are put into an Intensification Sequence which sweetens the offer with additional bonuses and provides additional proof and case studies. If they get through the Intensification Sequence and still haven't paid, they are offered a payment plan. The payment plan is only available for four days, and the deadline (Thing 2) is hardcoded into the contact record for each prospect.

Step 4: Upsells

Many business owners make the mistake of thinking that the sale ends when a customer buys. The irony is, that is often just the start. The hard work of turning a lead into a buyer has been done, and they are never more likely to buy than when they have just paid for something. The point of sale is a great time to upsell a buyer to further products and services. (Just ask McDonald's. "Do you want fries with that?" is one of the most profitable phrases ever spoken in sales.)

Todd has two upsells as the customer is buying (while they're still "hot"). The first is *Next Level Marketing Funnel Maps*, a set of 17 marketing funnel blueprints and an accompanying video training, for $199. The second is *Marketing Funnels Uncensored Annual Subscription*, a collection of 9 dissections of real marketing funnels for $670.

Step 5: Backend Sales

Another prime time to sell more products and services is just as the customer starts to use them, while they are getting their first real results.

Todd has a range of backend offers from $1,497 to $10,000 which are introduced from day 7 (after purchase) onwards.

They are used as backend offers for various products and services, so they each have their own campaign, and they are tracked separately.

Results

Since submitting his campaign, Todd has told me that his brand has evolved, and he no longer promotes this campaign on the front end with paid media.

While it was running, the Facebook spend for this campaign was $15,000/month, with an average cost per lead of $6, and 7,000 leads were put through the funnel. The campaign generated $772,667 in sales of the core product (not including upsells and backend sales). It has been one of the most effective customer acquisition campaigns Todd has used with cold traffic.

Why Is This a Great Campaign to Model?

In marketing, it pays to keep your prospects happy. Some prospects find dripped content frustrating, especially if they are highly engaged and simply waiting to find out how to buy.

At the same time, less engaged leads need to be nurtured, which takes time.

Allowing the prospect to control the speed at which they are progressing through your funnel is an OUTRAGEOUS way to maximize your income by keeping everybody happy.

An OUTRAGEOUS Way to Get People to Stay Three Times Longer on Your Webinars

---

Dr. Tom Orent is a dentist and runs a very successful program called GG12 which is a business improvement program for dentists that covers everything from operations to marketing, from customer service to finance. I first met Tom when we were both members of Dan Kennedy's Platinum group (the company was still just "KIC" at the time). After I sold GKIC, Tom reached out to hire me to help him grow his business, which I have done for the last six years.

The Campaign

This campaign was ultimately designed to get prospects on the phone, but it started with a five-email campaign to his house list to drive prospects into a live webinar.

Email 1: "You Are Losing $1/4 Million Per Year Due to Just 2 Patients"

That's an OUTRAGEOUS subject line, isn't it? But wouldn't you open that email up, just to find out WHO those two patients are? It turns out the two patients in question are the two existing patients the dentist could sell additional services to each month just by making three small changes to how they run their practice.

What are those changes? That will all be revealed in a 27-minute live webinar. It's a long email, but here's the part of the email where Tom introduces the webinar.

There are 3 CRITICAL FACTORS.

Get them right and you'll avoid harming existing relationships by embarrassing those who are happy with their chipped, stained or crooked teeth and prefer not to make it the topic of a discussion... Getting it right also means identifying those who would be interested in improving their smiles... even though they may never have brought it up on their own. Finally, getting it right means potentially adding 1/4 MILLION DOLLARS per year to your revenues... Right now you're missing out on helping 1 or 2 existing patients per month who would love to improve their smiles... you're missing out on as much as $250,000.00 per year by missing these two patients!

I will cover every detail of all three critical factors in just 27 minutes... or LESS!

Join me, Dr. Tom "*The Gems Guy*" Orent for a complimentary Colleague Appreciation Webinar.

Learn How to

"**Add $20,000.00 in Cosmetic Cases in the Next 30 Days ... and Every Month Thereafter...**

From EXISTING PATIENTS Already In Your Practice"

THIS IS a VERY SHORT 27 Minute Webinar - Tuesday 9/15/15, 8:30pm EDT   O
CLICK HERE TO REGISTER

YOU MUST BE WITH US LIVE. IT'S JUST 27 MINUTES.
This is a **FINAL ENCORE** PRESENTATION.
THERE WON'T BE A VIDEO REPLAY.

In just 27 minutes you'll learn

How to "Add 20,000.00 in Cosmetic Cases in the Next 30 Days, from EXISTING patients " Without ruffling a single feather of those who would prefer not to discuss

There are a few OUTRAGEOUS details here that you might want to swipe and deploy.

First, Tom emphasizes several times that this webinar is just 27 minutes long. Dentists are busy people. It's hard to get them to watch a 90-minute webinar. So, it's important to let them know that this is "only" going to be less than half an hour out of one day.

Second, this is a live webinar, and there is no replay. That's smart for four reasons. (1) A lot of the time, people sign up for webinars knowing they won't watch it live, but they'll watch the replay. However, life often takes over, and they probably never get to watch the replay. (2) Even if they do come back to the replay, if you have a deadline on your call to action, they may have missed it. (3) Remember, Tom wants to get people to book a phone consultation. That is much easier to manage if everyone signs up at the same time. You don't want people signing up slowly over several weeks. (4) When an event is live with no replay, it has a built-in deadline and urgency, and it's a deadline that doesn't need to be explained or justified.

Third, notice the positioning: this is a "complimentary Colleague Appreciation Webinar." In other words, this is one professional speaking to another as peers, and it's about showing "appreciation." That's an OUTRAGEOUS way to avoid the suspicion people often have about free webinars—it also works for in-person events and seminars, by the way.

Email 2: Your Handout: 27 Min. Webinar - Add 20k in Cosmetic Cases in the Next 30 Days from Existing Patients

Email number 2 included a handout that accompanied the webinar. Having a workbook or worksheet for your webinar and giving it to registrants ahead of time gets people excited about the webinar and is a great way to make sure they attend. If you're running webinars yourself, you should definitely start giving people a handout.

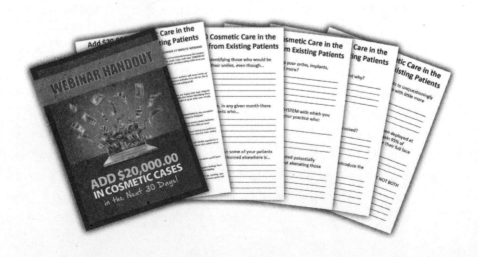

A handout also helps during the webinar in three key ways.

1. It keeps the audience engaged. If they're doing exercises, they're not checking Facebook or email.
2. When they're following a workbook, the audience members are no longer just watching—they're actively participating. It becomes an experience.
3. Once someone starts doing exercises, human nature takes over and they want to complete the workbook, which makes them more likely to stay to the end.

What made this completely OUTRAGEOUS, though, is that Tom sent it to all 70,000 leads on the list, *regardless of whether they had signed up for the webinar or not*. Read that again. If you were on Tom's list, you got the workbook even if you hadn't signed up for the webinar. The key thing here is these were leads who were already on his list. He wasn't spamming random dentists. If someone is on your list, you can send them whatever you want, even the workbook for an event they haven't registered for!

In effect, the campaign was both a way to get leads to register for the webinar and a stick campaign for those who register.

Of course, because it was going out to everyone, the main text was very much the same as the original email, but with a different opening.

```
PLEASE PRINT THE ATTACHED HANDOUT NOW, IN ADVANCE OF
OUR UPCOMING 27-MINUTE WEBINAR
During your 27-minute complimentary webinar I will re-
veal step-by-step exactly how you can measurably and
consistently increase the number of "Smile Makeover"
cases you perform. When you follow my simple protocol,
you could enjoy well over $200,000.00 increase in es-
thetic cases. Even if you fall short, adding more than
$100,000.00 in cosmetic dentistry will be EASY once you
understand the 3 critical factors currently holding you
back.
"You miss 100% of the shots you don't take."
```

> Wayne Gretzky's concept will help you help your pa-
> tients. This concept can change your dental practice
> and your lifestyle.

Email 3: Imagine if One Question, Asked at the Right Time, Could (Easily) Add 100k to Your Revenue

Email 3 is very similar to email 2. The handout is attached to the email, and it starts with a pitch for the webinar, but the messaging is broadly the same as in emails 1 and 2.

> There's really no need to imagine...
> There is one question proven to add 100,000.00 to
> $250,000+ per year in additional revenue.
> During this complimentary webinar, in addition to re-
> vealing the question, I'll share EXACTLY WHEN to ask it
> (critical to your success), and…
> HOW to ask it in order to AVOID CAUSING HARM with some
> of your patients who'd rather you not discuss this.
>
> PLEASE PRINT THE ATTACHED HANDOUT NOW, IN ADVANCE OF
> OUR UPCOMING 27-MINUTE COMPLIMENTARY WEBINAR.
> During your 27-minute complimentary webinar I will […]

The rest of the email from that point on is <u>identical</u> to Email 2. There's nothing wrong with repeating yourself in marketing. Indeed, you'll make a lot more money assuming people haven't seen, noticed, or read anything you sent in the past.

Email 4: Asked at the Right Time, This Question Could (Easily) Add 100k to Your Revenue

The fourth email restates the core ideas of the earlier emails: your patients only know about the services they already get from you, they will

probably go to other dentists for any other work they need, and it's dangerous to build a cosmetic-only dentistry practice. Yes, it's more repetition.

Email 5: TONIGHT: A Single Question, Asked at the Right Time, Could (easily) Add 100k to Your Revenue

This email went out on the day of the webinar.

Again, it's repeating a lot of the messaging of the earlier emails, but with a pitch for the webinar up front.

```
TONIGHT you'll discover the one question proven to add
$100,000.00 to $250,000+ per year additional revenue

TONIGHT I'll share EXACTLY WHEN to ask this question
(critical to your success), and...

TONIGHT You'll Learn HOW to ask it in order to AVOID
CAUSING HARM with patients who'd rather you not discuss
this

In the Next Thirty Days...

You Will Visit with at Least 1 or 2 of Your Existing
Happy Patients

Who I PROMISE YOU Would LOVE to Have a Beautiful
Smile...

But Will Never Mention it (or even think of it) on
their Own.

Unless...you know WHAT to ask, HOW to ask and most im-
portant... the EXACT MOMENT at which to ask...

During your 27-minute webinar, I will reveal step-by-
step exactly how you can measurably and consistently
increase the number of "Smile Makeover" cases you per-
form. When you follow my simple protocol, you could en-
joy well over $200,000 increase in esthetic cases. Even
if you fall short, adding more than $100,000 in cos-
metic dentistry will be EASY once you understand the 3
critical factors currently holding you back.
   YOU MISS 100% of the shots you never take."
```

> You've likely heard Wayne Gretzky's quote many times
> before. Learning how to USE this concept in your prac-
> tice will help you help your patients. This concept can
> change your dental practice and your lifestyle.

See how Tom starts with some new text, but then just goes straight back to the original message. If someone's already signed up, they're going to ignore the email. If they haven't, then this might be the one that tips them over the edge and makes them sign up. If they don't, you've lost nothing.

The Webinar

The webinar was billed as 27 minutes long, and he kept that promise. However, that was followed by 10 to 15 minutes of pitch for a free practice analysis, and then audience Q&A. In total, the webinar was roughly 90 minutes long.

The Q&As provide an opportunity for Tom to tell as many stories as possible about GG12 members. If a question can be tied to something in the program, Tom has a story for it. That's important if you do your own webinar Q&A: know your client success stories and look for opportunities to bring them into what you're presenting.

The Registration Page

The aim was to get attendees to visit a page (you can see it on the next page) where they could register for a free analysis of their business.

The Free Practice Analysis

The free practice analysis is done by one of Tom's sales team. It is a real analysis with real value, even if the dentist doesn't go on to join GG12. Before the call, the lead is asked to complete a questionnaire with about 100 questions about their practice.

"Who Else Wants a <u>Guaranteed</u> $250,000.00 Increase In 10 Months or Less?"

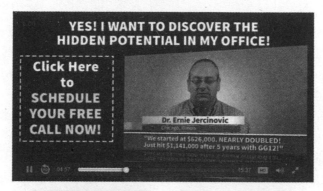

"Discover the Simple Path to Working Less and Making More" (a *LOT* More)

You're here for a reason... it might be that you want to make more money, make your time in your practice more productive, or your time with your loved ones more meaningful and fulfilling. Regardless of what the root-cause is, it's safe to say you're here because you want more from your practice. The good news is every dentist you're about to meet on this page joined GG12 for the exact same reason.

You're about to see the power that comes from combining proven strategies with desire and implementation. **The results are nothing short of miraculous.**

Below is a small sampling of the thousands of lives GG12 has radically transformed for the better. Unlike these wonderful doctors, your journey is just beginning. The next (and most important) step is to register now for your complimentary "RoadMap to Success" Strategy System. During this process, you'll **discover the hundreds of thousands of dollars in untapped opportunity just sitting in your practice** along with some of the most common roadblocks and mistakes that prevent dentists like you from enjoying the life you truly deserve.

There is no fee nor any obligation for your RTS journey, yet I promise you will find the process invaluable for your practice and your life.

Schedule your "RoadMap to Success" kick-off meeting now, and discover how you can easily add at least $250,000 to your practice.

First Name:		*
Last Name:		*
Email:		*

CLICK to SCHEDULE

Now, you might be thinking that 100 questions is OUTRAGEOUS, but anyone who takes the time to complete that questionnaire properly is clearly serious about their business, and the questions provide critical information to qualify the lead.

If you run free sessions in your own business, you probably find yourself spending a lot of time with unqualified prospects or people who aren't very serious. Getting them to complete an onerous task before the session is a great way to filter out those people.

The analysis call ends with a pitch for the GG12 coaching program. If the program is not right for a doctor, Tom's team can usually spot that after the first call. When someone is qualified, however, it sometimes takes another few calls after the initial call to satisfy the doctor's questions and concerns and to help them make the appropriate decision. Even at this stage, there's an A, B, and C pile (Thing 10) and it would be a mistake to stop marketing just because someone doesn't sign up at the end of the first call.

Results

For this particular webinar, 75 leads registered for the live event. Of those, 32 requested a Roadmap To Success call, generating four new GG12 members.

With membership of GG12 at $67,000 (or $97,000 for GG12 PLUS) for the year, that's a great result.

Why Is This a Great Campaign to Model?

There are a lot of valuable lessons that you can swipe and deploy in this campaign.

First, there's the length of the webinar. By focusing on the instructional part of the event, Tom makes it manageable. If someone chooses to stay for the Q&A, that's their choice. (Although the whole thing is designed to make sure they stay and register for the follow-up practice analysis call.)

Second, the campaign shows you shouldn't be afraid of repeating yourself in a campaign. Never assume someone has heard what you were saying the first time.

Third, use handouts to get people excited in advance of a webinar and keep them engaged during the event.

Fourth, keep marketing to people for as long as it takes them to make a decision.

If you're running any kind of live event—online or offline—this would be a great campaign to model in your own business.

Sending Outrageous Stuff Through the Mail Gets OUTRAGEOUS Results

Have you ever received an envelope with an unidentified lump—something solid that you can tell is inside the package, but you have no idea what it is? Doesn't it make you want to open the letter, just to find out what's in it? Even if you know it feels like a simple pen, you still want to know if you're right!

Turning 'flat' mail into 3D mail is an easy way to make your campaign just a little outrageous. (Or even very outrageous, depending on what you put in the envelope!)

I've known Travis ever since he and his dad (who also contributed a campaign to this book) were in my mastermind group, and his company, 3D Mail Results, supplies everything from rubber brains to plastic trash cans and shredded money for savvy marketers to use to grab attention and get their direct mail opened.

Naturally, Travis's outrageous marketing campaign uses the company's products to full effect!

The campaign is designed primarily for lead generation and lead capture. Leads come primarily from four sources (listed in order from most leads generated to least):

1. Links on referring websites
2. Teleseminars, webinars, podcasts, interviews, etc. with other coaches, consultants, and thought leaders. Some of those experts then also mention the offer in their newsletters, etc.
3. The company takes stands at trade shows and other events, or sponsors the event
4. Referral and other word-of-mouth

The Campaign

Step 1: The campaign starts when a prospect requests a free copy of Travis's book "How to Explode Your Advertising Results" and an accompanying DVD.

This is a physical book and DVD package, not a download, so the prospect gets an email confirmation that their request has been received and the items are on their way. A few days later, they get a follow-up telephone call.

Step 2: 14 days later, they get another package in the mail—a bank bag (which is one of the items the company supplies) with a personalized letter inside.

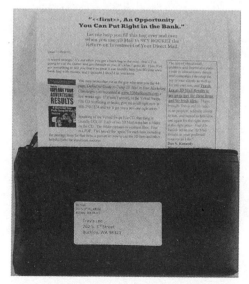

The letter points to an online special offer: 15% off twelve of the company's best-performing items, with a deadline at the end of the following week.

That's followed up with two emails and a phone call spaced a few days apart.

Step 3: Two weeks later, another mailer is sent. This time, it's a letter with a small bag of shredded money (another of the company's items). There's a picture on the next page.

This time, the offer is for smaller items that can be mailed at little or no extra cost (like this small bag of shredded money) with a deadline.

As before, there are two follow-up emails and a phone call, spaced a few days apart.

Step 4: Once the follow-up from step 3 is complete, non-buyers (the No and Maybe piles—remember, we need to keep selling to them!) are put into the company's standard engagement sequence

Results

6% of the people who request a copy of the book and DVD go on to place an order within 12 months, with an average order value of $1,500. Typically, Travis gets $10-$15,000 in sales each month from the campaign.

Why Is This a Great Campaign to Model?

This is a fun campaign that any business could implement. At its heart, you could sum it up as:

1. Offer a premium (here it's the book and DVD).
2. Follow up with a range of distinct offers (for this campaign, it's the time-bound discounts).
3. Stay in touch using a range of channels (in this case mail, email, and phone) until they buy or tell you to stop.

The key is that the follow-up uses the principles of OUTRAGEOUS marketing.

PART FOUR

The "Complex" Campaigns

In Part Three, you saw 35 campaigns that used a small number of media, had only a few steps, and were relatively simple.

The 14 campaigns you'll find here in Part Four make full use of a wider range of media. They have many steps, which allows for many touchpoints with the prospect.

It does mean that the cost is typically higher than the campaigns in Part Three, and they may take longer to set up. However, the potential returns are also higher.

Even if you don't have the time or the budget to implement a campaign like these in full, you'll learn a lot from how the campaigns are put together, and you can always take just one or two steps and add them to your own OUTRAGEOUS marketing campaigns.

An OUTRAGEOUS Way to
Sell Seats for a Conference

I met Bill Harrison when we were both members of Dan Kennedy's KIC Platinum Mastermind group. There were a few of us who lived relatively close to each other, and we created a small group that still gets together regularly for dinner to talk about what's going on with our businesses.

When I sold what by then had become GKIC, Bill was one of the first people to say he wanted to hire me. Once a month he and Steve would get on the phone with me and talk about any questions they had, or I'd talk about things I had done that they could use in their own business.

Bill and Steve run a business that helps non-fiction authors, experts, and entrepreneurs to get their message out (Steve is the "public face" of the company, while Bill is the "inside guy" who runs the business behind the scenes).

One of the key ways they get people into their programs is the National Publicity Summit, a conference that connects experts with top journalists and TV/radio producers who can feature them. Bill calls it "speed dating for people who want to be famous."

One thing I really like about how they've set up the business is that the website for the National Publicity Summit has a URL that is very easy to remember: www.NationalPublicitySummit.com. So, as long as someone can remember the name of the event, they can find the site. Anytime you can make life easier for your prospects, your conversion rates are going to go up!

The Campaign

Lead Sources

Bill and Steve have five key sources of leads.

a) House list of existing customers
b) House list of unconverted leads from previous events
c) House list of other leads
d) New leads generated by advertising
e) New leads from affiliates and Joint Venture partners

The Campaigns

Promotion starts six months ahead of the event, and there are four main campaigns.

1) Early-bird campaign
2) Alumni campaign
3) Main educational campaign (which educates prospects about publicity via a series of teleseminars/webinars, reports, and follow-up emails)
4) Direct mail campaigns to previous buyers of other offerings

Campaign Overview

It's easy to assume that successful marketers plan their campaigns out using expensive graphing tools to create perfect flow charts. Want to see Bill and Steve's flowchart?

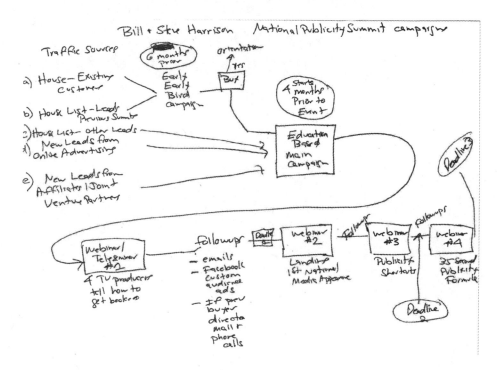

Hopefully, if you're the kind of marketer who doesn't feel they can get started until they have a perfect diagram of their campaign, this will encourage you to just get going.

Early-Bird Campaign

The early bird campaign is sent to existing customers and to unconverted leads from previous events. It starts while the previous event is still running. Think about that for a moment. A lot of business owners would think, "it's hard enough running an event. I'll wait and get this one out of the way before I start to think about the next one." But the current event is a great time to promote the next one because you can tap into the excitement surrounding the event.

Here's one of the emails that go out at this stage.

Subject: I wish you were here

Hi <Fname>—

Hello from New York City!

I'm here for my National Publicity Summit which is going great.

By the time we wrap up tomorrow, our attendees will have had the opportunity to meet face-to-face with more than 107 top journalists and producers who can feature them.

I wish you could be here!

While I'm disappointed you couldn't make it this time, the good news is we're doing another National Publicity Summit, April 25-29, 2017.

If you'd like to be interviewed on radio/TV shows and featured in leading magazines, newspapers and online outlets, you'll want to be with us in April.

The best news is that tomorrow (Saturday) at 1 pm Eastern (10 am Pacific), we're going to begin accepting applications to attend the next National Publicity Summit.

I'll be offering one of my best discounts for this "early bird" offer but can only offer 20 spots at this super-low price.

<u>Click here to get the Super-Early Bird Discount</u> by applying tomorrow (Saturday) at 1:00 pm Eastern (10:00 am Pacific)

Having a face-to-face meeting with an editor or producer dramatically increases the chances they'll write about you -- or put you on their show.

Here are some of the results previous Summit attendees have scored, including how:

• Gaby Cora became a regular on Fox News Channel.

• Connie Bennett got coverage in Time magazine.

• Ron & Lisa Beres appeared on the Today Show. So did Linda Franklin as well as Dave Farrow.

• Mark Amtower and Rory Cohen each landed a full-page story in Entrepreneur (and Rory also scored The View!).

- Steve Shapiro was the subject of a big story in O the Oprah Magazine after meeting the writer at my Summit.
- Lauri Loewenberg appeared on both ABC's The View and Good Morning America.
- Jim Vonmier got on the CBS Evening News and Early Show as a result of the training and contacts we gave him.
- Barry Spilchuk was interviewed on Fox News Channel within just five hours of meeting the producer at the Summit!
- Harrison Forbes got booked on Live With Regis & Kelly and also landed a major book deal.
- and many, many others!

Again, we'll begin accepting applications for only 20 discounted spots to attend the Summit at 1:00 pm Eastern (10:00 am Pacific) on Saturday, October 29th.

Click here to apply tomorrow at 1 pm Eastern and get the Super-Early Bird discount

I look forward to seeing you at the Summit and helping you get the media coverage you deserve!

Best wishes,

Steve Harrison

PS - Above links not working? You can also apply here <link>

Anyone who goes through this campaign and doesn't buy is fed into the educational campaign, along with other leads.

The Educational Campaign

Starting four months ahead of the next event, the educational campaign is designed to teach colder leads why publicity and media attention are so necessary for authors.

By this stage, hot leads (existing customers and leads from previous events) have already had a chance to buy, so anyone left is treated as a cold/warm lead and gets resold on the benefits of working with the media.

There are three kinds of email in the educational campaign:

- Inquiry generator emails
- Story emails
- Webinar/teleseminar invites

The inquiry generator emails are straightforward promotional emails, similar to the early bird email above. The aim is simply to get the reader to click on a link to the sales page.

The story emails are also designed to get the reader to click through to the sales page, but share a story-based resource like an interview with a past client.

Here's an example.

```
On one of my teleseminars on strategies for scoring na-
tional TV publicity, you may have heard me interview
Ron and Lisa Beres about how they got booked on The To-
day Show after meeting the producer at my National Pub-
licity Summit.

During that interview, they touched on four important
publicity strategies which you should bear in mind if
you want to get more big-time media exposure.

Listen to my interview with Ron & Lisa and discover how
they got on the Today Show plus 4 publicity tips for
you

Then, if too would like to meet major journalists and
radio/TV producers who can feature your book, product,
service or cause, get info on attending my upcoming Na-
tional Publicity Summit, October 26-29 in New York.

<link>    < == get info here

I look forward to seeing you in New York so you can
land the media attention you deserve!
```

Teleseminars and Webinars

For anyone who still hasn't booked their spot at the Summit, the education continues with a series of four teleseminars and webinars on various publicity topics such as:

- 4 Top National TV Producers Tell How to Get Booked as a Guest on Big Shows
- Landing Your First National Media Appearance
- Publicity Shortcuts: 7 Ways to Make the Media Love You
- The 35-Second Publicity Formula

Here's one of the invites.

```
SUBJECT LINE:   Want to be in major magazines?   6 top
journalists tell how

Hi <Fname>…

For all the talk about the decline of print media, the
fact is many major magazines and newspapers still have
HUGE reach.

A single article about your book, business or cause in
a top print publication has the potential to change
your life forever … sending your sales soaring and cre-
ating buzz around your work.

What would it take for you to get featured in a major
publication like one of these?

… New York Times (daily circulation 571,000)

… Cosmopolitan (circulation 3,011,848)

… Women's Health (circulation 1,511,719)

… Men's Journal (circulation 758,298)

… Parents (circulation 2,078,000)

… New York Daily News (circulation 516,000)

… Institutional Investor (circulation 101,000)
```

Ready to find out? <u>Join me Thursday for a free web class with six top writers who've written for those publications as well as major online media.</u>

They'll tell you exactly what you need to do to land major coverage not just in magazines and newspapers, but on the many rapidly-growing online outlets such as FoxNews.com and Huffington Post.

<u>Register for the free web class with the journalists</u> which will be held this Thursday (July 13th).

Hope you can make it, because I know you'll learn a lot!

See you on the web class,

Steve Harrison

If they don't register for a webinar, they get invited to the next webinar in the series. It's a very smart move—most businesses have a single webinar, and if someone doesn't want it, there's nothing else for them to choose. Having a series of different webinars on relevant topics gives you the greatest chance of getting people to sign up.

Follow-Up

Anyone who registers for a webinar gets added to a multi-channel follow-up sequence by email, Facebook retargeting, and—if they're a previous buyer—direct mail.

The aim is to get them to sign up for the summit, and again there's a mix of content: stories of client experiences, free reports and educational content, objection handling, and invitations to book a call to discuss attending the summit.

Piling on the Pressure

As you can see from the flowchart earlier, the webinars are scheduled to coincide with deadlines, and at each deadline the price rises.

Remember how I said in Thing 2 that every offer has to have a deadline? Well, I should have said *at least one* deadline. There's no rule that says you can't have multiple deadlines. In fact, it's an OUTRAGEOUS way to keep building the pressure to buy. Those deadlines turn up everywhere—in emails, in direct mail, even in Facebook ads.

And here's an excerpt from one of the follow-up emails:

> If so, I need to hear from you by today (Friday, Sept 16) at 6 pm EST (3 pm Pacific).
>
> I'm down to at most 23 spots to attend for my upcoming National Publicity Summit conference on Oct 26-29 in New York City, where you'll get to personally meet over 100 producers and journalists who do stories and shows for many of America's biggest media outlets.

Direct Mail and 3D Mail

As I mentioned above, the campaigns include an element of direct mail for existing customers. Segmenting leads like that is an OUTRA-GEOUSLY clever thing to do. If someone has already spent money with you, they're a much higher-value lead than someone who just asked for free information, and they've already generated profit for you. It's also much easier to get someone who already bought from you to buy again, so it's a no-brainer to spend a little more on marketing to those people.

For example, as part of this campaign, clients who have spent $1,000 or more in the past get a padded mailer with:

- A silver platter
- A three-page sales letter
- Eight pages of testimonials from attendees of previous events
- A list of all the media outlets that will be at the next event

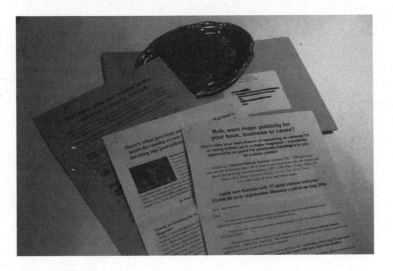

A lot of business owners would be tempted to put all the information into a single document, maybe a glossy brochure. Bill and Steve, however, split it into three documents, each printed on different-colored paper. Why? First, it just looks like a lot more—when the lead opens the mailer, there are three things to look at instead of one. Second, different people will pay attention to different things. If someone wants to know who will be at the event, they can see it immediately—they don't need to flip through a long brochure—so they're more likely to notice it and read it. They may not even read the rest, but if that's all it takes to tip them over into signing, you want them to get that immediately.

There are also postcards, like this one:

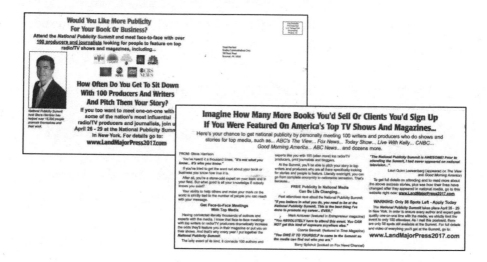

Results

The National Publicity Summit is limited to 100 attendees and, thanks to this campaign, each event is usually sold out, with an average ticket price of $6,200—that's $620,000 of revenue from the event alone.

At the event, attendees are offered the chance to upgrade to Bill and Steve's year-long Quantum Leap program, priced at $12,000 to $15,000.

80% of Summit tickets are bought by people who are already on the house list, so there's a very low cost to market to them. The other 20% of seats go to new leads, and this is where most of the marketing cost of the event goes: acquiring those new leads. To make that worthwhile, Bill and Steve are diligent in applying Thing 10: they keep marketing to the leads they've got, even if they haven't bought in the past. They have to keep putting them through this funnel every six months to make the cold leads worthwhile.

That's a big lesson that a lot of businesses need to learn. Most businesses waste a huge amount of money getting cold leads, but if the lead doesn't buy, they don't do anything with them.

Bill and Steve keep marketing to past buyers as well. Remember Thing 10: Just because someone has bought one product doesn't mean you should stop promoting other products to them!

Why Is This a Great Campaign to Model?

There's a lot of great lessons in this campaign for every business.

- Have different campaigns for different segments of your leads.
- Use multiple media, and have a variety of message types (stories, pitches, free stuff, etc.).
- Promote multiple offers (in this case, webinars) sequentially so that people will respond to the one they like the best.
- Invest more in marketing to people who've already invested in you.
- Keep selling to past buyers and unconverted leads.
- Use different deadlines to maintain the pressure to take action.

And don't assume that this campaign would only work for filling live events. It is really about how to keep selling to leads who haven't bought yet until they buy.

Anybody can run this campaign to their unconverted leads—their house list—but if you want to start adding new leads, you've got to invest. The key is to have a high-value upsell to make the upfront expense worthwhile.

An OUTRAGEOUS Way to Turn Potential Competitors into Clients

Bruce Hudson is a member of GKIC. He's been a professional photographer—not an industry that you normally associate with direct response marketing—since 1982.

Bruce built his business around the client lifecycle—people who have their photo taken in high school eventually get married and need wedding photos. Then they have kids, which means baby photos and family portraits, and the cycle starts again with a new generation. These days, he finds himself photographing high school seniors whose parents he photographed when they were in high school, and brides whose mothers he photographed on their wedding day.

Once someone becomes a client, they may stay a client for decades, which means a very high lifetime value. That first sale can lead to more business from future generations.

For many years, Bruce ran a very successful relationship marketing model built around that lifecycle. That worked well until the crash in 2008/2009. Suddenly, people weren't thinking about family portraits. They were more worried about paying the mortgage and keeping their kids in college. Business dropped by 75% in 2009, and another 50% in 2010.

Bruce's son Josh had joined the business in 2006 rather than going to law school. Shortly after the crash, he asked Bruce, "Dad, has it always been this hard to get clients?" The answer was no.

Their old high-school graduation photo clients weren't going to keep them afloat. They needed to do something FAST, or the business was going to go under.

In fact, what they created works so well that Josh and Bruce have built an additional revenue stream from teaching it to other photographers.

The Campaign

When your business is built on referrals and repeat customers, it's easy to fall into the trap of thinking you don't need any more leads because you have all the business you need in your address book. But at some point, you can't just rely on relationship marketing: you have to implement some new client acquisition strategies.

Josh came up with the idea of running photography classes for amateurs in their studio in Seattle.

Initially, Bruce was totally against the idea. Ever since the advent of digital photography, any clown with a smartphone thinks they are a master photographer. As a result, studios up and down the country have gone out of business because happy couples are getting amateurs to photograph their big day as a way to cut costs. Why would Bruce want to add to the problem by training even more snap-happy amateurs? Why create more competition?

Josh's point was that they needed to get new people through the door. This way, people would come in and have a direct experience of the quality of their work.

It turns out Josh was right. Five-and-a-half years on, 50% of the studio's new portrait clients come from the classes they are running. But there are other OUTRAGEOUS benefits, as we'll see!

Daily Deals

The crash coincided with the rise of the daily deal platforms like Groupon and Living Social, and Josh wanted to create a deal to get new customers. Bruce had major reservations. He has always seen the business as "high end" and hardly ever offers discounts, even to long-term customers, so he hated the idea of practically giving things away on a mass platform.

In the end, Josh convinced Bruce to offer an on-location portrait session and a 9x12 portrait—normal value $500—for $67.

The first three clients who took the offer ended up spending over $10,000 between them.

Bruce was sold!

Classes

The offer was so successful that Groupon approached Bruce about offering a class. They had experienced great success with similar offers in other cities and wanted Bruce to do the same thing for them in Seattle.

Running classes was bad enough, but cheap classes?

Bruce overcame his resistance. The first offer sold 489 classes in the first 24 hours. More than that, Bruce and Josh got 50,000 hits on their website, which sent their Google rank sky-high.

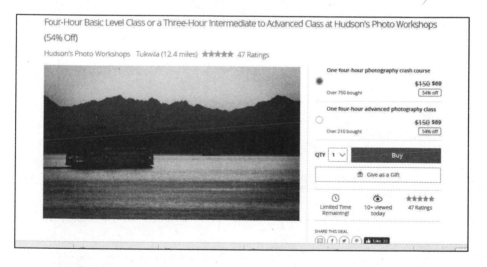

Costco

One of Bruce's best clients was an executive for Costco at their corporate offices in Seattle. He saw the Groupon deal and saw potential, so he hooked Bruce up with the key buyer for the Seattle region.

Getting into Costco is not easy. The vetting is intense. Bruce and Josh got through it, though, and their classes were put into three stores.

If you've ever bought an "experience" at Costco, you'll know that what you actually buy is a gift card which you can then redeem for the service. Bruce had never sold gift cards, but once they'd created the card for Costco, it was easy to repurpose it. He now sells the gift cards online, which has created another great source of revenue throughout the year.

The House List

One of the advantages of running a relationship marketing strategy for 35 years is that you do build a great house list.

Bruce is very good at keeping in touch with his list. He sends out monthly email newsletters, and a print newsletter twice a year. Josh also actively promotes the business on social media every day.

That's a smart way of making sure you maximize contact. Different people like to connect in different ways, so having three ways to make contact means your messages are three times more likely to be noticed.

Organic Search

Despite all of that activity, the most powerful source of leads for the studio is people searching on Google for photography classes in the Seattle area. All those amateurs that used to really annoy Bruce are constantly looking for classes to improve their technique.

Josh and Bruce created a separate website for their photography classes and optimized it for search, even down to the URL (seattlesbestphoto-class.com). The site also has some opt-in offers to get visitors to join the mailing list.

You might be wondering why someone would pay for a photography class when you can learn it all for free on YouTube. Bruce wondered that, too, so he asks all the students who come through the door. They have all tried online videos, but in the end, they want to learn from a real human being. That's a valuable lesson if you've been putting off running live events because you think no one will want to come.

Bruce and Josh also run Facebook ads and Google PPC ads. Recently, they've also started a radio show.

Step by Step

1. The campaign begins in several different ways:
   - Online search for photo classes
   - Facebook ad
   - Groupon
   - Email marketing to the house list
2. Prospect visits the website and watches testimonial videos.
3. Prospect buys a class.
4. Prospect takes the class.

Of course, that's only the beginning. The ultimate aim is to turn those people into paying portrait clients, so students are put into a follow-up campaign to convert them.

1. **Two days after the class:** They get a thank-you email with more info about the studio.
2. **One week after the class:** They get a surprise gift in mail—$100 gift card towards portrait services.
3. They get a $25 gift card in the mail towards the next class
4. They are added to the general database for relationship marketing

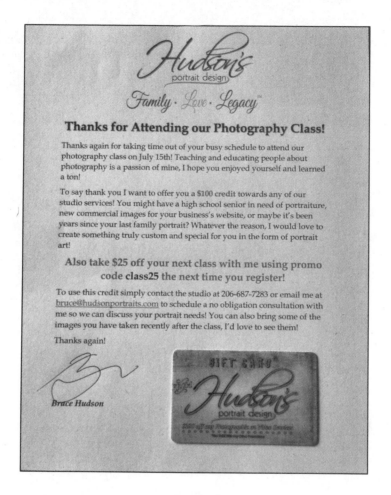

Results

Bruce and Josh have mastered the art of getting paid to generate leads.

The published price of their 4-hour Seven Steps class is $125. The Groupon deal sells for $69, and thanks to Josh's negotiating prowess, they net $50 of that.

In a typical class, there will be 30-35 students, 60% at full price and 40% Groupon participants, so Bruce will net $2,800 to $3,350—not bad for four hours' work, and that doesn't include future revenue from photo students who become studio clients.

Why Is This a Great Campaign to Model?

This is a brick-and-mortar business acting like an info-marketing business. They have even successfully applied the paid seminar marketing model to a normal, everyday business. Bruce is teaching people how to do photography, and they are learning how good he is in the process and building a relationship.

Better yet, Bruce and Josh are getting paid to bring in clients.

When things get tough in your business, you have to think of other ways to build it back to where it needs to be, and beyond. The point of this campaign is not just to get clients, but to get new clients in an OUTRAGEOUSLY innovative way.

An OUTRAGEOUS Way to Make $2,000 From Every "Free" Customer

Dr. Kelly Brown was a member of GKIC, and I've known him for more than a decade. For as long as I've known him, he has been a hard worker. Building his business wasn't easy, and it took effort, but he is someone who really knows his marketing—as you'll see from this campaign!

Kelly is a dentist, and also the founder and chairman of Custom Dental, a company that partners with young dentists to run the back-end operations—everything from HR and marketing to Accounts Payable and Accounts Receivable—in exchange for equity in the practice. The concept is simple—Custom Dental helps the doctors "load the chairs" so that they can focus on doing what they love.

The company currently has twelve offices in three states, averaging $1.4 million per year in revenues each, with relatively young dentists. That's in an industry where the national average revenue per office is just $600,000 a year!

The Campaign

This campaign is designed to help the dentists fill their chairs by getting people into a free seminar. I haven't included flowcharts for most of these campaigns, but there's a lot happening in this one, and sometimes a picture really does say a thousand words, so here it is. And don't worry: I'm going to walk you through it.

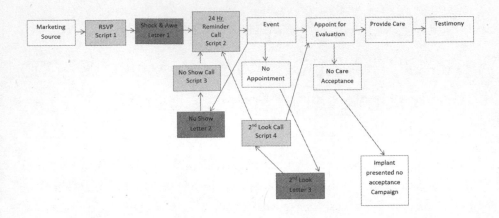

Marketing Source

The campaign is triggered by an inquiry generated from one of several sources: newspaper inserts, print ads, TV, and radio, depending on the market. (There's a different, more highly automated campaign for social media prospecting.)

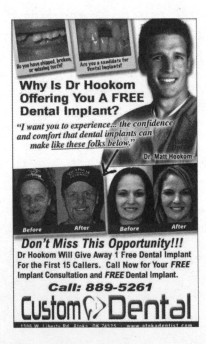

It's a direct response ad that tells the prospect to call a number to reserve a seat at an upcoming seminar about dental implants. There's a bribe to encourage fast action—the first 15 registrants get a free implant.

The RSVP Script

When the prospect calls the office, the receptionist has a script to follow that ensures they get all the information they need. For example, a mailing address is critical for this campaign, so the script has wording for that.

Implant Seminar No-Fault Campaign Inbound Call for Reservation Script

1. Regular Greeting

Inquiry about Seminar

2. Yes, we will be holding the seminar here at our office (date & time of event). I'm so glad you called. We still have a few seats left. Would you like for me to reserve you one?

"Yes"

3. Perfect. Could I have your full name?

4. Dr. XXXXXXXX wants to send you your Free Dental Implant Certificate that can be redeemed at the seminar and directions to our office. Can I have your mailing address?

5. I will be calling you as a reminder a day before the event. What would be the best number to contact you?

6. In case I miss you by phone, I will be sending your reminder by email. What is a good email address for you?

7. I am looking forward to meeting you (repeat the date & time of the event). Good-bye.

The Shock and Awe Pack

That mailing address allows the office to send out a shock and awe pack-age (see page 141). Along with the certificate, the prospect gets a 4-page introductory letter with photos, testimonials, case studies, etc. Of the six offices that use this campaign, four have also written a book which they include in their shock and awe pack to provide additional credibility and authority.

As you can imagine, people have a lot of fears around dental work. The pack is designed to calm their fears and tell them exactly what to expect. Since the company introduced it, the show rate has increased dramatically, from 20% without the pack to 50% with it.

24-Hour Call

By the time a prospect walks into the seminar, they've already had four touches—the ad, the RSVP script, the shock and awe pack, and a reminder call 24 hours before the event.

Free events typically have very low show rates, so anything you can do to increase that is critical. A nudge the day before is a great way to make sure people are coming, and allows you to rebook them if something has come up.

Hi Mary, this is XXXXXXX from DR. XXXXX's office. I'm calling to confirm your reservations for the Free Dental Implant Seminar on (date & time) at our office. Can we count on seeing you then?

Excuse: Well, I'm sorry to hear that. Do you want me to put you on the list for our next seminar?

Confirms coming: Great, we will look forward to seeing you then. There are 2 things I need to tell you. First, you are welcome to bring a friend, relative or spouse to the seminar with you if you like. Do you think you will be? Next, please let us know if anything changes and you can't make it. We try to hold the seminar up until everyone is present. Looking forward to meeting you (date & time). Goodbye.

The Event

Everyone who attends gets their coupon for a free implant, which is only valid until the next month's seminar (an offer with a deadline).

At the event itself, the offer is a free appointment to assess whether the patient is a good candidate for implants or other work. About 50% of attendees take the appointment.

One problem that arose early on was that people came for their appointment expecting everything for free, so now the presenter warns them at the event that they are getting a $1,898 credit for the implant, but there will be other costs of about $2,000.

Another problem was that people were booking the appointment out of curiosity: they had no intention of getting work done. So, the patient now has to make a $200 deposit for their appointment, which will be credited towards any future dental care they take (implants or anything else). That filters the applications down to people who are serious and are willing to put money down to reserve a slot.

Any time you're offering a free consultation, it's an OUTRAGEOUSLY smart move to ask for a deposit that will either be refunded or credited against future purchases, in order to discourage people who are just curious.

The Assessment

If someone attends their appointment but doesn't accept further care, they are put into a separate five-step "implant presented no acceptance campaign" in Infusionsoft.

If they do accept treatment, they are asked for a testimonial afterward (typically on video), which is used in front-end marketing and during the seminars. If they are willing, they are also asked to come to a future seminar to share their experience live, which is even more powerful.

Seminar No-Shows

With any free event, there are inevitably some no-shows, even with the 24-hour reminder call.

No-shows get a letter and a phone call offering them a second chance to attend the following month's event. If they register, they get their 24-hour reminder call.

For people who made an appointment, there is a Second Look Call Script to see if they want to come in and see the seminar again.

The same offer is also made to anyone who attended but didn't make an appointment—they are invited back to the next seminar.

Results

Some offices run the campaign every month; others run it quarterly. Results for the campaign vary widely across different markets, but on average an office can expect 40 responses to their initial ad, of which 20 will attend the event, and 10 make an appointment.

For example, one of the offices runs a seminar every month, and over the last 12 months has generated 268 new patients with a typical lifetime value of $4,000—a total of $1,072,000. To get that, they spent around $36,000 on marketing. That's a 2,978% ROI: every $1 spent on marketing turns into $30 of revenue.

Why Is This a Great Campaign to Model?

The seminar sales model is great for a business that has a high-value front-end sale: in this specific campaign, even if the patient only takes the "free" implant, they still spend $2,000 on that initial treatment. Having a high-value back end after that initial sale makes this an even more profitable approach.

It also works well if your business model is built on lots of regular low-value transactions with a high overall lifetime value, even if the initial sale isn't that high.

Kelly and his doctors work very strategically to get leads, targeting the specific sources that work best in each market. That takes effort, but it massively increases the ROI.

The initial call to the dental office is critical, and the script makes sure that it doesn't matter who takes the call. They'll get the registration, and they'll get all the information they need.

After the call, the shock and awe package to answer objections/fears and the 24-hour reminder call are important steps to increase the attendance rate, and something that anyone running a free event could implement.

Seminars are a great way to build trust for a professional services sale: doctors, lawyers, accountants, consultants, etc. They are also a great way of educating a potential customer in industries where you need a well-informed customer in order for them to make a decision.

This is one of the more complex campaigns in this book, with a lot of steps and a lot of setup. That said, if you have the resources to back it up, and the lifetime customer value to justify it, this could be an OUTRAGEOUSLY profitable way of doing business!

How to Profit OUTRAGEOUSLY from Event Sponsorship (Even If the Cards Are Stacked Against You)

Dustin Mathews was a member of my mastermind group and is a client of my mentor, Dan Kennedy. Dustin and his business partner, Dave Vanhoose, run Speaking Empire, a company that teaches business owners and professionals how to present and how to sell from the stage and online.

In any kind of sales, control is critical. If you lose control—of the conversation, the questions, the situation, even the environment—you risk losing the sale. Nowhere is that more true than when you're selling from the stage.

This campaign was created for a situation where Dustin started with almost no control. The campaign gave him control and allowed him to sell and keep selling.

The challenge

Dustin is always looking for opportunities to speak—not a huge surprise, given the business he's in. When he sponsors an event, he's not interested in turning up and sitting behind a table in a booth. He wants to speak from the stage, whether it's the main stage or a breakout room.

Many events don't even advertise that there are opportunities to speak, but if you simply ask, "How could we speak?" you'll be surprised by the answers you get. There are a lot of up-front costs for event organizers, so they'll take any opportunity they can to get money in from sponsors ahead of time.

The problem with speaking at someone else's events—especially conferences—is that it's not an ideal environment for selling.

First, they may not allow selling from the stage, even though you're giving them money for sponsorship.

Second, even if they do let you sell, you may not have enough time. That was the challenge Dustin faced with this campaign. The offer was for a five-figure training package—that's a tough sale in just 60-90 minutes with a cold audience.

Third, when someone else is running the event, they're also controlling what happens, when, and where. In this case, Dustin's breakout room was well away from the main conference room, on a different floor of the building. So, without a little extra help, no-one was going to be finding their session by chance.

The campaign

The first hurdle to overcome was getting people to the talk. When you're presenting on the main stage, your challenge is simply to convince people to stay for your talk. When you're in a completely different room, you've got to hustle to fill the room. Most people would simply turn up and play the cards they were dealt. Not Dustin.

The Program

Driving traffic started with the event program. Dustin negotiated a full-page ad on the inside front cover.

Here are some key points to pay attention to when you look at that ad.

1. **Authority by association:** The ad includes some serious social proof, starting with the headline. The event was a GKIC conference, so mentioning Dan Kennedy in the same sentence as the Speaking Empire brand right at the top was a very smart move. Equally smart is the list of Dustin and Dave's clients on the lower half of the page, which includes people who were speaking at the

event and others whose names would be instantly recognizable to the GKIC community.

2. **Advertising the advertising:** Details of the breakout session hadn't been finalized when the program went to press, so the time and location were printed on a separate "ticket" (which we'll talk about in a moment) inside the event bag. Some people might not notice it, or might wonder what it was, so this ad drew their attention to it. There's even a picture of the ticket at the bottom, so they know what to look for.

3. **Deadline/scarcity:** The red headline at the top also tells you that this is an "Exclusive" session. It's a simple fact that as soon as you tell people something is exclusive, they start to worry about being excluded. The big yellow sticker on the ad also says that the first 50 people who show up will get a free lunch. At events like this, that's a big draw.

4. **Everyone wins:** The problem with scarcity is that, while it encourages people to take action, people may decide not to act simply because they think they've missed their chance. In this case, it might discourage someone from turning up to the session if they thought they wouldn't be in the first 50. The easy fix is to give everyone a gift in addition to the scarcity bonus. So, the yellow sticker also announces an additional free gift for *everyone* who attends.

The Ticket

As I mentioned above, details of the room and time for Dave's session had to be printed on a separate red ticket.

Even though this is "just a ticket," it's also a fully-fledged piece of OUT-RAGEOUS marketing.

1. The ticket was oversized, to stand out in the event bag.
2. The time and location are mentioned several times on the ticket, so you can't miss them.
3. The GKIC logo is on the ticket again to reinforce the association started in the ad.
4. Clear commands tell the reader what to do ("see other side" "RE-DEEM – Use this ticket").
5. There's an alternative response in case you can't make it to the event ("Stop by the booth").

6. The text on the ticket is efficient, attention-grabbing, and creates a fear of losing out. It's good copy, despite being short.
7. Just like any OUTRAGEOUS marketing, there's plenty of bold text, capitals, text at odd angles, and other tricks to guide your attention.

Footprints

One of the biggest challenges was that the room was so far from the main auditorium. Dustin's solution to this problem was brilliant. He had dozens of footprints printed on adhesive paper and stuck them on the floor leading in a "Path to Profits" from the event room, all the way down the hall and stairs, to the breakout.

People loved the footprints and followed them just to see where they led.

Reminders

Anyone who visited the booth before the breakout was invited to register for SMS reminders about the session.

Notice that there are multiple reminders, not just one, and the messages use video as well as text. Also, notice how the footsteps make the instructions in the message simple: "Just follow the footsteps."

> ROOM, downstairs. Text STOP 2 stop
>
> Oops, forgot to include this Video in my last text: http://goo.gl/b1iO4l.
>
> Dustin, see you in PINE ROOM, downstairs at 11:30. Text STOP 2 stop
>
> Dustin, it's time. PINE ROOM downstairs. Just follow the foot steps. The room is filling ip. Get here fast to get your FREE LUNCH.
> Text STOP 2 stop

Conversion

It wasn't just about getting people to attend the presentation. The aim of the exercise was ultimately to make sales. Except that Dustin wasn't allowed to sell during the event. How do you deal with that?

Dustin and Dave decided to offer a free consultation. Even though it's a free session, it still has to be "sold," so they created a full offer stack with a value of $1,691

- How to Use NLP (value $995)
- The Profitable Speaking Manifesto (value $199)
- Confidence for Public Speakers (Value $497)
- Rapid Results Strategy Session ("priceless")

Conversion Reminders

Events are chaotic, and it's easy for people to lose track of time. With other speakers to see, they'll forget about you as soon as they leave the room. To counter that, Dustin set up more reminders by SMS and email—with both text and video—for people who signed up for the free session.

They used reminders to get people to the event, and again to get them back to the room. To make sure the prospect came back, they emphasized the fact that the sessions were overbooked and asked people to confirm they were coming as someone else wanted their spot if not.

Sat, Nov 7, 8:35 AM

Dave from Speaking Empire asked me to send this video to you Dustin.

http://cllp.co/1Nzk8TE

Text STOP 2 stop

Dustin - looking forward to getting together today. Dave asked me to send this video to you http://cllp.co/1Nzk8TE.

Text STOP 2 stop

Sat, Nov 7, 6:36 PM

Hi Camille - I've got you down for a strategy session today at 5pm to talk about you upcoming speaking gig. Please meet at our booth. We had an overwhelming number of sign ups so please show up on time.

Hi Camille - just checking to see if you are coming as we have someone who wants to take your spot.)

Delivered

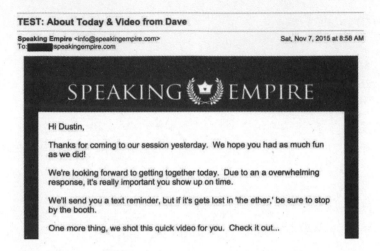

The Strategy Session

The real close came in the strategy session, where the sale was made.

The session was scripted from start to finish and was designed to get the prospect to sell themselves as a suitable client for Speaking Empire rather than trying to get them to buy. That's another really smart strategy, by the way! Here's the script, exactly as the sales team used it.

There are a few interesting things to note in this script.

• The critical point is step 9, where they ask for permission for the close. A lot of the time, if people aren't used to selling, they'll dance around the subject in a sales meeting, and try to slip it in without anyone noticing. If you ask permission to sell ("Would it be OK with

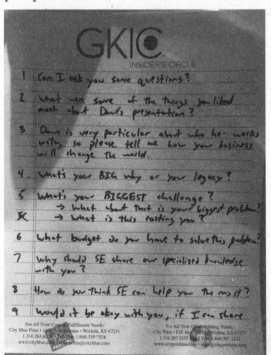

you if I share how we can help you?"), there's no need to be evasive. They are telling you it's all right to sell to them.

- The key is asking the prospect to justify why they should be allowed to work with Speaking Empire. That's the direct opposite of the way most people sell ("Please hire me...").

- There are three offers, priced at $10K, $10K, and $20K. The closing question is not, "Do you want to buy or not?" Instead, it's "which package works best for you?"

- Step 12 is a work of genius. In the previous question, the prospect simply said which package they prefer, but they haven't yet said, "I want to buy." Now, without being asked,

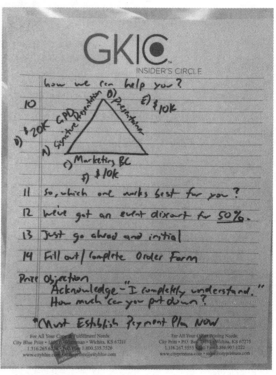

the interviewer offers a 50% "event discount." Since the prospect has already decided that this is the package they would take *if* they were buying, that saving will tip most people over the edge. And notice that it's an "event discount"—in other words, after the event, it's gone.

- Finally, if money is still a problem, they will take a down-payment now and set up a payment plan that makes it affordable.

Results

Filling the Lunchtime Session

The first task was to get people to the breakout room.

The room itself had a capacity of 81 people. Thanks to all the traffic strategies, 110 people turned up—there were people standing in the doorways to watch. That's an outstanding result, especially when you think about the challenges they had with location.

Closing Registrations for the Strategy Sessions

The room was so full that Dave, who was doing the close, couldn't do a table rush; instead, he had to close people in waves, starting with the most qualified prospects first, and ending with people who were just there for the free gift.

In the end, 40 out of the 100 people in the room registered for strategy sessions. Of those, 7 cancelled and 33 showed up.

Paying Customers

Of the 33 strategy sessions that went ahead, 16 people paid in full at either the $5K or $10K level, and 2 set up payment plans, resulting in a total revenue on the day of just over $117K (plus, of course, the future payments on the payment plans).

Why Is This a Great Campaign to Model?

There are aspects to this campaign that you can use anytime you have to pitch with very limited time. You could use this approach, for example, when you give a 10-minute presentation at a networking event.

There are also aspects that you can use to get over difficulties with your location. If your business is off the beaten track, away from a main street and passing trade, think about what your equivalent of the cutout footprints could be to lead people straight to your door.

Ultimately, this campaign teaches one very simple OUTRAGEOUS principle that we can use for ANY business. In any sales situation, the question to have at the back of your mind is, "How can I take control of the process?"

How to Generate an OUTRAGEOUS 273% ROI with Facebook Ads

I first met former Marine fighter pilot Ed Rush when he ran one of our local GKIC groups. He then joined our mastermind group, originally as the 'plus one' for one of his own clients who had joined the group, and later in his own right. Over the years, I have seen him grow into one of the most successful motivational speakers in the country and build a highly lucrative consulting business. He also works closely with Mike Koenigs (who you'll hear from later in this book).

The Campaign

Ed's campaign feeds clients into a funnel to sell a $2,000 training product called "Consult and Profit" which teaches you how to close high-end consulting clients. Ed finds his prospects through Facebook but quickly moves them onto platforms that he controls.

Step 1: Facebook Ad

The sales process starts on Facebook, with an ad inserted into the prospect's timeline.

Facebook gives you a lot of control over who can see your ads. In Ed's case, the ads are shown to existing clients of the company, people who follow other thought leaders in the coaching and consulting industries, and followers of other top marketers.

In addition, the ad is 'retargeted'—if you visit the sales page for the product but don't buy, you'll see the ad again. —remember, as I said in Thing 10, we keep marketing to the B and C piles.

Step 2: Webinar

The Facebook ad drives the prospect to a lead capture page where they sign up for a webinar.

A webinar is a really smart way to sell, because it allows you to sell to groups of people without the hassles associated with live seminars. The prospect doesn't have to travel, they can attend from their desk or their home, and you don't have to rent a room or hire staff.

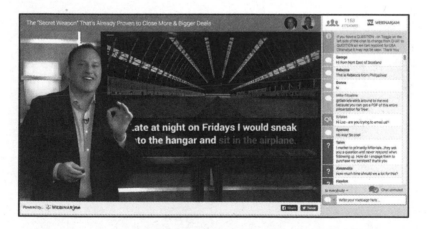

Webcasts are great because they engage the viewer in multiple activities at one time, so you keep their focus. Ed and his partner Mike call this "eyes, ears, hands." The person watches with their eyes, listens with their ears, and is constantly engaging in live chat with their hands.

Even better, the webinar was recorded as it was being delivered　Anyone who missed it (or just wanted to watch again) could watch the replay, and the campaign can be rerun in the future as an "evergreen" webinar. Ed did the work once, and he can keep getting paid into the future. It's not free money, but it's pretty darn close!

The webinar gives great value and information, but more importantly, it is packed with social proof in the form of case studies and testimonials (Thing 3). At the price point Ed is working with, that is a critical component of the sale.

Step 3: Sales Page

The webinar is designed to sell the Consult and Profit product, so the final step is to tell viewers how to buy. During the close, Ed tells viewers to click on a sales button on the webinar page which takes them to a long-form sales letter that restates the offer and the urgency.

Remember: the sales page isn't simply a mechanism for taking the order. It's a continuation of the sales conversation. As you scroll down the page, there are ten bonuses/premiums to make the offer more irresistible, and dozens of testimonials to provide additional social proof.

Step 4: Follow-Up

Once they sign up, the prospects receive email reminders to watch the webinar. In the days after the webinar, they also get sent a link to the replay, reminders to buy, and an invitation to contact the office and talk to a real person if they have any questions.

The key is not to let someone off the hook just because they didn't take action immediately.

Results

So how well is this campaign working?

In total, over a period of nine months, Ed (and his partner Mike) invested $337,000 in running ads. That sounds like a lot, but let's revisit that in a moment.

At the time of writing, 94,248 people had visited the webinar signup page, and 23.26% (21,928) registered to watch.

9,960 of those people (45.42%) attended the webinar live, and another 4,007 (18.27%) watched the replay.

That's almost 14,000 prospects who not only raised their hands by registering but also followed through by watching.

Of course, it's not about getting people to watch a webinar; it's about getting them to buy.

The campaign generated 461 new clients. At $1,997 per sale, that's just over $920,617 of additional sales. Even though Ed had to invest $337,000 in running the ads, they generated a 273% ROI.

I want you to remember one thing—unsuccessful business owners ask, "How much?", while successful business owners ask, "What's the ROI?"

What Happens Next?

A lot of businesses would be more than happy to take nearly a million dollars of revenue and leave it at that, but there's a chance they'd be leaving money on the table.

Consult and Profit is no different, and the kind of person who buys it is an incredibly well-qualified prospect for the company's other products and services. It would be almost criminal, and not very OUTRAGEOUS, to leave things here.

Ed and Mike have a range of services, products, and live events that focus on building a celebrity brand for consultants and other advisers. As part of their purchase of Consult and Profit, clients are invited to come into the office for a live small group training session with Ed and Mike. That gives them an opportunity to cross-sell other products and services as part of the delivery.

Why Is This a Great Campaign to Model?

This is a smart business that has figured out how to get new leads using Facebook and get an offer that converts in front of them.

It's not a cheap process, but when you have a high-converting offer with a high price, it works very well. So, this kind of campaign is ideal for high-ticket training products, and it would work equally well for consulting services and personal services.

GKIC

An OUTRAGEOUS Way to Sell from the Stage at a Live Event Without a Table Rush

It's over six years since I sold Glazer-Kennedy Insiders' Circle and it became simply GKIC, but it still holds a soft spot in my heart, and I am still closely connected with them.

When I spoke to GKIC about a campaign for this book, I wanted something that would be different from the other campaigns already included. In the end, we settled on a presentation given by Ed Rush (who you met in his own campaign in this book) at GKIC's 2017 Info-Summit event to sign up clients for membership of their Platinum mastermind group.

The Campaign

Selling high-ticket coaching from the stage is very different from selling a high-priced product or service. Likewise, there's a big difference between making a $2,000 offer and making a $13,000 offer.

With lower-priced offers, its normal to aim for a "table rush," where you send a frenzied crowd of buyers to the back of the room. As a result, the focus of the presentation is the close, which makes up a substantial part of the presentation. The close itself is designed to make people want to buy, whatever the cost. You want the audience already on their feet when they hear the call to action.

You can't do that at the higher end of the price scale. If you tried to create a table rush with a fast-action bonus and no one ran, you'd be killing your sales. Instead, the presentation itself is the focus. The close still has to be clear and powerful, but it's a much smaller part of the whole presentation. Your job is to get their mind ready for the $13,000 price tag. You want the audience sitting on the edge of their seats as the close begins.

People attend these events because there is some result they want that they haven't been getting—it might be income, impact, lifestyle, work-life balance, or whatever.

The presentation is designed with surgical precision to get them to self-diagnose the aspects of their business that are most lacking; then in the close, you show them that your program is the solution to all the problems they have just told themselves they have. If you don't do that, when you get to the close and tell them about your mastermind, the response will probably be, "I don't need a mastermind."

The opening

The first slide of the presentation focuses on two key promises: speed and certainty. People don't want to pay for "it depends" or "this should work." They want someone to look them in the eye and say, "This will work."

The next slide is completely black because Ed wants attention focused on his story. In fact, every time he tells a story during his talk, Ed brings up a black slide. Those stories can each end up being ten minutes long, not because they're long stories, but because Ed will use points from the story to agitate the audience's pain or get them to imagine having their problem solved—he wants them focused on that.

He's also constantly probing. In effect, he's saying, "Can you see that you don't have this right now, but it's okay because, down the line, you can have this?"

Every story also has a point. For example, the opening story Ed tells is about losing control of a fighter plane and getting it back by following a system. The point? As Dan Kennedy frequently says, "Really great businesses have really great systems."

Building Desire

Next, Ed tells the audience what most business owners want.

> ### The GOAL...
> - A **Consistent**...
> - **Repeatable**...
> - **Revenue** Stream...
> - That **Doesn't Require You** To Be There All The Time

The reality is that these are things every business owner wants, but usually, they are missing at least one of them.

He also points out that most business owners assume they can get these with "superhuman speed." The reality is that they can't, which plants the seeds for coaching.

Working Back to the Offer

The next section of the presentation builds up the offer. When you're making a sales presentation, you can't just teach something interesting and then switch to the pitch. You have to work backward from the offer and figure out what you need to teach the audience for them to want it.

In this case, the mastermind is all about systematizing, so the teaching focuses on systems.

The Systems Six-Pack

- **Lead** Generation
- **Customer** Acquisition
- Customer **Delivery**
- Getting **Reviews**
- Getting **Referrals**
- Getting **Repeat Customers**

There isn't time for detailed instruction. All you can do is build awareness of what's missing from their business, the impact it would have, and proof that it's possible. Each point is backed up with hints, plenty of stories about how Ed built them into his own business, and the results he achieved.

The final slide of this section is designed to build frustration with the status quo.

One More Thing...

- "...Without YOU Having to Be There All The Time."
- Your Time Value
  - 2,000 Hours / Year (50 weeks x 40 hours)
  - 6-Figures = $50 / hr
  - 7-Figures = $500 / hr

The point here is to make them diagnose their own problem. If Ed simply said, "You're never going to make $1M," they'd resist and tell themselves he's wrong. Instead, he shows them some simple math—if you want to make $1M, then every hour you spend at work you need to make $500, or you won't reach a million. Now the audience member is asking themselves if they make $500 every hour they're at work, and they realize *for themselves* that they're not going to make it.

Building Proof

At this point, many audience members are starting to make excuses. "Of course Ed can do this. But I'm not Ed, so it won't work for me." To counter that, Ed brings up a panel of coaching clients and asks them questions about their experience in the mastermind. The aim is to have as diverse a group as possible—all ages, genders, industries—so that every audience member can find someone they can relate to.

Here are the questions Ed typically asks.

1. Tell me what your business was like before you joined the Platinum Mastermind?
2. What is the biggest piece of advice you have implemented that you got out of Platinum that has made the biggest difference in your business?
3. Tell me what your business is like now a year after joining the Platinum group.
4. For someone on the fence potentially thinking about doing coaching, what would you say to them?

The Close

At this point, the presentation is done, and it's time to move into the close.

The close starts with two transition slides that set out who the program is for, and who it's not for. Of course, the qualities of people the program is for are all positive, and those of people it's not for are all negative. The point is to get good prospects to self-select for the program, and also to set up the behaviors they will be expected to show while in the program.

Who Is Platinum Coaching Right For?	Who Is Platinum Coaching NOT Right For?
• You want to dramatically grow your Info Marketing Business while freeing up time in your schedule and life • You want to make an extra 6- or 7-figures this year • You are abundance minded and recognize the value of good advice and speed of implementation	• You consider yourself a whiner, complainer, or you are unwilling to share good ideas. • You have demonstrated zero willingness to implement good ideas in your business. • You have a scarcity mindset and believe the government should provide for you (and others like you).

These are followed by slides that show everything they get if they join the program. At this point, a lot of speakers make a massive mistake: they focus on the features. No one cares how many sessions there are, or what products they get as a bonus. So, Ed goes through each aspect of the program and translates it into benefits. Ed uses the word "imagine" a lot while he's doing this: he wants the audience members thinking about what it would be like to be in the program.

Next, Ed builds up the financial value of the program so that he can contrast it to the cost later.

A Little Math...	
• Product Bundle	= $50,179.00
• IMA Membership	= $1,880.00
• Diamond Membership	= $3,119.64
• Super Conference	= $997
• Info Summit	= $997
• TOTAL Value of Bonuses	= $57,172.64

At this stage, everyone *knows* it's not going to be that much, but it anchors the price in their brain.

The Drop

Having established the full value of the program, Ed works his way down to the actual price.

The first drop is to $25,000. Could one idea you got in the program make you an additional $50,000? If so, then the program pays for itself twice over. "Where else could you get that return?"

However, even though Ed has just shown that the program would be worth investing in at $25,000, there's another drop to the actual price— $12,997 or four payments of $3,749.

For the audience members that may still be thinking that's too much, Ed turns the tables. If you can't make $13,000 from at least one idea you get in the mastermind, he tells them, then you don't have a business.

The Call to Action

The price justification and the price go together, leading straight into the first call to action. The sales team are set up at the back of the room, waiting, and Ed tells the audience what will happen when they go to them. This is not a rush; rather, it's an invitation to go to the back and have a conversation.

You can't just pay and join. There's an application form to complete, which we'll discuss in a moment because the structure of a mastermind application is a critical element of the marketing of the program.

You do still need urgency, however (Thing 2), so Ed introduces some fast action bonuses (Thing 5). To reinforce the urgency, there's a kick-off event that evening for anyone who gets an application form.

That only creates urgency around asking for an application form, so Ed adds some urgency to joining by introducing an extra bonus for the first three people to join.

Finally, Ed puts the investment back on the screen and goes to the back of the room to answer questions.

The Application Form

As I said above, when you're selling a mastermind group, the application process is a critical element of the marketing. The process serves two main purposes.

First, it creates desirability by telling people that they may not get in. Nothing makes people want something more than telling them they can't have it.

Second, it allows you to select only the clients who are going to fit in well and get real results from their membership.

The Platinum Application form has three main sections.

Section 1 is designed to find out how deeply embedded the prospect is in the world of info-marketing and GKIC. The questions focus on what involvement they have had with GKIC's products and events, and what aspects of info-marketing they have already implemented or want to implement.

Section 2 is designed to learn about the individual. It's about figuring out whether they have the right mindset, what they bring to the group and what they want to get from it, and their business model.

Finally, Section 3 is the order and payment form.

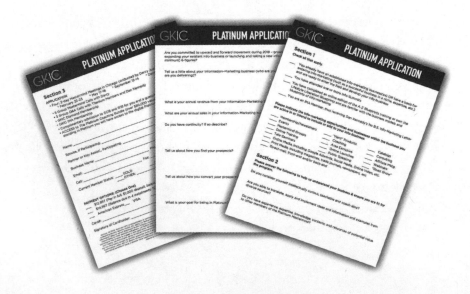

The Event

Remember that although the event is positioned as a kick-off event, it's actually for people who have applied—they haven't yet joined the Platinum mastermind group.

In reality, it has a dual purpose. First, it's designed to give the prospects an experience of what it's like to be in the group, and start to bond with other potential members and with Ed and the team. It's the equivalent of being taken for a test drive in that Ferrari you have your eye on.

The second purpose is to allow more filtering. Ed is there to answer questions, but also to ask questions. One of the best ways to kill a group program is to let the wrong person in. Anything you can do to filter out unsuitable prospects is going to improve the experience and the longevity of your program.

Sneaky Reminders

Ed presented Platinum on the second day of the event. On day three, GKIC scheduled me to give a presentation on the value of belonging to a mastermind group. Many event organizers are great at seeding the sale before it happens. But never forget that you can also seed after the pitch—keep reminding people of the value of joining your programs all the way to the end of the event, and then carry on selling.

Post-Event Follow-Up

When you're selling a high-ticket offer like a mastermind, some people are going to have to go away and think about it. It's easy to leave huge amounts of money on the table if you let them leave the event and you don't follow up with them. In the days after the event, GKIC's team followed up by phone with everyone who had applied.

Results

In the end, GKIC filled sixteen slots, and at the time of writing, there is one more applicant still considering the mastermind group. Of the people who did join, three came in directly after the presentation, six more came from the sales team following up during the event, and another seven joined as a result of the phone follow-up in the days after the event.

Why Is This a Great Campaign to Model?

I've already highlighted the key points that make this campaign work. The big one—and this applies to any high-ticket sale—is the power of follow-up. Almost half of the sales were made after the event. That's $91,000 of revenue that would have been lost if GKIC didn't pick up the phone.

An OUTRAGEOUS Way to Blitz Amazon

Matt Bacak has abandoned lead capture pages, a brave—you might even say OUTRAGEOUS—move in the world of online marketing!

What drove him to take such a bold step?

A couple of years ago, Matt was talking to a client about the importance of list building, and the client commented, "You know, it's not a real lead unless they're a buyer."

It's an idea that hit home, and Matt turned off all his optin pages. Today, the only way to sign up for one of Matt's lists is with a credit card, and he has a number of low-priced products precisely for that purpose. Once someone has taken that first step, they are ideal prospects for higher-end products and services. The result is a much smaller list, but one that is far more responsive.

This campaign was designed to launch a book, *Everyday Heroes*, and promote it to bestseller status on Amazon.

Getting ready

The Name

Long ago, Matt worked out that it's not just the name of your product or service that matters. The name of your campaign can have a major influence on whether people buy in.

This campaign was about using affiliates to "blitz" the top of the Amazon bestseller tables. Amazon's algorithms work in a very specific way, and Matt knew he needed to create a rush of sales in a very tightly defined space of time. He could have called it the Amazon Rush, but Matt used to play football, so instead, the campaign became the Azon Blitz. ("Azon" was used to avoid any possible trademark issues with Amazon.)

Key Messages

The message behind the campaign was simple: "We are launching a book called *Everyday Heroes,* and we are going to be doing the Azon Blitz. I need every able man, woman, and child to come on board to help me.'

The book was a collaborative project with 35 co-authors, and another key part of the message was that this wasn't just about promoting the authors or selling copies of the book—it was about the thousands of people who would be helped by the book.

The diversity of authors also raised an interesting challenge: what to do with the royalties? The answer was simple and made the launch even more appealing: all the royalties were donated to Children's Healthcare of Atlanta.

Signing Up Partners

Although there were 35 co-authors and therefore, in theory, 35 lists that the book would be promoted to, the big question was how responsive those lists would be, and whether they would buy the book. Partnerships would be critical to the success of the campaign.

Matt set up a sign-up page for joint venture partners, affiliates, and all the co-authors to register to promote the book.

Here are two emails Matt used to get people on board:

Subject: attn: jv's and affiliates

On November 11th, 2016 you're invited to CHANGE THE GAME and in turn GET LEADS...

...through the Azon Blitz

->> http://azonblitz.com

Get your bonus gift in ASAP so you get leads.

Find out more.

Best Regards, Matt Bacak

> **Subject: The world votes on Friday.**
> The US is voting today for president of USA.
> The world votes on Friday for bestseller on Amazon.
> Join the blitz:
> http://azonblitz.com
> Bonuses need to be in by Wednesday at midnight.
> You Rock!
> Matt Bacak
> P.S. Save this link for this Friday at 7am EST:
> http://everydayheroesbook.com

Matt knew that people who had signed up and actively promoted the book were also the most likely to buy, so it was important to get them engaged and promoting as soon as possible. He came up with a strategy he called "Buy and Tell." Throughout the run-up to the launch, promotional activities for the book were built around the following concept: "On November 11, 2016, we Buy and Tell."

That phrase—buy and tell—was repeated over and over again. It became the mantra of the campaign. On launch day, everyone was posting on their Facebook pages, "Go buy this book, and tell other people." They were leading by example, saying "I bought this, you should buy it too."

Stacking the Bonuses

Another key element of the launch was the bonuses that people would get for buying the book. Matt collected bonuses from each of the co-authors. With 35 participants, that created a bonus stack that made buying the book a no-brainer.

Here are the first sixteen of the 47 OUTRAGEOUS bonuses readers were able to claim (with a total value of $5,222.89).

- 12 Steps to Building a Better Business
- Free Insider Access for Monetize It! Business building Program & The Monetization Summit Pre-Launch
- FREE BOOK: Approach – Discover the Game-Changing, Rejection-Free Way to Reach Your Ideal Clients, Have Them Clamoring to Work with You, and Grow Your Business With Multiple Streams of Revenue
- Free Report: Discover How to Get Your Book to the Top Charts in Record Time
- 32 Topic Ideas for Subscription Websites and A Profit Potential Calculator
- Freedom Lifestyle Academy MP3 and PDF Download
- Insider Secrets to Attracting Customers and Boosting Sales
- Free E-Book: An unofficial guide for app creators on how the king of gaming makes $700,000 a day
- How to Kick your Customer Service Up A Notch
- Free Conversion Map & Direct Mail Building Blocks
- Free Report: 7 Simple Ways to Grow Your Business Online
- Benefits of Alkaline Water
- Top SEO Mistakes Marketers Make & Top Adwords Mistakes Marketers Make
- A Beautiful Desktop Screen Saver
- The recipe for success on Instagram, Twitter, and Facebook
- Video Marketing Package Includes: Marketing Video, Logo Stinger, 15-min Consultation

Election Fever

The launch happened the same week as the US presidential election. That was used throughout the promotion (which, of course, is an application of Thing 6).

A second fortunate coincidence was that Donald Trump had a book in one of the categories that *Everyday Heroes* was in. Matt contacted the co-authors and told them, "We have to beat Trump. Tell everyone you know to buy, because then you can take a screenshot and tell the world that your book beat Trump's." It was an idea that everyone bought into, whether they love Trump or hate him.

The campaign

Step 1: Building anticipation

The campaign started with email and social media promotion. In addition to the 35 co-authors, who naturally promoted the book to their own lists, there were joint ventures and affiliates, as well as many other people, friends, and family who jumped on board to promote the launch because it was for a worthy cause. At the same time, Matt knew that some of those people might not follow through, so he also promoted it to his own list.

Everybody—authors, partners, and Matt—emailed their lists three times to warm them up for the launch.

Subject: Blitzing Amazon

The Election is over (thank goodness). BUT, the "Everyday Heroes" Book blitz is happening on Friday (11/11) ...at exactly 7am EST.

Please help us take this exciting new book to the top of Amazon.

Details here: http://everydayheroesbook.com

So far people have donated $5,222.89 in Bonuses that will be given away for Free with your proof of purchase of the book.

100% of the proceeds are going to Charity.

This is getting bigger and bigger.

Together we are blitzing Amazon on Friday at exactly 7 am EST.

http://everydayheroesbook.com

Come join the party :-)

You Rock! Matt Bacak

Subject: My New Book.

This Friday 11/11/16 I have a new book coming out called "Everyday Heroes".

This is a book that I co-wrote with some other amazing entrepreneurs and people from all over the world.

We are hoping to hit International Best Seller Status on Amazon, but in order to do that, I need your help!

Please block your calendar to take 2 minutes out of your morning on Friday 11/4/16 and buy this book on Amazon (between 7am-8am) if at all possible.

Tell your friends to please buy one too.

Here's why... 100% of ALL royalties for this book will be donated to the Children's Hospital, because the Children are the real heroes of the future!

I'm going to buy a book during this time, and I would greatly appreciate your support for this Best Seller Book Launch Effort!!

To learn more go to: EverydayHeroesBook.com

Thanks for supporting my new book and for supporting a great charity!

You Rock.

Matt Bacak

Subject: Don't buy Everyday Heroes without getting the best deal possible!

This is a book that I co-wrote with some other amazing entrepreneurs and people from all over the world.

We are hoping to hit International Best Seller Status on Amazon, but in order to do that, I need your help!!

Please take 2 minutes out of your morning on Friday 11/11/16 and buy this book on Amazon (between 7am-8am) if at all possible.

Tell your friends to please buy one too.

100% of ALL royalties for this book will be donated to the Children's Hospital, because the Children are the real heroes of the future!

> I'm going to buy a book during this time, and I would greatly appreciate your support for this Best Seller Book Launch Effort!!
>
> To learn more go to: http://EverydayHeroesBook.com
>
> Thanks for supporting my new book and for supporting a great charity!
>
> Buy & Tell.
>
> You Rock.
>
> Matt Bacak

Social media was also a major channel for this promotion, with authors and partners using text and video to get attention.

Matt created a Facebook banner image that a lot of the authors and JV partners set as their profile picture.

Step 2: The Push

The focus on social media and email carried through to the day before the launch and the launch itself. On the day before the launch, there was a big push. Matt created images for people to post, as well as pre-written emails for them to send out, or they could write their own if they preferred. As an aside, when you're relying on other people to promote something for you, it's always a good idea to do as much as you can for them: promotional images, suggested social media posts, emails, etc.

Everyone is Blitz Buying "Everyday Heroes" Book Tomorrow at 7am EST. =>>
http://azonblitz.com/buy/ Luv all the help we can get! Everyone wins! Over
$5,222.89 in Bonuses. 100% Of Royalties Go To Children Charity.

 Jocelyn Jones 😊 feeling excited with Gary Kissel and 3 others.
November 10 at 12:22pm · 🌐 ▼

TOMORROW is the Day! 11/11/16 to ALL My Friends in Facebook Land:

Please help support a WORTHY Cause by going to
http://everydayheroesbook.com at 7 am EST and follow instructions on how
to purchase your copy and get access to over $5000 in Bonuses.

You will also have the opportunity to read all the Inspirational Entrepreneurs
Stories from around the world. If We can do it, so can You! 😊

 **Everyday Heroes Book – Everyday
Heroes Book**
Everyday Heroes Book Launch With Bonuses

 Kathleen Gage
November 10 at 3:59pm · 🌐 ▼

Most people have causes they believe in. Many of those causes have to do
with children. Tomorrow, November 11th, I'm involved in a very important
cause that's the brainchild of Matt Bacak. Be watching for information and
when you see it, jump on board.

Here is one of the prewritten emails:

Subject: Holy Cow!

So far, people have donated $5,222.89 in bonuses that will be given away for free with your proof of purchase of my new co-authored book: "Everyday Heroes" Tomorrow!

We need your help! Join in for a great cause and purchase this book on Amazon.com tomorrow (11/11/16) between 7am-8am EST.

Buying at this time is very important, because we are shooting for an International Best Seller. Your purchase of this book at this time could literally put us over the top!

AND...100% of book sale proceeds will be donated to the Children's Healthcare of Atlanta (CHOA).

All details are explained here: www.EverydayHeroesBook.com

Thanks for your support in my new book launch!

Best Regards,

NAME GOES HERE

Step 3: Launch Day

On the day of the launch itself, everyone "blitzed" their email lists at 7 a.m. with the following email:

Subject: Everyday Heroes Book is Live!

We need your help to make this book an International Best Seller!

Your purchase of this book right now could literally put us over the top!

AND...100% of book sale proceeds will be donated to charity.

All details are explained here:

http://www.EverydayHeroesBook.com

When you grab the book right now, you'll enjoy immediate access to tons of free bonuses ($5,222.89 value already donated) as our way of saying thank you for

supporting our book launch and for supporting the children.

Thanks for your support in my new book launch!

Best Regards,

NAME GOES HERE

The emails and social media posts were designed to drive traffic to a launch page which listed the bonuses they would get for buying the book and asked them to opt-in to get instructions for claiming the bonuses.

Afterward, they were taken to a second page which repeated the bonuses and gave them the instructions.

Later in the day, a follow-up email went out.

Subject: #1 Best Seller!

Wow, what a day!

We are still crushing it with book sales as we speak.
The momentum has been through the roof, and I'm blown
away and grateful for all the support.

Check it out...see that orange "Best Seller" banner?

Best Seller

Everyday Heroes: A Collection Of Motivational & Inspirational Stories From Around...
by Matt Bacak
Paperback
$14.95 *Prime*
Get it by **Monday, Nov 14**
FREE Shipping on eligible orders
6 offers from $11.79
⭐⭐⭐⭐⭐ (11)

...yep, hard work pays off.

I couldn't have done it without your support, and it's not too late if you still want to get your copy and spread the word. More book sales equals more money for our charity, the Children's Healthcare of Atlanta.

Please consider getting a copy of my new book if you haven't already done so, and tell your family and friends to do the same, because all proceeds are donated to children in need. It's only $14.95, and shipping is free if you are a Prime member with Amazon.

All details about getting the book and $7,508.92 in free bonuses can be found here: www.Every-dayHeroesBook.com

Best Regards,

Matt Bacak

Step 4: Buyer Opt-in

In order to claim their bonuses, buyers opted into a second list by entering details of their Amazon receipt. Note that this was a list of buyers, which (as I say elsewhere in this book) is far more valuable list than a list of leads. After entering their receipt details, the buyer was sent to an upsell page.

Step 5: The Upsell

Because the key messages that attracted partners were about collaboration and support for charity, Matt felt that upselling a product would be inappropriate. It would also be difficult to find an appropriate product for a book with such a broad theme.

Instead, the upsell was an invitation to apply to collaborate on a follow-up book, *Everyday Heroes 2*.

Step 6: Social Proof

On launch day, Matt bought a copy of the book himself and posted a screen print of his receipt on social media to show that he had bought it. Then he asked everyone else to do the same.

It was taking "Buy and Tell" to the next level—getting people to lead by example.

The Unexpected Bonus

The promotions on launch day had the desired effect, but Matt spotted another spike in sales the day after. What happened was that people got the book shipped to them on overnight delivery, and when the book arrived they were so excited they started to post pictures of themselves with the book on Facebook. No-one asked them to do it, but that kickstarted a new bunch of buyers.

That second spike inspired one final push. Matt sent out an email to all the buyers who had registered asking them to post a screenshot on Facebook of the shipping confirmation from Amazon. It was another excuse for telling people about the book, and another "Buy and Tell."

Results

We can look at the results of this campaign in two ways.

First, over 1,000 copies of the book were sold on launch day. In a world where the average non-fiction book sells just 250 copies a year, selling 1,000 copies in a single day is a huge achievement.

It also put the book on several Amazon bestseller lists:

- #8 in Self Help
- #6 in Success
- #4 in Motivation
- #3 in Movers and Shakers
- #1 in Philosophers
- #1 in Hot New Releases

Second, as a result of the upsell, all of the author slots for *Everyday Heroes 2* sold out.

In both respects, the campaign was a success.

Finally, don't overlook one really valuable part of this campaign. The list of JV partners, affiliates and other promoters can be used for future books and products, and so can the list of buyers.

Why Is This a Great Campaign to Model?

Although this was a book launch, the core of the campaign could be used to launch any kind of product or service.

One of the things that made this campaign so successful was the "Buy and Tell" theme, supported by screenshots and selfies. This would work just as well with a digital product—just have people screenshot the receipt, or add a physical component to the product (as you'll see in Yanik Silver's campaign) and encourage people to post selfies when the package arrives.

Of course, if you're selling a physical product, then those photo opportunities are already there.

An OUTRAGEOUS Way to Sell a High-Ticket Offer by Investing OUTRAGEOUSLY!

Back in 2009, when I was getting ready to write my first book, Bill Harrison told me, "If you're getting ready to write a book, you need to know Mike Koenigs." Bill was right. Mike told me that if I came to his studio, he would record a series of videos for me and put them online to get people to purchase my book. So, I went to San Diego, and we created the videos.

I've since invited Mike to speak at several of my events, not only because I wanted to help him, but also because he did a really great job of speaking and people really like his style!

The Campaign

Mike's company, You Everywhere Now, has a range of products, services and live trainings that help professionals to position themselves and create a celebrity brand in their industry. One of those events is a 3-day workshop called Publish & Profit where clients become #1 bestselling authors before they leave. Mike has also created a "home study" info product version of the program.

This campaign is designed to teach leads the power of being a published author before offering them the information product or the live event.

Lead Generation

Leads for the campaign come from a variety of places.

The first is Facebook ads to cold leads. Mike uses long-format text ads and video ads to drive leads to the webinar. When someone clicks on the ad, they are taken to the registration page which has an OUTRAGEOUS piece of social proof: a photo of Mike sitting next to Hollywood star Richard Dreyfuss on a plane thanks to his book.

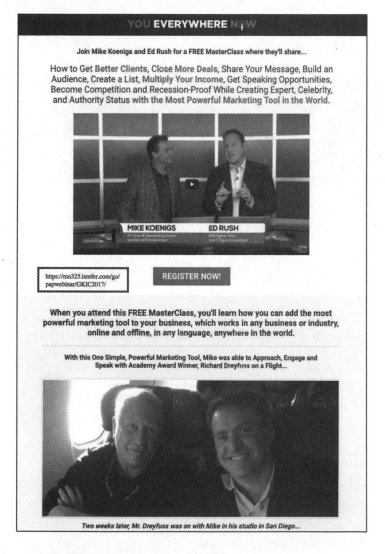

The second is Mike's *house list*, who are already well indoctrinated. The list is engaged through emails and retargeted with Facebook ads. Getting existing community members onto the webinars is critical for Mike because during the broadcast they are often the ones who start interacting with each other and with Mike and his team. That creates a real family atmosphere that gets everyone else involved even if they've never seen Mike before.

Third, Mike uses the same presentation as a platform speech to sell Publish & Profit directly from the stage. (As you can see, he's not afraid to be OUTRAGEOUS himself!)

Finally, Mike has turned the webinar into a content-rich book which he uses for lead generation and sends directly to potential candidates.

If you have high-value content that your audience loves, repurposing it into other media is an OUTRAGEOUSLY smart way to leverage the time and energy you've already invested.

The Webinar

The webinar is a prerecorded evergreen webinar, but it is configured so that viewers don't realize that it is not live. Comments from previous runs are displayed in real time as though they were being entered by a live viewer. If someone asks a question while they watch, it is forwarded to Mike's team, and they email a response.

The webinar includes a large number of testimonials and case studies of past students to provide social proof and to show the viewer that the results are possible for them too.

Immediate Follow-Up

After the email, there are two follow-up emails with a link to the replay and a three-day deadline to take action.

The first email goes out on the Friday after they watch. The structure is something you might want to model for your own OUTRAGEOUS follow-up.

It starts with teaser copy for the webinar to get anyone who hasn't watched to watch—and indeed if someone has watched but not bought, then it's good to get them to re-watch.

Then there's a minute-by-minute breakdown of the content of the webinar, all copy-written to get the reader to want to watch the replay.

```
The LIVE Event Invitation
• 33:10 - Mike walks through the 3-day event that GUAR-
ANTEES you will walk away a bestselling author. Just
show up with an idea, and you'll leave a bestseller!
```

- 37:15 - Get answers to your questions on launching (and re-launching) a quality, brand-building book.

The Price and Guarantee

- 37:45 - Guaranteed Ways Becoming a Bestselling Author!

Training - Continued

- 48:12 - What do a Rolex and your iPhone have to do with getting and keeping an audience's attention?
- 52:29 - A brand-new tech example of how you can stream LIVE into the computers, cars, laptops, and devices of everyone on the connected Planet...for less than $300.
- 54:16 - Mike demonstrated the You Everywhere Now Principle to show you how to get seen, heard, read, viewed on any device...anywhere on the Planet!
- 57:00 - Mike tells the story of how his bout with cancer led him to crack the code on the publishing world...and create 10 straight #1 best sellers.
- 1:01:10 - How Mike answers the question "Can I pick your brain?" and how you can copy and paste these same words to (finally) get paid what you're worth.
- 1:03:45 - With this one powerful marketing tool, Mike was able to approach, engage and speak with Academy Award-winner Richard Dreyfuss...and just two weeks later, Mr. Dreyfuss flew to San Diego to meet and work with Mike in his studio.

The second email goes out on Sunday morning (the morning of the deadline). Again, it has teaser copy and a link to the sales page, to get the reader to either watch or invest.

The third and final email goes out Sunday evening and is short and to the point.

Subj: DEADLINE. TONIGHT.

Hey there-

The deadline to get in on the new Publish and Profit LIVE Event is in just a few hours.

This is the event that guarantees you'll walk away a bestselling author in 3 days.

```
You heard that right.
You have until Midnight tonight to lock in your dis-
count and guarantee all the Bonuses.
Get It All Here.
(DEADLINE: Tonight at Midnight)
Reminder: Not only will you become a bestselling author
in 3 days, I will also create and launch a SOLO /
STAND-ALONE promotion to my entire Facebook following
for you and your book.
Boom.
See you inside the system.
Mike
```

Long-term Follow-Up

If a lead doesn't buy, they are retargeted with Facebook ads (assuming they came from Facebook to start with) and other relevant content that may generate their interest.

Mike also follows up by email to invite them to register again for the webinar.

Leads from other sources (e.g. live presentations) are given an opportunity to speak to a strategy coach—a sales-minded professional who will talk to the prospect, learn about their business and find out what their outcomes are, what their challenges are in their business, and guide them toward either the digital product or the live event. For a high-ticket sale like this, introducing a live sales team to follow up with unconverted leads is an OUTRAGEOUSLY good idea.

Results

The campaign has generated millions of dollars of sales of this product. Mike's aim—which he achieves—is a cost per sale of $700 or less, giving him a 3:1 gross ROI.

Many business owners would balk at spending that much to get a customer, but let me ask you an OUTRAGEOUS question: if you knew that for every $700 you spent you were going to get back either $1,997 or $4,997, how many $700 investments would you make? The key is to focus on the return rather than the cost—when the stakes are that high, and you have a proven funnel, it's worth spending to get the sale.

Why Is This a Great Campaign to Model?

This is an OUTRAGEOUSLY good way to sell a high-ticket offer. As Mike has proven, it works both for live events and for info products, and it works with both warm leads and cold traffic. The secret is to be willing to invest what it takes to get high-quality leads. And that should make you want to do an OUTRAGEOUS jump for joy just like Mike!

An OUTRAGEOUS Way to Sell a High-Ticket Offer Without a Sales Team by Getting OUTRAGEOUSLY Personal

I first met Oli Billson when we were both speakers at the GKIC spring Super Conference in 2017. As I listened to his presentation, I remember thinking he was teaching the audience some very smart marketing strategies.

As well as running several very successful "real" businesses, Oli also teaches other entrepreneurs how to market their business, or they can just outsource the whole thing to Oli and his team.

The Campaign

This campaign presents the prospect a high-ticket business opportunity. Most of the time, selling anything with a high price requires a sales team to build trust, answer questions, and ultimately close the prospect. When you're offering a business opportunity, that sales team becomes even more critical. Oli's campaign was designed to make an (expensive) human sales team unnecessary. OUTRAGEOUS!

Lead generation

Leads for the campaign came from two sources.

1. New leads generated offline through direct mail.
2. Reactivating unconverted leads on the house list.

Direct Mail to the Cold List

The campaign used several direct mail pieces. Here, for example, is a postcard.

You'll recognize quite a few things here from Thing 4. First, font and color changes create a double readership path. Then there are CopyDoodle arrows to take your eye to the URL. And then there's the URL itself: join.black-code.co.uk/David.Bellwood. It's what's known as a PURL (Personalized URL), and it has the name of the recipient coded into it. Who could resist visiting a web page that has their own name in the address? That's an OUTRAGEOUS way to get people to visit your landing page.

Another of the direct mail pieces was a tear sheet that looks like a newspaper cutting with a yellow sticky on it that says, "Saw this and thought of you… J" It's the first thing most people see when they open the envelope.

Who is J? Who knows! But the prospect is going to read the article just so as not to disappoint the mysterious J who kindly sent them the cutting.

Both the card and the tear sheet were designed to take leads to a landing page to download a free report.

Emailing the House List

Unconverted leads on the house list got a series of emails that drove them to the same landing page and free report as the direct mail.

The OUTRAGEOUS Landing Page

Here's the landing page all the traffic was sent to. Look carefully and see if you can spot what makes it OUTRAGEOUS.

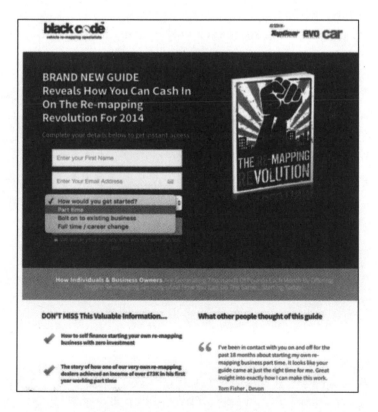

Did you spot it? At first glance, it looks very similar to the other lead pages you've seen in this book. The secret is at the bottom of the optin form:

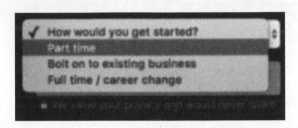

This segmentation question is the key to the whole campaign, and it's what made it possible to sell a high-ticket offer without human salespeople.

The answers to the question correspond to three types of ideal client that Oli and his team had identified.

The difference between these three ideal clients (marketers call them *avatars*) is in how they think about their current situation, what they want from a business opportunity, and how they see their future progressing.

What makes that so important is that if you can create messages that are tailored to how someone thinks, what they want, and their aspirations, it can sound like you're talking to them personally. And if you can get your online marketing to sound like it's been created for the lead personally, then why would they need to talk to a human being?

Think of it like this. Imagine your name is Bob and you're looking for a part-time business opportunity. Which of these messages are you more likely to respond to?

1. "Would you like to make an extra $20,000 next month?" or
2. "Bob, would you like to make an extra $20,000 next month, working part-time?"

Number two is going to win every time. And the lead page was set up so the rest of the campaign would be exactly like that.

Once the lead chose an answer and clicked the button, they were taken down separate paths, depending on how they'd answered the question.

Dynamic Expiration Dates

It's really hard to have deadlines in an evergreen lead generation campaign and enforce them. Why? Because you either have to close the campaign down after the deadline, in which case it's not evergreen, or you have to open it up again after the deadline, which teaches your list that your deadlines aren't real and they can ignore them.

Oli solved that by setting deadlines dynamically in Infusionsoft. When a visitor signs up, the system creates an early bird deadline 14 days later, and a final deadline 28 days after the initial opt-in. Those dates were used in all the communication that followed.

Address Capture

Oli wanted to be able to follow up by mail as well as email. As we've seen in several campaigns, Oli split the opt-in over two screens to maximize completion rates.

In keeping with the theme of OUTRAGEOUS personalization, the lead's name was used at the top of this second page.

One other thing to note is that Oli collected the address from people on the house list as well as cold leads. Why? Because your

leads don't always remember to tell you when they move, so it makes sense to validate the information in your database when you get the opportunity, especially if you're about to spend money based on that information.

Conditional Follow-Up

Once the lead had provided their address, they entered a multi-step, multi-media sequence of online and offline follow-up designed to get them to visit a sales page. All of that follow-up—by email and mail, as well as the sales letter copy used—was driven by the response the lead gave to the segmentation question when they opted in.

Offline Follow-Up

1) Shock and awe pack: sales letter, testimonial sheet, FAQ sheet, CD
2) Early-bird reminder postcard
3) Micro sales letter + "A day in the life" press release
4) Final deadline postcard
5) Final deadline follow-up sales letter

Email Follow-Up

Email follow-up started 72 hours before the dynamic Early Bird deadline, and five emails were sent: "72 hours left," "48 hours left," "24 hours left," "closing today," and "last chance." A similar sequence started 72 hours before the dynamic final deadline.

Flexible Sales Letter

Based on the segmentation response, Infusionsoft modified multiple elements of the sales letter:

- Pre-Headline/Headline
- Video Sales Letter
- Sub Headline
- Opening
- Testimonials
- Bullet Benefits
- Close & P.S.

These elements were inserted around a core message to tailor it with pain points, challenges, and obstacles that spoke directly to each of the three avatars in a way that a single generic message never could. Even the testimonials used echoed the specific situation, objections, and desires of the lead.

Here's the sales letter for someone bolting the opportunity onto an existing business.

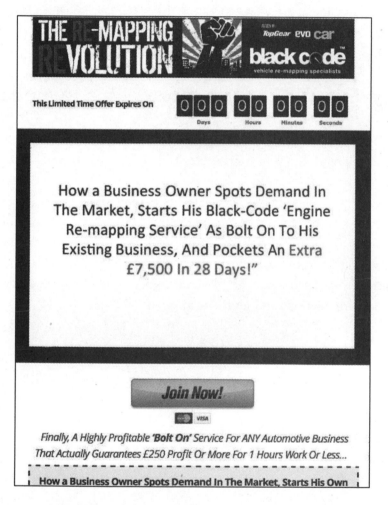

The video sales letter for someone who wanted to do this part-time started instead with a screen that said, "Who else wants to earn an extra £2,000 per month re-mapping vehicles part-time?" while the video for someone who was going to switch jobs and run the business full-time said, "Can full-time 'Vehicle Re-mapping Technicians' earn £250+ per hour?"

Results

The campaign was run seven times. In total, Oli and his partners invested £2,840 (around $3,750) and generated revenue of £66, 877 ($88,400) for a total ROI of 2,255%.

Why Is This a Great Campaign to Model?

The higher your price point, the more connection you need to build with a prospect. That's why high-ticket sales tend to rely on salespeople to close the deal.

This campaign gives you a very effective alternative. It relies on the facility Infusionsoft gives to personalize many aspects of the campaign.

It's particularly effective in situations where the early stages of the interaction would be spent qualifying the leads. Rather than pay someone to spend time with a prospect who ultimately goes nowhere, you can automate those early interactions and let the lead qualify themselves.

How to Harness The Power of People to Turn a Really Bad Idea into an OUTRAGEOUSLY Great One

What would you do if you ran an event with ten speakers, spent $100,000 setting it up, and only three people turned up to watch? You probably wouldn't turn around and do it again immediately, and you probably wouldn't try to get other people involved as well. But that's exactly what Ron Seaver did.

I first met Ron when he was a GKIC member, and I got to know him even better when he later joined the Peak Performers Group.

Back in the 1980s, Ron worked in Major League Baseball as Director of Sponsorship and Promotions for the San Diego Padres. His job, in his own words, was to "get people to part with their good money… to come watch some pretty bad baseball." (Apologies to any Padres fans reading this!) And bear in mind that this was in San Diego, so his biggest competitors were the beaches!

Every year in the Fall, Ron would head to Arizona and spend three days with his counterparts at other major league baseball teams, finding out what they'd been doing to get fans to their ballparks. Then he'd head home and figure out how to use the same techniques for the Padres.

Now, if you've read this far, you can see the flaw in that: yes, everyone was swiping and deploying (Thing 1), but they were only swiping from each other.

As much as Ron loved those sharing sessions, the madness of it was brought home by one veteran of the baseball wars who told Ron, "There are only six original ideas out there. Everything else is a variation on those six."

That set Ron thinking. If baseball had six ideas, what six ideas did the NBA have? And NFL? And NASCAR?

The problem was that the leagues in pro-sports simply don't talk to each other. Members talk to other members of the same league, but you wouldn't catch a football team talking to a hockey team. You won't even find someone from the business side of a Major League Baseball team talking to a Minor League Baseball team—and they've got the same commissioner.

When you think about it, they're all in the same business—the "selling tickets to fans" business. There's a lot they could learn from each other.

That's when Ron had his OUTRAGEOUS idea: someone should put on a meeting and bring ALL of the ticket sales, marketing, promotions and business development people together from across the world of sport.

Introducing …the National Sports Forum. A GREAT idea. Or so you'd think.

The National Sports Forum

When Ron first took the idea to his boss (and mentor) at the Padres, his reaction was, "Are you crazy?" He didn't stop there. He told Ron that of all the incredibly stupid idea's he'd come up with over the years, this was easily the dumbest.

Ron was unfazed. And so, in 1995, he launched his (not quite overnight) success, the National Sports Forum (NSF). Today, it's one of the largest annual sports business conferences in North America, gathering league teams and property executives from the NFL, MLB, MBA, MLS, NASCAR, UEFA, the minor leagues, NCAA, auto- and horseracing, and many more.

The road to success wasn't smooth, however.

First Steps

For the NSF's inaugural event in Colorado Springs, Ron brought together ten leading industry figures—the presidents of the Golden State Warriors, Anaheim Angels, and New Jersey Nets, the owner of the Colorado Rockies and top sponsorship guys from Coors and Coca-Cola. And an audience of…three. Not three thousand. Not three hundred. Just three people.

What do you do when you've spent over $100,000, and you don't bring in any money? (Apart from wondering how you're going to pay back the $100,000?)

If you're Ron Seaver, you turn right around and plan to do it all over again. Only this time was going to be *different*.

Harnessing the Power of People

While he was putting together the 1995 National Sports Forum event, Ron had run the idea by various senior people in the sports industry, and they had said that they liked the idea (although none of them had attended!). Trusting that they were sincere, Ron decided that the second time around he would see if he could harness the power of others.

He asked them again whether they still thought the idea had merit; whether they still saw the value in getting all of their peers from other sports together to share their best ideas for selling tickets. This time, when they said *yes*, he asked them whether they would join his steering committee and help get the movement off the ground. In exchange, they'd get free access to the 1996 event.

He got nine people on board. As you'll see, it's grown OUTRAGEOUSLY since then.

Committee Life

Most voluntary boards—whether they're called an advisory board, executive committees, steering committee, or whatever—operate much the same way. You meet once a year or more simply to rubber stamp whatever the chairman has decided. Often committee members don't know much about their fellow members beyond first names.

That wasn't the kind of committee Ron wanted.

His big challenge was convincing people to attend, so what he wanted was an oversight committee that would do the heavy lifting for him.

That's exactly what he got, and you can have it too if you structure your organization the right way.

How to Build a Steering Committee That Works OUTRAGEOUSLY

Twenty-three years on, the executive director at Ohio University—an institution that has the oldest, and one of the most distinguished Sports Management programs—has commented that they should be offering a master class on how the NSF built and manages its steering committee!

But you don't need to sign up for a Masters at OU to find out. I'm going to break it down for you.

1. **Make it very selective**. Serving on the committee needs to be an honor. If someone doesn't buy into your vision, they are welcome to attend the event, but there's no seat for them on the committee.
2. **Have a beginning and an end**. Most committees are an open-ended commitment, with no fixed end. NSF steering committee members serve a fixed term from June to May.
3. **Keep your winners**. At the end of the term, Ron calls each committee member to discuss their experience and performance. Those who did a good job and enjoyed their time are invited back. That allows him to hold on to achievers and let go of the rest (although problem performers can be let go mid-year if necessary).
4. **Set clear objectives**. Committee members must be told what's expected of them when they are first invited. There are only TWO rules that must be adhered to if you'd like to come back for another year on the NSF Steering Committee:
    *   **"Get Your Six"**—also known as "the Skins." This is a sporting analogy, in keeping with the sports motif of the NSF (in golf, a "skin" is a designation you get when you get the lowest score on a hole during a round). Steering Committee members must have six skins on their scorecard by the end of their year. They earn them by bringing in an attendee (1 skin), a trade show exhibitor (2 skins) or a sponsor (the number of skins varies according to the level of sponsorship).
    *   **You must ATTEND**. If you organize an event and recruit people to come, but you don't attend yourself, it's like a chef going to eat at the restaurant across the street. So, unless there is a grave family emergency, committee members are not invited back if they don't attend that year's Forum.
5. **Make it something people WANT to be a part of**. Ron wanted the NSF event to be the "Gold Standard" that other sports conferences would be compared against. When you set yourself an objective like that, the committee members "get it," and they either live

up to it, or they move on (which is fine, because there are dozens of industry executives who would welcome the opportunity to replace anyone that falls short).

6. **Stay involved**. Even though the event is only once a year, it's critical to keep committee members involved all year. In Ron's case, he couldn't wait until December to get people engaged. He needed them as involved in July as they would be in January.

- **"Springtime in San Diego"** Each year, in May or June, the committee meets in San Diego to discuss how they can make that year's Forum even better than the year before. Spouses are also invited, along with top-level sponsors. They spend a long weekend together meeting, mixing, and getting to know one another better. It costs money to put together, but it's money well spent!

- **Founders Dinner**. The Forum starts on a Sunday. On the Saturday night before, there is a special invitation-only dinner for Steering Committee members, sponsors, and hosts from that year's city. With well over 1,000 people attending the NSF, the "Founder's Dinner" acts as the "calm before the storm," and provides an opportunity for Steering Committee members to catch up with one another before they jump head first into the following morning.

7. **Communicate…Communicate…Communicate**. Keep everyone involved and engaged by communicating frequently with your Committee members. NSF does that in three main ways:

- An annual **one-on-one phone call** to discuss their standing on the Committee.

- **Update memos** to keep everyone involved and on top of the latest news.

- **Monthly Steering Calls** to bring committee members up to date on the agenda, get progress reports, and answer questions.

8. **Let their voice be heard.** In addition to recruiting, the NSF Steering Committee serves an equally important role in giving input both before the Forum and at the event itself.

- At the start of each new year, members are asked to complete an Agenda Ballot to identify topics and issues for the breakouts and panels and to nominate speakers.

- NSF gets major sports figures to speak by taking advantage of the network of Steering Committee members.

- Committee members have key roles (session leaders, moderators, panelists) during the NSF itself, which enhances their standing as an industry leader.

9. **RECOGNITION.** Last, but not least, is giving recognition. The key is to recognize that these people are special, and to do so wherever you can. NSF does this in various ways, including

- At the Conference, Steering Committee members get immediate recognition in the first session when they are brought onto the main stage to introduce themselves.

- Outside the Conference, their names and titles are prominently featured on the NSF web site, in issues of the quarterly newsletter, and in the main Agenda brochure.

- At the annual board meeting, a series of Steering Committee awards are given to NSF employees: Rookie of the Year, the Spirit of the Forum award, Most Improved, and the big award, the Steering Committee MVP Award, presented in front of all of the Committee members, Sponsors, and Employees. The winner also has their name engraved on a permanent plaque recognizing all the great MVP's who have been hon-  ored down through the ages of the Forum. It is also the reigning MVP who opens the next conference.

Why Is This a Great Campaign to Model?

Look beyond all this information about the inner workings of a Steering Committee, and you'll see that it is, in effect, a referral strategy on steroids.

Few business owners would think of an advisory board or steering committee as a marketing opportunity. Yet, the board is the engine that drives ticket sales and sponsorship for the NSF event. I wish I'd thought of this when I ran GKIC!

You could get creative with this. For example, you could invite clients onto a steering committee to help you grow your business. Or imagine creating a mastermind group in which members can only stay by bringing in new members for the group, or by bringing attendees to your annual conference.

Even if you don't have a steering committee and you don't run a mastermind, you could use several of the ideas in this campaign as stick strategies for rewarding clients so they want to stay with you: running award ceremonies; or creating different tiers of clients, for example an inner circle of your top clients nominated by the other clients with conditions for staying in the group.

The key is to make membership of any group you create so desirable that people want to be part of it and want to stay in it.

In general, I'm not giving out contact details of the entrepreneurs who contributed campaigns to this book. However, if you want to create something like this for your own business, you can email Ron at R.Seaver@sports-forum.com.

An OUTRAGEOUS Way to Get People to Pay $340.00 for a Free Book

Russell Brunson, the founder of ClickFunnels (and other businesses), was in my mastermind group when I owned GKIC. I knew he was a smart guy, and I am very proud of him for building such a successful business.

Russell has written and published two very successful books, *Dotcom Secrets* and, more recently, *Expert Secrets*. The campaign below is the steps he took to launch *Expert Secrets*.

The Campaign

The "Dream 100"

Russell launched the book as though it were a product. That applies not only to the funnel he created but also to how he promoted it: joint venture partners and affiliates.

Lining up partners is one of those things that often gets left to the last minute in a launch. You prepare the product, you build the funnel, and then you go out and form joint ventures to promote it. The problem is, the most desirable partners get the most requests to help in a launch, and they also have their own businesses to run. This means they may only give 10% of their promotional space, energy, attention, and budget to partner launches. Their calendars fill up months in advance.

Knowing this, Russell knew he had to get in early, so he made a point of starting to nurture relationships 14 weeks ahead of his launch. He started by identifying the key influencers he wanted to get on his side—a list he referred to as his Dream 100—and sending them a quick message to ask for a shipping address so he could mail them "a gift." The campaign used

Facebook as its primary platform, so Russell looked for influencers with a large following on Facebook.

Over time, the Dream 100 grew to 400, and Russell started to notice that a lot of minor influencers who weren't on the original Dream 100 list were getting big results in the affiliate contest. That's a key takeaway—don't pre-judge how you think affiliates will perform just because they're less well known or have a smaller list.

Dream 100 Gift #1

Russell is a big Batman fan, so all the gifts followed a superhero theme.

The first box that arrived contained a comic book called *Clickfunnels Avengers*, a Batman figure and a copy of the book.

The book wasn't finished, so it was actually just a cover wrapped around 200 blank pages. (OUTRAGEOUS!) The blank book was more effective than if it had been finished—people called the office to find out what was going on, which naturally led into a conversation about JV promotion. Total cost: $20-$25 per person. Russell also set up a Facebook group for the JV partners, and the blank book created a lot of buzz in the community that got people immediately engaged.

Dream 100 Gift #2

The first box was followed closely by a second box which contained a note to get people excited about the affiliate contest and what they could win. It also contained a "sneak peek" edition of the book with just the first four chapters. It was the perfect cliffhanger and made everyone who saw it want the whole book.

Dream 100 Gift #3

A few weeks before the launch, a third box arrived containing a copy of the finished book (this time with words in it), another comic featuring the top two affiliate Avengers, and a bat light. It also introduced another prize for the top affiliate— a Batman suit of their own (I told you Russell loves Batman!).

The overall aim of the three boxes was to build excitement and to convince the influencers to take part in a virtual book tour.

The Virtual Book Tour

Another element of the launch was a "virtual book tour." Russell arranged interviews with major influencers (people like Tony Robbins and Grant Cardone) and promoted the interview to their lists. The way Russell did this is OUTRAGEOUSLY sneaky.

Most entrepreneurs launching a product ask their partners to promote

the launch on the basis that they'll make their money back in affiliate commissions. The problem with that approach is that the partner has to make a judgment call on whether they think they'll make enough money to justify the trouble and expense of the promotion. A lot of JVs never make it past that initial question.

To sidestep that objection, Russell logged onto the partners' Facebook advertising accounts, entered his own credit card details, and paid for ads to drive traffic to the interview. All the partner had to do was take part in the interview and wait for their commission checks. And they also got the benefit of lots of free traffic.

Grant Cardone's interview had 578k views and over 600 shares. The Tony Robbins interview had 3.6 million views.

Flat-Rate Week

About half-way through the launch, Russell knew he needed to do something OUTRAGEOUS to keep the momentum going. He wrote to the Dream 400 (as it had become) and told them that for the next seven days they would get $20 for every book sold (which was $12 more than the shipping and handling fee Russell was charging for the book). At that point, the affiliate contest took off.

How could he afford to give more in affiliate commission than he was making in sales? Because he knew his numbers. He knew that on average, every book sold would turn into $35 in sales. He could afford to give away $20 and still be profitable.

That's a very valuable lesson—when you have a campaign that works predictably, you know how much money you can spend and still make a profit.

The Funnel

The aim was to drive traffic to a sales funnel where visitors could get a free copy of the book for $7.95 shipping and handling.

The first page was a two-step order form which asked for the buyer's name, email, and shipping address on the first screen and payment details on the second. Why split it? Online shoppers often click away from a transaction before completing it. By asking them to submit their contact details first, Russell can put them into an abandoned cart sequence to recover the sale if that happens. It's an OUTRAGEOUSLY good idea, and something every business owner should be doing on their sales pages.

Look at the page running down the side of this page, and you can see it's a full sales page. It starts with a way to buy the book immediately (for anyone who comes ready to buy), but then there are case studies and testimonials from clients in many different industries—fitness, real estate, social media, dentistry, and even hot dog stands!

Below that, there are three call-to-action buttons in the body of the text. If someone is ready to buy halfway down the page, don't force them to keep reading all the way to the bottom!

The second page (below), where payment details were taken, was the first "bump." Buyers could choose just to have the book for $7.95 shipping and handling, or they could upgrade to $46.95 for a 'Black Box' bundle of books and products.

OUTRAGEOUSLY, the upgrade was pre-selected on the page, so the buyer had to select the $7.95 option deliberately. I know that Russell split tests *everything*, so I'm prepared to believe that increases the conversion rate!

The next page had the first one-time-offer (OTO): the audio version of Expert Secrets (bundled with the audio version of Dotcom Secrets). Even here, Russell had an OUTRAGEOUS trick up his sleeve. There were three options: first, the digital download only for $47, an MP3 player loaded with the audiobooks for $97, and both (digital download and the physical MP3 player) for exactly the same price ($97).

That's an interesting pricing strategy when you think about it. It makes the physical + digital bundle look much more appealing than either of the alternatives.

On the next page, there was a second OTO for a $197 information product (Expert Secrets Evolution Masterclass) with extra bonus content to help the reader implement the strategies in the book.

By the time they get to this point, the most motivated buyers have purchased the following:

- The book
- The Black Box
- The audio versions of Russell's books
- The Expert Secrets Evolution Masterclass

That's a total of $340 for a free book! That's the OUTRAGEOUS power of "free"!

And affiliates were earning commission on everything those buyers purchased (except when the $20 flat-rate promotion was on).

The Live Event

Even then, the funnel wasn't finished. The final thank you page after all the upsells and one-time offers was an invitation to register for a free three-day live web class (value $197).

Each day, Russell presented on YouTube Live and Facebook Live to an audience of over 10,000 people. That was the sales event for a $297/month (or $1,997 for life) high-end program (the 2-Comma Coaching Club). Affiliates loved it because they were still earning commissions.

The Re-Excitement Phase

There's a challenge with selling physical products online. When someone clicks "buy," they're at the peak of their excitement. Then they have to wait, and by the time the package arrives in their mailbox, the excitement has worn off, and buyer's remorse may have set in.

To counteract that, Russell implemented a strategy he learned from my friends Joe Polish and Alex Mandossian: the envelope had a big red sticker on the outside that said,

> "STOP! Don't open this box until you've heard an important message about Expert Secrets from Russell Brunson.
>
> Text the word 'Expert' to the number below."

The Launch Stack

The final sale—and the ultimate aim of the whole campaign—was to turn buyers into users of Russell's Clickfunnels software. Buyers were also invited to register for Russell's evergreen "Funnel Hacks" webinar that pitches 6-months' Clickfunnels access for $997.

Maintaining Momentum

After a book launch, it's easy to let things go quiet. But ongoing sales of your book rely on keeping the momentum going. In Russell's case, he's using Facebook, Instagram, and YouTube. However, he has some advice to anyone just starting out on this.

> Pick a platform you know your ideal reader is on and start there! Study the platform and find out what type of content works. Then drive everyone into your book funnel once you know the average cart value and have enough data to get it optimized.

Results

Over the four weeks the launch was running, this campaign generated $1.5 Million in sales.

Why Is This a Great Campaign to Model?

This is a BIG campaign, with a lot of OUTRAGEOUSLY good ideas.

The idea of creating a Dream 100 of your ideal JV partners is very smart, especially if you follow through and start to build relationships with them before you need them (Russell calls it "digging your well before you're thirsty").

You should also pay attention to the smart way Russell takes a lead through a whole ascension funnel in one go. There is no better time to sell to someone than while they have their wallet open.

And notice that the longest sales page was actually for the lowest-priced offer (the free + shipping book). Why? Because the first sale is the hardest!

These are all ideas that many businesses can implement. You don't have to be selling software or coaching programs like Russell. You could equally be selling a service or a high-end product, or filling a sales event.

The critical point is, you need to know your numbers so you know how much you can spend. Russell knew that every book buyer was worth $35 on average, so he could spend up to that amount to get them to buy. As long as the cost to acquire the customer is below that, the offer is "self-liquidating" (it pays for itself). After that, all the other sales (the software and the coaching programs, which also happen to be the highest-value offers) are pure profit.

An OUTRAGEOUS Way to Add 2940% to Your Revenue with a Simple Checkbox

Ryan Deiss has been a client and friend for many years. Ryan attended the very first GKIC InfoSummit. He had recently graduated from college, and he had an offline business. At the Summit, he asked to join the mastermind group I was setting up, and he was part of the group from then until I sold the company.

Initially, he wasn't interested in running an online marketing business, but I kept telling him that with the knowledge he had, he should be helping other businesses to market themselves online, set up masterminds, run live events, and so on.

Today, he is one of the most successful—and best known—online marketers, and his company, DigitalMarketer, helps tens of thousands of clients from 68 countries to scale their business online.

The Campaign

A common challenge for most businesses is how to identify the highest-value leads from among all the leads in their funnels. For Ryan and DigitalMarketer, that distinction is critical.

Customers for the company fall into three broad categories: entrepreneurs, small business owners, and digital marketing agencies. The company's products appeal to all three groups, but digital agencies are the most profitable customers.

Why? Because while all three customer groups will invest in the company's core product—a continuity program that sells for $387/year—only agencies will invest in becoming a certified partner, which has an annual value of $10,000. Segmenting leads to find out which ones are agencies is OUTRAGEOUSLY valuable.

DigitalMarketer makes extensive use of lead magnets—valuable resources you give away as a bribe to a lead in exchange for their contact details. Here is a typical lead capture page.

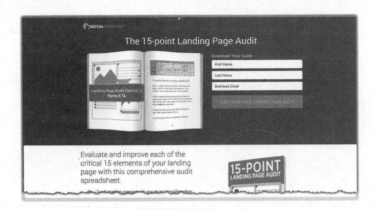

As you can see, the lead capture form is very simple—just first name, last name, and email address—and that's deliberate. The fewer questions you make someone answer when they opt in, the higher your conversion rate will be.

Want some proof?

When Ryan's team added questions (see the picture on the right) to help them identify the *type* of lead, the conversion rate fell from 37% to 30%: an 18.9% drop!

And that's not surprising. Would you want to fill out this form? The extra questions make it too much like hard work.

Unfortunately, the extra data they were gathering didn't make up for the drop in conversions.

Back to the drawing board.

Eventually, after a lot of A/B split testing[4], Ryan's team found a way to identify the highest value leads—the agencies—without affecting conversions using a simple "Yes/No" question.

Now that you have the background, let's go through the campaign step-by-step.

Step 1: Facebook Ad

Ryan uses colorful images in his ads to make sure prospects notice them. Here is an image that suggests you can get your emails out of Gmail's "Promotions" tab and into your prospects' main inbox.

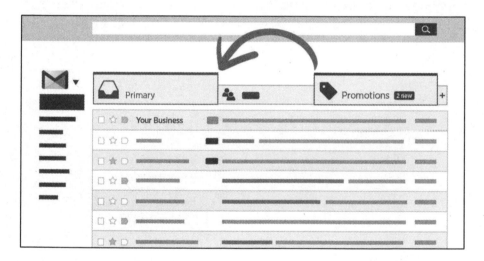

---

[4] A/B split testing involves creating two versions of a marketing piece and comparing the conversion rate for each. Eventually, you'll identify which version works best and you can stop using the less effective version. The key to good split testing is to only change one thing at a time, so you know what's making the difference.

Here's another colorful image that represents an envelope (great for an ad about email conversions) with a simple, appealing promise:

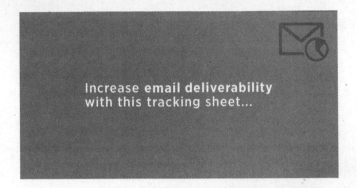

Clicking on the ad takes you through to a landing page that offers a free download: *The Ultimate Email Marketing Metrics Guide (& Tracking Sheet).*

Step 2: The Landing Page

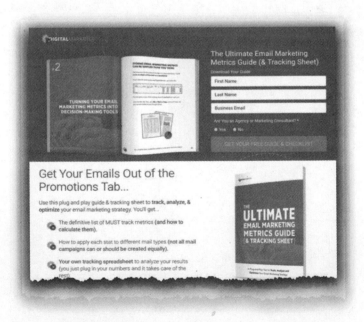

It looks very similar to the first landing page I showed you. You probably can't see the subtle change, so let me make it larger for you.

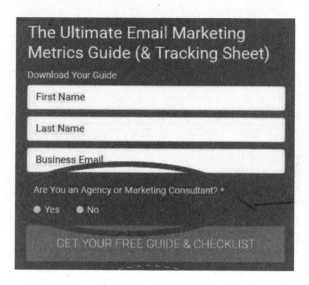

Anyone who picks answers "yes" to "Are you an Agency or Marketing Consultant?" is a high-value lead. And the best part? *The conversion rate was the same with or without this question.*

Step 3: The Sales Page

After a lead opts in, they are taken to a sales page for the *Email Marketing Specialist Mastery Class & Certification Program,* which they can buy at a 90% discount for the next few days (as I said in Thing 2, every OUTRAGEOUS offer has a deadline).

One thing you won't be able to see if you're reading the black and white print edition is something that I've mentioned in a few other campaigns in this book—visual consistency. Every image in this campaign has a big splash of orange—the envelope, the pages of the free guide, and the shield for the certification. As I've said elsewhere, keeping design elements the same between different stages of your funnel makes people comfortable and lets them know they're "in the right place." Using a consistent color is a simple way to achieve that.

Step 4: Email Follow-Up

This is where things start to get interesting. After all, Ryan and his team have gone to a lot of effort to get information from the lead without hurting conversion rates, so what do they *do* with that data? They use it to tailor the email follow-up sequence.

Leads who answer "no" to the segmentation question get the standard follow-up sequence. Leads who answer "yes" (the agency leads), however, get that sequence and an additional sequence focused on the certified partner program.

The second sequence comes from a separate email address, attributed to a named member of the DigitalMarketer team, and feels a lot more personal in tone.

Results

Adding the checkbox and the tailored follow-up sequence to the campaign has allowed Ryan to increase sales of the certified partner program without affecting sales of the lower-end core offer.

Identifying agency leads allows his team to sell to them more effectively, and in particular to sell them on the benefits of joining the Certified Partner program. That raises the value of those leads from $387/year to $10,000/year: an OUTRAGEOUS 2,490% increase!

Why Is This a Great Campaign to Model?

When a business owner wants to raise revenue, their instinct is to spend more on lead generation. What Ryan has done with this campaign is to make better use of the leads he was already getting, and it doesn't cost him anything.

With results like that, Ryan has added the checkbox to every lead capture form on DigitalMarketer's site. Any time you find something that's working in your marketing (or of course in someone else's marketing), you should automate it and replicate it. You can Swipe & Deploy from yourself! It's a simple way to increase the effectiveness of your marketing, but so many business owners forget it.

As Ryan himself likes to point out, the best part about this simple checkbox strategy is that anyone can do it.

If you have a group of customers who are especially valuable to your business, think about how you could get them to quickly and easily identify themselves in a lead form—and it would be smart to try a checkbox first, since you have seen that work so well in this campaign!

Once you get those high-value leads to raise their hand, you'll be able to customize everything else in your marketing campaign—from your landing page to the follow-up emails they receive—to maximize the revenue you get from those high-value leads.

48 - SHAUN BUCK

If Something is Working OUTRAGEOUSLY, Don't Fix It!

Shaun Buck has taken something many people use to support their business and turned it *into* his business. His company, The Newsletter Pro, writes, prints, and sends *done-for-you* newsletters for other businesses.

The campaign below is Shaun's main lead magnet, designed to educate and indoctrinate (typically cold) prospects, and lead them into the conversion funnel.

99% of the company's leads go through this campaign at some point in their relationship with The Newsletter Pro. The campaign has been running since 2013, and Shaun will keep it going because it works.

The Campaign

Lead Generation

The leads come from online ads, promotions through partners, direct referrals from clients and business affiliates, the company's own print publications, and links at the bottom of all their blog posts. Another major source is Shaun's booth at trade shows (right).

The Book

The campaign starts when someone opts in for a copy of Shaun's book, The Ultimate Guide to Newsletters. That might happen at a dedicated lead page, or just on the company's homepage.

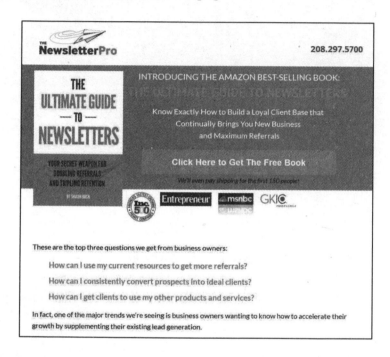

It's a three-step optin. Why three steps? The less someone has to do up front, the more likely they are to do it. If they had to enter all their information immediately, practically no one would opt in. An OUTRA-GEOUSLY simple way to increase the optin rate on your site is not to ask for all the information at the same time.

Once someone signs up, the book is sent out in a bright orange padded mailer. Not only do they get the book, but they also get a cover letter, five sample newsletters, and two CDs that explain why you should have a newsletter. The ultimate aim of the cover letter is to get the prospect on the phone, so it includes an invitation to schedule a meeting. The fact that they're not expecting any of that is OUTRAGEOUSLY clever. It creates that effect of shock and awe that is going to make people want to call in.

Step 2: Multi-Step Follow-Up Sequence

After the book mailer goes out, the lead gets put into a multi-step follow-up sequence.

1. The lead gets an immediate confirmation email to say that the book will be sent in the next 24 hours.

> **Subject: Your book, Bill**
> Bill, thanks again for requesting a free copy of the book The Ultimate Guide to Newsletters. It will be rushed to you within 24 hours via UPS.

The email includes a photo of the orange mailer, which is a very smart move. It makes the prospect look out for the envelope, so when it arrives, they're going to put it on the top of the pile.

2. In the first week, the lead gets another four emails with stories relating back to the book.

3. At the end of the week, they get a phone call to check they got the book.
4. Over the next 2-3 weeks, they get six more emails with highlights and insights from the book, and five check-in calls.

Step 3: Ongoing Engagement

The lead then enters the company's ongoing contact sequence, which has two main elements.

1. Each Friday, a "Weekend Reading" email goes out with helpful articles.
2. Each month, there's a printed newsletter with content written by Shaun Buck himself.

Results

On average, 550 leads enter the campaign each month. 20% (110) of prospects who get the book go on to request a consult, and about 30% (33) of those prospects convert to become clients.

Why Is This a Great Campaign to Model?

This is a campaign designed to keep Shaun and his company "top of mind." Sending a print newsletter each month is an obvious step for The Newsletter Pro. The weekly email newsletters ensure that the prospect doesn't forget in between.

It could be run by any business in any industry; all you need is a book to send out!

An OUTRAGEOUS Way to Keep Customers in a Long-Term Program or Service

I originally met Yanik Silver at a Dan Kennedy event. We very quickly became good friends, and we have stayed friends ever since.

This campaign is what we call a "stick" campaign for Yanik's Maverick 1000 program.

Stick campaigns are a really useful tool in marketing. If there's any kind of delay between when someone places an order and when they get the product or service, there's always a risk that they might get buyer's remorse and cancel.

In services that are delivered over time—memberships, software-as-a-service, monthly subscriptions, etc.—of course, you're constantly in danger of a customer wanting to cancel their account. A stick campaign is designed to minimize those cancellations.

The Campaign

Yanik describes Maverick 1000 as an invitation-only global network of top entrepreneurs and industry leaders. It's a higher priced program and members of the group pay yearly or quarterly to stay in the program, so keeping them in the membership is very worthwhile.

There's an online element through a membership site with training and resources. Members also meet in person throughout the year for retreats and experiences where they get to rub shoulders with iconic business leaders like Sir Richard Branson, Tony Hsieh, Tim Ferriss and many others.

The campaign was created with the help of one of the members of the program, Joey Coleman. It was designed to get them engaged as soon as they join, and keep them engaged and taking action for the first 100 days of their membership.

That's critical in any membership program. However exciting and valuable the program is, it's no good if someone joins and then sits for a few weeks waiting for something to happen. Things have to start happening immediately.

100-Day "Stick" Campaign

The campaign is designed to make sure things are happening all through their first hundred days in the Maverick 1000.

Throughout the campaign, members receive regular emails. An email might contain video, a task that involves interacting with other members, a story about some social contribution that the program has made, or some educational content.

For example, the email for day 13 includes a video in which a puppet (yes, a puppet—everything can be OUTRAGEOUS) shares what it truly means to be in the program—the core values—by talking through the MAVERICK DNA Acronym.

The idea is to help new members realize that this is not just another mastermind group: they are part of something far bigger.

In addition to the emails, new members also receive a series of physical mailings—effectively, a shock and awe package (see page 141) spread out over three months.

MAVERICK DNA

M - I am a Multiplier
A - I am Abundance Minded
V - I am a Visionary
E - I am Extraordinary
R - I Re-imagine, Re-invent and Re-Create
I - I am Impactful
C - I am a Connector, Catalyst and Co-Creator
K - Kiss Kiss, Bang Bang

Day 1 – New Member Kit

New members are sent a welcome kit immediately after joining—a big box packed with items like

- A custom Maverick vest
- Three copies of Yanik's books *34 Rules for Maverick Entrepreneurs* and *Evolved Enterprise*, with a Post-It note inviting the new member to pass the books along
- A postcard welcoming the new member to the program

Day 17 – Leather Journal

Journaling is one of the processes Yanik encourages as a way to process the issues and challenges business owners encounter, so members receive two journals early on in their membership. The first is custom-imprinted and leather-bound. For those who are new to journaling, the second is a gentle introduction called *The 5-Minute Journal.*

With the journals comes a letter from Yanik explaining the benefits of journaling and how to get started.

The letter also sends the member back to the membership site for additional resources (and to get them to engage with the program).

Day 40 – Learning Content

Forty days into their membership, the member gets a pack of DVDs. These are sessions recorded by four of the celebrity entrepreneurs who

contribute to the program, such as Richard Branson, motorcycle mogul Jesse James, Tony Hsieh, and Chip Conley.

As well as providing massive value, these serve another major purpose: they provide huge social proof. *These are my peers*, the DVDs say, *and now they're your peers, too.*

With the DVDs is a note from Yanik suggesting the best material from each DVD and again, pointing the member to more videos inside the membership site.

Day 50 – Superhero

"Fun" is a big part of the ethos of Maverick 1000, and their day-50 gift certainly lives up to that. It's also a great demonstration that a shock and awe package doesn't have to have lots of parts. Sometimes, even a single item can create the shock and awe effect.

In this case, that item is a custom-made superhero doll of the member. How does Yanik pull it off? A few weeks before, the member is invited to take part in a "secret mission" for which they have to send in a set of photographs of themselves. In due course, the doll arrives.

Other gifts that the members receive during their first 100 days include a passport cover made by a social enterprise in Africa which is supported by Maverick 1000, and Maverick-branded aluminum luggage tags. Both of those gifts, of course, are inspired by the travel that members undertake as part of their membership.

Referrals

I also wanted to point out an aspect of the Maverick 1000 that's very clever, even though it doesn't fit into the "first 100 days" campaign. I mentioned that the members of the group get together many times during the year. At many of those events, they are encouraged to bring another entrepreneur as a guest.

While they are there getting great value, and meeting the other members and experts, Yanik takes the opportunity to stand up and invite anyone who wants to be part of the group to join. Of course, most people who attend a meeting as a guest do end up joining.

It's a great way to encourage referrals and let your clients do the selling.

Why Is This a Great Campaign to Model?

Any time you're asking people to pay you over and over again, there's a risk that one day they'll decide to stop. Anything you can do to put that day off for as long as possible is a huge benefit to the business.

Any business that runs a subscription model would benefit from this. In Yanik's case, that's a mastermind group for business owners, but any business can introduce some form of monthly subscription. In this book, you'll find examples from many industries, and membership programs are used successfully by professionals like dentists and lawyers, haircare (Wen haircare products), razor blades (Dollar Shave Club), food (Graze), and many others.

Stick campaigns also work well in industries where there's a long lead time between when a customer pays you and when they get their product or service, or where they buy from you multiple times, but with a long gap in between (e.g., an accountant doing annual tax returns).

Here are the key points that make this stick campaign work so well.

1. It crosses media. While most of the communication is by email, there are physical packages too, and the program itself has both an online component (the membership site) and a physical component (the events).

2. The packages always contain something special, so when a package does arrive with the Maverick 1000 branding on it, the member is curious and excited.

3. The focus of the campaign is on maintaining engagement between events—get the member to the membership site and get them doing an activity.

4. Communication is regular. Maverick 1000 members are used to getting something daily, so they remain engaged.

Pulling ALL the Pieces Together to Change Your Good Business into A GREAT Business

Phew! You made it to Part Five.

You've seen 49 OUTRAGEOUS campaigns from some of the most successful marketers and entrepreneurs in the world. All of them share one major characteristic: their marketing is making them money—which is something most businesses struggle to achieve.

You may be wondering, "Why only 49 campaigns, Bill? Why not a round 50?"

Simple. Campaign #50 is <u>yours</u>. It's the OUTRAGEOUS CAMPAIGN you're going to build with everything you've learned in this book.

Before I tell you how you can pull all the pieces together, let's recap what you've seen so far.

In **PART ONE**, I explained why you should run your business OUTRAGEOUSLY, whatever business you're in. If you don't agree, then I strongly suggest that you reread *The 7 Steps to Apply SUPER OUTRAGEOUS Marketing to Your Own Outrageous Business* on pages 31-34).

In **PART TWO**, I explained **Why You're Leaving OUTRA-GEOUS Amounts of Money on the Table If Your Marketing Isn't OUTRAGEOUSLY "Multi-Step."**

In **PART THREE**, you saw 37 CAMPAIGNS that are relatively simple—they only have a few steps, or use just one or two media.

In **PART FOUR,** you saw 12 CAMPAIGNS that are more complex—they have multiple steps, use many different media, or run over a longer period than the campaigns in Part Three.

Before You Go Any Further!

Yes, it's unusual to see a "STOP" in the middle of a book, but I want to check: have you read Parts 1-4 fully? Because if you haven't, then you're going to be missing a lot.

For Part 5, rather than me just telling you how to pull all the pieces together and change your good business into a GREAT business, let me ask you some questions which will tell you how to put together everything you've learned and create CAMPAIGN #50.

The Questions

Question#1: Which of the following are you using?
- ❑ Offline Marketing
- ❑ Online Marketing
- ❑ Both

If you checked "both," then congratulations! You never know where you're going to find your leads, or what marketing they will respond to.

If you only checked one then consider that half your audience may be missing your messages. There are many simple ways to get started mixing online and offline strategies. One easy starting point is with a free book offer like the ones in the campaigns by Ben Glass and Sean Buck.

Question #2: Where do you get your leads? (check all that apply)
- ❑ House list (existing leads and customers)
- ❑ Generated leads
- ❑ Purchased lists

It's great if you have an existing list of leads and customers, but leads are the lifeblood of your business, and eventually, you need to start bringing in some "new blood."

At the same time, every lead has a cost, so once you have someone in your house list, you should continue to market to them until they tell you they're no longer interested. Otherwise, you're wasting all the time and money you invested in getting them onto your list to start with.

For campaigns about generating new leads and marketing to existing leads, just about every campaign in the book will show you how to do that.

For campaigns that use purchased lists, take a look at Chip Kessler, Michael Thibault, and Demetrios Tzortzis for some great examples of how to make these work best in your business.

Question #3: How good are you at getting customers/clients to come back, keep buying, and refer their friends?

Be honest! This is OUTRAGEOUSLY important. Depending on your industry and who your customers are, getting an existing customer to buy again from you is typically around six times cheaper than convincing someone who has never bought from you to try. Just as important, those returning customers will typically spend around 3x more than a new buyer. Put those two together, and you have a recipe for making your business 18x more profitable!

Take a look at the campaigns from Dr. Sean Tarpenning, Richelle Shaw, Bent Hansen, and Julie Boswell to see how this is done.

Question #4: How could you track the results of every piece of marketing you do?

Look back at the campaigns in Parts Three and Four. Every contributor was able to tell me what they spent and how many customers they got. Many of them also discussed how they tracked, adjusted, and improved their campaigns as they went along.

That's because they monitor their results. Tracking is critical in marketing: you need to know what's working and what isn't. You need to know when results change, so you can get out of a channel that's not working anymore or put more money into something that's working well.

Question #5: How could you segment your leads, so you don't treat them all the same?

One of the biggest mistakes entrepreneurs make is that they send exactly the same marketing campaign to everyone. But think about it. Some of your customers respond more to some information than others; some spend a lot more than others; some are more loyal than others; some are more likely to refer than others. If you can figure out who's who, you can save yourself a lot of money by targeting the right messages to the right people.

Look at the campaigns by Ryan Deiss, Oli Billson, and Bill and Steve Harrison to see examples of brilliantly segmented and targeted marketing.

Question #6: On page 360, you'll find a list of all the media used in the campaigns. Now that you're ready to add multi-step campaigns, what additional three media do you want to begin with?

1) _____

2) _____

3) _____

When you've picked your media, go back to the list and look up the campaigns that use them. See how the marketers applied those media, and what their results were.

And maybe the most important OUTRAGEOUS question ...

Question #7: Think about each CAMPAIGN you saw in Parts 3 and 4. After you looked at the headlines, did you decide to skip some of them if you thought they wouldn't apply to your business or they wouldn't be helpful to you? Be Honest.

_____ YES

_____ NO

The reason I ask is that at the end of every campaign I show you how to model it for your business, whatever your business might be. If you didn't read every CAMPAIGN, then you'll miss a lot of opportunities. I strongly advise that you go back and read the ones you skipped. In fact, go back and read EVERY CAMPAIGN at least twice, because there's bound to be some detail you missed that will make you slap your forehead and shout, "How did I miss that? That's OUTRAGEOUS!"

Planning your CAMPAIGN

You're going to build your CAMPAIGN around a specific business objective or set of objectives that you want to achieve.

To run a CAMPAIGN, you need to get clear on a few things.

1. The CAMPAIGN objectives
2. Where the leads will come from
3. Which leads you'll be marketing to
4. How you want people to respond
5. The steps that will get someone to respond that way

How do you put it all together?

CAMPAIGN Objectives

It's easy to assume that marketing CAMPAIGNS are about getting new customers, but there are a lot of ways that we can use marketing.

Here are some other objectives you should consider.

1. Gaining new customers for an existing product or service
2. Launching a new product or service
3. Persuading past customers to come back

4. Making sure current customers stay loyal (what we call a "stick" CAMPAIGN)
5. Getting current customers to spend more or buy more often
6. Going back to people who inquired in the past, but didn't buy
7. Building a list of prospects that you can continue to market to in the future

In Parts Three and Four of this book, you saw multiple examples of CAMPAIGNS built around each of these objectives.

Where the Leads Will Come From

If you look back at the list of business objectives above, you'll see that some of these objectives are about closing new leads, but a lot of them are about selling to the leads you've already got. Business growth isn't always about finding new people to sell to. The leads you already have can be some of your best resources.

You need to decide whether you're going to market to people on your list, generate new leads, or both.

Which Leads to Focus On

Not all leads are created equal. That's especially true when you're marketing to an existing list, but it also applies to new leads that you generate. You'll need to plan what criteria you'll use to decide whether to put someone through your CAMPAIGN.

For example, in marketing to past customers, you might choose to focus on those who have bought in the last three months. Or you might only target people who *haven't* bought in the last three months. You might run a CAMPAIGN specifically for men, or for women, or for people in a certain age bracket. You might focus your CAMPAIGN on people in a particular geographical area. Or who work in a particular industry.

There is an infinite variety of ways you could narrow down your CAMPAIGN, depending on the business you are in and the objectives you are working toward.

You might wonder why you would want to narrow down your CAMPAIGN? After all, if you're promoting something, doesn't it make sense to get it in front of as many people as possible? The answer, as in so many aspects of business, is time and money.

Let's say you run a CAMPAIGN in a national daily newspaper. It sounds great, doesn't it? "I got my ad in the New York Times!" But, what if you're in Philadelphia and can only serve customers in that area? You're paying to get your ad in front of millions of people that you can't sell to.

Even if your business is national, is everyone who reads the paper going to be interested in what you are selling? Let's say you sell high-end, high-priced audio equipment. While you might *want* every reader of The Times to be interested in your products, the reality is only a small minority actually are, but you're paying to get your ad in front of all the other readers, too.

And finally, even if you do have mass appeal and can service people anywhere, can you handle the level of inquiries you'll get? If your switchboard suddenly started getting two hundred calls a day from prospective customers, could you handle it?

Being clear on *exactly* whom you're going to market to can save you *major* headaches (and cost)!

How you Want People to Respond

The next thing you need to consider when planning your CAMPAIGN is the action or actions you want people to take as they go through the CAMPAIGN. Knowing the first and last responses people make is critical.

The first response is simply a way for someone to hold up their hand (literally or metaphorically) and say, "I saw your CAMPAIGN, and I'm interested." This could be something obvious, like walking into your store or office, or it may be something less direct, like calling a recorded information line, visiting a web page or watching a webinar.

The last response is whatever you need them to do to meet your business objective. A revenue generation CAMPAIGN is going to lead someone to buy. A lead generation CAMPAIGN, on the other hand, will take them toward some way to qualify the lead.

As you read the CAMPAIGNS in this book, you'll have seen examples of many different kinds of response, using many different media.

The Steps to Get Someone to Respond That Way

Between those two responses—the first and the last—the lead will go through a series of steps. Remember, I said people often need 7 or more touches with you to get to the point where they're happy to buy. So, each step corresponds to some form of contact that the lead has with you: a letter, an email, a call, etc. How many—and what kind—will depend on many different factors.

One major factor is how much they have to invest—whether in money, time, energy, or some other resource—in the final step. The more they have to do or spend at the end of the CAMPAIGN, the more steps you're likely to have to get them to go through.

Another factor is the relationship you already have with the lead at the start of the CAMPAIGN. Broadly speaking, the colder a lead is as they enter the CAMPAIGN, the more steps you'll need to warm them up. If the lead knows you very well—an existing client, for example—then you may only need one or two steps.

You have seen examples in this book of CAMPAIGNS for stone cold leads, red-hot leads, and everything in between. You have also seen CAMPAIGNS for low investment offers and for much higher investment offers.

Results

Once the lead has been through the CAMPAIGN, you'll be able to gauge how successful it was by how many responses you got. When I asked the marketers featured in this book to submit their CAMPAIGNS, I also asked them to tell us what the results were, whether they would use it again, and what was special about their CAMPAIGN.

As you went through the campaigns, I'm sure you enjoyed knowing that these were CAMPAIGNS that truly work, and that really make money.

OUTRAGEOUS Media

OUTRAGEOUS multi-step marketing CAMPAIGNS need OUTRA-GEOUS ways to reach potential clients, and the campaigns in the book use many different media to get clients and to get *to* clients. Here is an index of the media you saw in the CAMPAIGNS in Parts Three and Four. The Numbers refer to the campaigns in which they were used.

MEDIA	USED IN CAMPAIGNS #
Advertorials	15
Affiliate marketing	36, 42, 46, 48
Awards ceremonies	4, 45
Contests and prize draws	8, 25, 27, 32
CopyDoodles®	2, 3, 17, 18, 23, 24, 30, 32, 44
Coupons	2, 9, 38
Cross-selling to current clients	2, 5, 7, 8, 14, 16, 17, 23, 27, 32, 33, 36, 37, 40, 43
Customer appreciation events	28, 34
Customer testimonials	1, 7, 8, 10, 15, 17, 19, 21, 23, 24, 25, 28, 29, 32, 36, 37, 38, 40, 43, 44, 46
Direct mail: 3D mail	3, 19, 20, 21, 25, 26, 27, 32, 35, 36, 46, 49
Direct mail: postcards	7, 13, 18, 19, 25, 27, 31, 32, 36, 44, 49
Direct mail: sales letters	2, 3, 4, 5, 7, 9, 13, 17, 19, 22, 23, 24, 26, 27, 29, 32, 35, 36, 38, 44, 48, 49
Email marketing	1, 2, 5, 6, 7, 8, 10, 11, 12, 14, 15, 16, 17, 18, 23, 28, 29, 30, 31, 32, 33, 34, 35, 36, 37, 38, 39, 40, 42, 43, 44, 45, 46, 47, 48, 49
Events/seminar: free	28, 31, 38
Events/seminar: paid	28, 37, 45, 41
Every Door Direct Mail	9

Facebook ads	9, 11, 14, 16, 21, 23, 31, 33, 36, 37, 40, 43, 46, 47
Joint ventures	11, 23, 28, 42, 46
Lead capture/squeeze pages	1, 21, 23, 31`1, 33, 34, 37, 43, 44, 47, 48, 42
Magazine ads	15
Newsletters	5, 8, 9, 26, 27, 29, 30, 34, 37, 45, 48
Newspaper ads	31, 38
Newspaper inserts	9
Pay-per-click ads	10, 23, 31, 37
Pre-recorded dial-in messages	46
Radio ads	38
Referral contests	27, 46
Sales pages	5, 11, 14, 21, 23, 28, 30, 33, 35, 37, 40, 43, 44, 46, 47
SMS/text messaging	25, 33, 39
Social media	16, 28, 42, 46
Speaking at others' events	4, 11, 25, 39, 43
Special reports	10, 22, 36, 44
Sponsoring a booth, breakout or meal at live events	19, 25, 35, 39
Sponsoring a non-profit	4, 45
Sponsoring an event	31
Telephone calls	6, 11, 12, 22, 23, 30, 32, 34, 35, 36, 38, 41, 43, 45, 48
Web TV shows/ livecasts	43, 46
Webinars/teleseminars	11, 21, 34, 36, 40, 43
Writing a lead generation book	1, 19, 21, 22, 26, 28, 35, 42, 43, 46, 48

OUTRAGEOUS CAMPAIGNS LIVE

Do you want to see the entrepreneurs in this book
WALK YOU THROUGH their campaigns in person?
Do you want to learn how they've updated their campaigns
to make them EVEN better?
Do you want to meet HUNDREDS of business owners
just like you, and make friendships and partnerships for life?

I'm running a LIVE workshop in sunny San Diego,
and I'd love to have you join us.

All the proceeds from this book and the live event
will be going to Veteran's Affairs, and you'll be able to see me
hand over a MASSIVE check LIVE on stage.

You can find out all the details at
www.outrageouscampaigns.com/live

I hope we'll see you there!

Bill Glazer

More Praise for Bill Glazer's
OUTRAGEOUS Multi-Step Marketing Campaigns

"I've always been amazed at Bill Glazer's brilliant campaign strategies that create massive results. This will be the go-to book for anyone wanting to do outrageous marketing that works." ● **NINA HERSHBERGER**

"With Bill, you get the best of both worlds: an outstanding marketer, and someone who has demonstrated in his own business background that he knows what it takes to achieve success. What a treasure to have Bill Glazer available. Best of all, he's still giving us quality material as found in his newest book." ● **CHIP KESSLER**

"Bill really walks you through exactly what you need to run a successful multi-step marketing campaign. I highly recommend this book to any business owner who wants to make sure they're getting the most out of their marketing." ● **CRAIG SIMPSON**

"Renowned marketer Bill Glazer's new book is a rich compilation of 49 superbly-constructed marketing campaigns from Bill's handpicked group of the top marketers and business owners in the country. Bill breaks down the key components of each campaign, deconstructing the key elements that made them outrageously effective." ● **DR. DAVID PHELPS**

"Bill Glazer's first book changed my life and became my marketing and advertising bible. The first book was fantastic, but this book is next level mastery in taking an idea and implementing it with step-by-step guidance and commentary from Bill. These are campaigns that have actually produced millions of dollars in sales for business owners." ● **JEFF GIAGNOCAVO**

"If there's one thing you can do to stand out from the crowd it's STAND OUT FROM THE CROWD! Bill's new book reveals exactly how to make that happen in a way that generates not only interest, but bottom line results as well. It's exactly the kind of book on marketing every small business owner/entrepreneur needs to have in their library: practical, inspirational, and a blast to read." ● **JACK TURK**

"We small business owners have to fight the Goliaths of our competitors who have huge advertising budgets. Bill Glazer's tried-and-true OUTRAGEOUS methods and examples help us beat the competition with agility and style." ● **KEVIN CARTER**

"Bill Glazer's OUTRAGEOUS Multi-Step Marketing Campaigns is the perfect book for the busy entrepreneur, business owner or private practice owner because it is full of valuable resources from every business category. What Bill has assembled here is worth a ton of money." ● **DAN CRICKS**

"In 2006 I was introduced to a completely unique type of advertising and marketing: Outrageous Advertising. The person who introduced it to me was Bill Glazer. Bill epitomizes the concept of Outrageous Advertising, making marketing fun, exciting, anything but boring, and most of all, productive. When Bill speaks, I listen. You should, too." ● DR. BRIAN BERGH

"Only one marketing guru could get the most successful marketers in the world to pull back the curtain and reveal their top grossing campaigns, and that's Bill Glazer. Bill's latest book is another home run, chock-full of money-making marketing information and OUTRAGEOUS campaigns that will generate millions of dollars in sales for those that get their hands on it! If you want to take the shortcut straight to the bank, you need this book in your marketing arsenal." ● MICHAEL THIBAULT

"Bill Glazer has been a pioneer in bringing people into action. His thought process is something that every business will greatly benefit from. It's not just an ad, it's the philosophy behind the ad that makes his ideas so valuable. If you are looking for down to earth, easy promotions that will make your customers respond quickly, this book is a must!" ● HOWARD ANDERSON

"If you want to grow your business or professional practice, you need this book! You'll get so many great ideas, it'll be the most profitable book purchase you ever make. Even if you only implement one of the many proven strategies, you'll pay for the book 1,000 times over." ● BILL HARRISON

"I highly recommend anyone starting a business or running a business to study what Bill Glazer teaches in this book as his outrageous, proven and tested advice will be transformational to the success and profitability of your business. Bill genuinely cares about his readers' and students' success. Most marketing books are published to make the author rich and famous. Bill does this for the benefit of others and the satisfaction of knowing he was able to help someone else." ● DAVID LINTON

"The biggest misconception in marketing is that it is a one-time event, ad buy or social media posting. So you put in all this work, then get nothing. Frustrating! *OUTRAGEOUS Multi-Step Marketing Campaigns* reveals how to create marketing that generates customers with easy to follow examples you can quickly use within your business, bringing relief and new customers." ● ROBERT SKROB

"Bill's book is a quick study in how to bring in money quickly and efficiently for your next big project, with just enough info to get the job done! Think of it as a 'money recipe book,' tried and true by outrageously nimble pros!" ● CESSALY D HUTCHINSON

"Whenever I get stuck and need some inspiration I always reference Bill's Outrageous Advertising book. It immediately gives me great ideas that I can implement and helps take my work to the next level. Thank you, Bill!" ● DEMETRIOS TZORTZIS